WHY ARE OUR BAB

Why Are Our Babies Dying?

Pregnancy, Birth, and Death in America

Sandra D. Lane

Paradigm Publishers
Boulder • London

Copyright © 2008 by Paradigm Publishers

Published in the United States by Paradigm Publishers, 3360 Mitchell Lane, Suite E, Boulder, Colorado 80301 USA.

Paradigm Publishers is the trade name of Birkenkamp & Company, LLC, Dean Birkenkamp, President and Publisher.

Library of Congress Cataloging-in-Publication Data

Lane, Sandra D.
  Why are our babies dying? : pregnancy, birth, and death in America / Sandra D. Lane.
    p. cm.
  Includes bibliographical references and index.
  ISBN-13: 978-1-59451-440-1 (hardcover)
  1. Infants—Mortality—United States.   2. Social problems—United States.
I. Title.
  HB1323.I42U644 2008
  304.6'40973—dc22

                                                                2007045743

Printed and bound in the United States of America on acid-free paper that meets the standards of the American National Standard for Permanence of Paper for Printed Library Materials.

Designed and Typeset in New Baskerville by Straight Creek Bookmakers.

12 11 10 09 08   1 2 3 4 5

To Robert
To Helen
and in the memory of my parents, Mae and Fred Lane

Contents

Preface

Shortly after arriving in Syracuse in 1996, I learned that the infant mortality rate in Onondaga County was historically one of the highest in the United States. Moreover, the infant mortality rate for people of color in the county was so high that the rate approximated what might be found in a developing country. Two months later, I was hired by the county health department with the charge to write grants to support infant mortality reduction. My contract for this employment was run through Syracuse Model Neighborhood Facility, Inc. (SMNF), a comprehensive community agency operated by and serving the Syracuse communities of color. In the now eleven years since, I have worked closely with and benefited greatly from the friendship of the SMNF staff. My enormous respect for their work led me to allocate my author's royalties for this book to the SMNF.

When I began to fulfill the health department assignment of writing grants to reduce infant mortality, I approached the task as would any anthropologist arriving in a new place. I went into the field. I met with community groups, nonprofit agency staff, and county employees. I led a team that wrote a successfully-funded federal Healthy Start grant and became the founding director of Syracuse Healthy Start, a project that still provides needed services to prevent infant death. After five years I left Syracuse Healthy Start to join the Department of Obstetrics and Gynecology at SUNY Upstate Medical University. I wanted to study in greater depth the intersection of imbedded racism, discrimination, poverty, and premature mortality in Syracuse. I am now part of a research team of some twenty faculty, students, and community members that not only searches for risk factors and potential solutions to health inequalities, but also communicates our findings to community members, elected officials, and policymakers.

In 2005, I became chair of the Department of Health and Wellness, in the College of Human Services and Health Professions at Syracuse University, where I have found numerous colleagues who also bridge analysis and activism on the gap in health and survival.

My perspective in this work comes from my doctorate in medical anthropology and master's degree in epidemiology, as well as more than a decade of work as a registered nurse in the beginning of my career. I also lived and worked in Egypt for five years, where I developed expertise on maternal and child health in developing countries, first as a doctoral student, then as a Ford Foundation program officer. In my Syracuse research I have been struck by how similar the problems are in the developing and developed worlds. Inadequate education and low literacy—barriers to healthcare posed by poverty, discrimination, and misguided policies made on the basis of short-term fiscal analysis—wreak havoc in both settings.

A second major finding of our work led me to question the individual responsibility model that guides a wealth of public health interventions. We found that, considering such health risks as the use of illicit drugs or alcohol, pregnant white women were quite similar to pregnant women of color in Syracuse. Pregnant white women, moreover, smoke cigarettes at higher rates than women of color. Findings like these forced us to go beyond individual-level risks to look at disease-inducing environments. In several cases described in this book, we found that such environmental risks as lead poisoning, lack of supermarkets, and disproportionate incarceration seem to account for much of the health inequality of African Americans and Latinos. Our findings do not indicate that individual-level risks should be ignored. Indeed, we should all try to avoid smoking, eat healthful food, and wear our seatbelts. But individual-level risks do not fully explain the racial/ethnic health gap.

With numerous co-authors I have published eleven articles based on our analysis of health disparities in Syracuse. I wrote this book to bring together and describe in one volume a decade of work on unequal health and survival for babies (and people throughout the life span), caused by poverty and structural discrimination. I have tried to write as simply and clearly as possible, not an easy task for an anthropologist at the turn of the second millennium, in which our profession increasingly values impenetrable prose. I hope this book will be useful to community members in their efforts to improve the conditions in which they live. I have also written the book for students of anthropology and other social sciences, medicine and other health professions, and bioethics.

Sandra D. Lane
Syracuse, New York
August 2007

Acknowledgments

U<small>NTIL NOW</small> I <small>HAVE FULFILLED</small> the "publish or perish" academic mandate by producing articles, which I co-author with university colleagues, students, and community collaborators. Most of my research team members become friends with whom I work on project after project. Some of my students have become like family members; I have attended their graduations, weddings, and sometimes even the births of their children. Many of our grant proposals and study designs have been drafted around my kitchen table over food and wine. I wanted to write this book to tell the story of our work on infant mortality in Syracuse and to integrate into one volume the results of the studies and programs that we have accomplished together. This work is theirs as well as mine.

I hold appointments in two universities: Syracuse University and Upstate Medical University. At Syracuse University I want to thank Chancellor Nancy Cantor, whose commitment to university-community linkages, social justice, and support for our efforts is invaluable. The dean of the College of Human Services and Health Professions, Diane Lyden Murphy, is another leader for social justice and I am very grateful for her support. Rob Keefe, Michael Freedman, Don Mitchell, Jonnell Allen, Ambika Krishnakumar, Jo Thomas, Kim Jaffee, Carrie Smith, Deborah Monahan, Arthur Paris, Vennie Cowart, Kelly Pettingill, Lisa Mignacca, and Eric Kingson have all contributed their efforts to improve community health in Syracuse. At Upstate, I want to thank my chair, Shawky Badawy, for his mentoring and encouragement. Department of Obstetrics and Gynecology colleagues Richard Aubry, Martha Wojtowycz, Linda Newell, Phillip Ferro, Rob Silverman, John Folk, John Nosovitch, Maria Czerwinski, Pam Parker, Mary

Marone, Mary Ellen Hane, Anne Marie Seller, and Elizabeth Chapman have worked tirelessly to provide the highest quality obstetrical and reproductive care to the Syracuse community. Jerrold Abraham, Gerry Hall, Theresa Hargrave, Judy Crawford, Paula Rosenbaum, and Chien-Chih Liu, my colleagues on the asthma triggers study, are incredibly dedicated. Other health care providers, Steve Blatt, Anne Barrash, Anne Botash, Larry Consenstein, Celeste Madden, Cathy Patrick, Joan Vincent, Daphene Johnson, Tanya Paul, George Stanley, Marge Ostrander, Rhonda Sussman, Janet Press, and Gerry Galaresee devote time and attention, well beyond their official duties, to reduce infant mortality in Syracuse.

I am grateful for the years of camaraderie and shared hard work of Don Cibula, Stacey Barone Cibula, Florence Schweitzer, Maizie Shaw, Llamara Padro Milano, Amanda Nestor, Miguel Perez, Diane Rothermel, Gerry Christie, Lee Quinlin, Barbara Bourgeois, Jean Reilly, and many others with whom I worked at the Onondaga County Health Department. We are fortunate to have such capable women as Chief Medical Examiner Mary Jumbelic and Commissioner of Health Cynthia Morrow. Both of these committed leaders have shared their expertise with me, for which I am very appreciative. I also thank Lloyd Novick, our former health commissioner, for giving me the chance to direct Syracuse Healthy Start.

I have worked with stellar students in the past ten years at Syracuse who have become valued colleagues. I am most grateful to Noah Webster, Brooke Levandowski, Kelly Polinsky, Priya Sharma, Olabisi Dele-Michael, Darlene Carter, Adrienne Socci, Andrea Shaw, Jessica Brill, Beth Dawson, Danielle Yerdon, Suzanne Morrissey, Sally Huntington, Jobe Jamerson, Shirley Obioha, Tina Nguyen, Silvia Shenouda, Svetlana Peshkova, Deborah Ellerbee, Aaron Kingson, Johanna Kingson, and Zaki Badawy for their idealism and enthusiasm in addressing the intersection of social justice and health.

My colleagues at Lemoyne College, with a grant from the Health Resources and Services Administration, have led the way in developing a curriculum that teaches health care students about health disparities and cultural competence. The writing of this book was partially supported by that grant. I am so pleased to be part of this work with Linda Allison, Mark Archambault, Lynne Arnaull, and Mary Springston. I have also had the great good fortune to work with Emilia Koumans of the CDC's STD branch and Kathy DeMott, once the Healthy Start nurse midwife, now Dr. DeMott, a graduate of the London School of

Hygiene and Tropical Medicine. The Health Resources and Services Administration also funds Syracuse Healthy Start; Mary Beth Badura, Donna Hutten, David de la Cruz, and John McGovern of HRSA's Maternal and Child Health Bureau were endlessly supportive and knowledgeable in assisting our project during my time as director. At the New York State Health Department, Donna Cashman was always more than helpful and I thank her for her patience and kindness. Mindy Thompson Fullilove of Columbia University came to Syracuse five times as a consultant and every time astounded me with her analyses. Her theoretical influences resonate throughout this book. I am grateful for her friendship as well.

My most fond appreciation is expressed to the many community members who welcomed me, with my overly academic charts and statistical analyses, into their networks of friendship and activism. Jesse Dowdell, Barbara Dowdell, Jenny Penningston, Tarah Tapley, Pam McKenzie, Silky, Xenia Becher, Mary Martha Wilson, Sister Ida Gregoire, Marsha Weissman, Alan Rosenthal, Michelle Galvin, Maritza Alvarado, Liz Crockett, Anne Andrianos, Sharon Jack-Williams, Louella Williams, Fernando Ortiz, Linda Hall, Minister Mark Muhammad, Win Jones, Courtney Ramirez, Tanika Jones, Sandra Teeter, Nessa Vercillo, Jim Wiggins, Cara Steiner, and many others have given so much time, good humor, and support to me. Two dear colleagues, Joan Kingson and William Cartwright, died prematurely while working on behalf of the community. I am deeply grateful for their examples of how to live. I became quite close to Joan, first when she analyzed the translation needs of non-English speaking clients and, later, while she stood up to the cancer that finally took her. She was one of the most generous and kind people I have ever known, who cared about this work even on her deathbed.

I have also benefited from the mentorship of some leaders in anthropology and in the intersection of infectious disease, health, and behavior. Joan Ablon, Fred Dunn, Chan Dawson, Julius Schachter, Art Reingold, and both Nevin and Susan Scrimshaw meant more than I can ever say in shaping my work. George Foster, the father of the sub-discipline of medical anthropology, died while I was writing this manuscript. Even into his 90s he took the time to read and comment on my work and I miss him so very much.

One of the best decisions I ever made was to marry Robert A. Rubinstein, a fellow anthropologist and my best friend. He collaborated on much of the research described herein and continually encouraged me to write this book. He brings me coffee in bed every morning and often served me dinner at my computer while I wrote. Both Robert and I would say that our greatest collaboration is being parents to Helen Lane Rubinstein, our daughter. Helen acted in infant mortality prevention television commercials my colleagues and I produced, pre-tested our health education materials for reading comprehension, and assisted with research on the types of food available in corner markets in Syracuse. I am blessed, indeed, to have these two in my life.

Finally, I am most grateful to Dean Birkenkamp, Beth Davis, and Dianne Ewing for their incomparable editorial guidance.

Chapter One

Introduction

She was seventeen, two months pregnant, and he was nineteen when the police battered down the door of her apartment to arrest him. They were both from loving families, who worked hard, attended church, and were well known in the community. Syracuse at the end of the 1990s had the twin tragedies of a collapsed legitimate economy combined with swelling illicit drug markets, in which her boyfriend became entangled. She was attracted to his "thug" swagger, sporting diamonds and the confidence that cash can provide. But he was also smart and caring, values that she knew her family would appreciate. She had become pregnant after his first arrest, in her adolescent denial not believing that either pregnancy or prison was a real possibility. When she told them about her pregnancy, her parents said they would support whatever decision she would make, but in their clear-eyed assessment of the difficulties ahead of her, they offered to pay for an abortion. Her baby's father, via a collect call from the county jail, begged her, "Please don't terminate my baby." She continued with her pregnancy, beginning with making an appointment for prenatal care. For a seventeen-year old she was remarkably capable, working part time while attending high school and visiting her boyfriend, first in the county jail and then the state correctional facility, every week. Her mother attended the birth of her child, while her baby's father listened over the phone from prison, where he remains today. Her baby was full term and healthy. Her baby's father never had his name entered on the birth certificate, because, being unmarried, to enter his name would require his notarized signature or his presence. Neither he nor his family has provided any financial help to her, but she has accepted an average of $200 in collect phone calls from him each month of his incarceration. She feels that the love and support he has given her in those telephone calls, and the frequent visits she makes with her child to him in prison, have kept him involved as a father to her child for the past seven years.[1]

The case study, above, is the story of an African American woman in Syracuse, New York. The woman, who I will call Mae and who is remarkably resourceful and intelligent, currently works, attends college part time, and supports her child single-handedly. Mae's success in mothering her son—despite poverty and an incarcerated partner—is evidenced by his health, early reading ability, wide vocabulary, and self-confidence. Many of the young single mothers I have met—like Mae—struggle heroically to provide for their children's emotional, social, and financial needs. Despite the mothers' efforts, high infant death, violent neighborhoods, dilapidated rental housing, failing schools, and missing fathers are often insurmountable obstacles.

Syracuse, in central New York State, has been characterized as a "typical ... American mid-sized city," and is routinely used as a test market for consumer goods.[2] Casual visitors often remark on the lush green summer foliage, the parks, the beautifully preserved nineteenth-century architecture, and even the quality of our restaurants. Hidden from view, invisible even to many long-term residents, is the poverty and unequal mortality of people of color. Syracuse has spiraled downward economically in recent decades, with the loss of industry and concomitant loss of jobs. These fiscal problems have hit worst the communities of color, which make up about one third of the city.[3] African Americans and Latinos have been pushed out of their former homes due to urban renewal, into decaying neighborhoods without grocery markets, with the highest lead poisoning in the city, and that are served by inadequate schools.[4] Many residents of these impoverished parts of the city see their only economic hope in the state-run lottery, on which they spend an inordinate part of their meager earnings.[5] Some younger males find employment in the illicit drug markets, which draw customers from all parts of the city and the suburbs. Less than one third of students get their high school diploma in June after four years of education; some graduate high school later, some earn a GED, and some never finish.[6]

Following urban renewal and increasing unemployment, in 1973 New York State implemented the "Rockefeller Drug Laws," mandating lengthy prison sentences for possession or sale of illicit substances.[7] Incarceration rates among African Americans have tripled since that time and female-headed households have doubled.[8] Young males of color began experiencing arrest and jail time as a rite of passage to adulthood. Today's incarcerated adolescent males are the second, and in some families the third, generation of children who were brought to the correctional facility on visiting day to meet their fathers.

Rather than being deviant, incarceration of males of color between age sixteen and thirty has become normal. As a result, people of color are facing the "prisonization" of their communities.[9] Prison fashion can be seen among young males, who favor clothing several sizes too large. Young women say that they are attracted to the "thug" look in males and especially the "buffed" bodies of the newly released.[10] Large numbers of the community cannot vote, due to the felony disenfranchisement penalty.[11] Women are often the main bread-winners, because males have not gained marketable job skills in jail. Disproportionate incarceration may also be the key risk factor in the alarming rise of HIV and hepatitis B and C among African American women and Latinas; all of the behavioral risks for transmission of these blood- and semen-born infections occur in prisons and jails, where the usual public health protections are illegal and where the rate of infection among inmates reaches between five and ten times that in the community.[12]

African American and Latino babies die two and one half times as often as white babies in Syracuse.[13] Infant mortality is too often addressed as if it were an isolated problem, rather than part of a repeating pattern of higher mortality throughout the life span, inadequate education, disproportionate incarceration, substandard housing, and unemployment. The stories and the data in this book center on Syracuse, New York, from 1997 to 2003 and show that low birth weight, premature birth, and infant death are a part of life patterns resulting from systemic discrimination in all of our social institutions. This unequal treatment increases the accumulation of risk over a lifetime and, in some cases, is passed on to the next generation.[14]

In an analysis by the Commonwealth Fund, comparing the 2002 infant mortality rates (IMR) of twenty-three developed nations, the United States ranked last.[15] Compared with Iceland's IMR of 2.2 infant deaths per 1,000 live births, the lowest of the twenty-three countries, the United States's rate was 7.0. The study showed considerable variation among states in the United States, which ranged from 5.3 to 9.1. By 2004, the U.S. rate had inched down to 6.78 per 1,000 live births, with New York State's rate nearly matching that in Texas, Kentucky, and Arizona.[16] UNICEF, which in 2007 ranked the United States next to last among twenty-two "rich countries" in measures of child well-being, said, "Significant in itself, the infant mortality rate can also be interpreted as a measure of how well each country lives up to the ideal of protecting every pregnancy, including pregnancies in its marginalized populations."[17] Social scientists and international health specialists use the infant mortality rate of a region either alone or grouped with other measures to evaluate the socioeconomic development, as well as the degree of social inequality, in that region. By this measure, Syracuse, New York, faces serious problems, which it shares with many other United States cities.

The conceptual framework for this work is structural violence, a theory elaborated by Galtung[18] and further defined by Weigert,[19] as "preventable harm or damage … where there is no actor committing the violence or where it is not meaningful to search for the actor(s); such violence emerges from the unequal distribution of power and resources or, in other words, is said to be built into the structure(s)." Structural violence encompasses institutional racism, relative deprivation in food or health care, disease-ridden environments, and stigmatizing social norms. The "search for actors" to blame obscures the *preventable harm* in macro-level elements—bureaucracies, institutions, environments, policies—that form the context in which disproportionate illness and death occur. Steven Steinberg argues that racism is "imbedded in major institutions" and that "liberal" analysts have ignored the racism that is built into the social fabric of society.[20] As children on the schoolyard we often chanted, "Sticks and stones can break my bones, but words can never hurt me," when a classmate would shout insults. Too often racism, if considered at all, is conceived of as overt behavior of one individual toward another, typically in the form of insulting language. Structural violence in Syracuse—more sticks and stones than words—is a form of racism that is less visible, but more pernicious than overt verbal insults. Census data indicate profound economic and educational disparity among people of color in Syracuse; criminal justice data indicate that African Americans and Latinos are many times more likely to be incarcerated than their white neighbors. This inequality forms the context of higher African American and Latino infant death and poorer health for many of the survivors.

Who Gets Sick? Who Dies?

As one of his top five priorities, former Surgeon General Dr. David Satcher called for research and intervention to eliminate disparities in health and survival related to race and minority status. In response to Dr. Satcher's call, a landmark study by the Institute of Medicine, *Unequal Treatment,* documented in a wealth of detail how people of color are treated differently by physicians, clinics, and hospitals in ways that are detrimental to their health.[21] Among the physicians, nurses, and other health professionals with whom I work in Syracuse, this study is receiving serious consideration, as it should. Access to and receipt of quality healthcare are critically important. But health is a bigger issue than healthcare. While access to good quality healthcare cannot be overestimated, healthcare alone cannot make up for disease-inducing environments. Syracuse, a city of fewer than 150,000 residents, has five hospitals providing world-class medical care. Three of these hospitals offer labor and delivery services, and two of them feature neonatal intensive care units. Yet, within two miles of these sophisticated medical facilities sit neighborhoods with among the highest rates of infant death in the United States. Clearly, we need to look beyond the clinic and hospital, to the neighborhoods, schools, correctional facilities, and policies that create the context in which lives are lived. It is this crucible of disadvantage and discrimination that makes people of color sick. The stories and statistics in this book focus on the neighborhood and environmental risks that lead to disproportionate infant death among the impoverished residents of Syracuse. I do not address the many healthcare and clinical interventions—from prenatal care to testing for gestational diabetes—that also help women to deliver healthy babies. A plethora of books and articles cover prenatal and obstetrical care and few scholars doubt its value.[22] Very few published works describe the impact of ecological and social disadvantage on infant death. This book fills that gap.

Although this policy focus on health disparities only began at the turn of the millennium, unequal health of the poor, and most profoundly people of color, has been recognized at least since public health's beginning in the nineteenth century. I became aware of the issue in 1972, as a first-year nurse on the pediatric ward at Boston City Hospital. There, I cared for children whose reoccurring admissions for lead poisoning resulted from their repeatedly being returned to the same apartments where lead-based paint crumbled into powder around doors and windowsills. Children were admitted with multiple fractures from being hit by cars while playing on city streets and others were nearly killed by gunshots. Two Puerto Rican sisters—ages three and five—could not escape the blaze in the tenement that was their home because the fire escape door had been nailed shut, blocking their escape from the burning building. Third degree burns—covering the faces, hands, and nearly three quarters of the skin on their bodies—healed into thick bands of scar that contrasted shockingly with the colorful ribbons tied in their tightly curled pigtails.

Most of the school-age children were barely literate, stumbling over simple words in the books we encouraged them to read. The Puerto Rican children were also unable to read the Spanish-language comic books we obtained for them, thinking that perhaps they were better educated in their native language. In an effort to coax their mastery of arithmetic, I taught the children blackjack during slow periods on the ward. It was during that year that I realized that medicine, surgery, and advanced technology were often missing the point, coming too late, and patching up children damaged by their environments, only to send them back to those environments. I had grown up in what at that time was an all-white, largely working class suburb of Boston, which was both fewer than ten miles and a whole world away from the Roxbury, Mission Hill, Dorchester, and South Boston neighborhoods served by Boston City Hospital in that era.

Leaving Boston for California, I returned to school, earning a doctorate in medical anthropology and an MPH in epidemiology. I lived and worked in Egypt for five years, conducting research on gender and health, while serving as a Ford Foundation Program Officer for Child Survival and Reproductive Health for the Middle East. Since 1992, most of my work has been in the United States, with brief consultancies in the Middle East. I was part of a team that evaluated needle exchange programs for injection drug users in the United States and Canada, spent six years as a behavioral scientist in a county health department, and conducted research and designed programs to eliminate the gap in health and survival facing people of color in Syracuse, New York. I gradually realized that the differences in the causes of poor health between Egypt and Syracuse—between the so-called "developing world" and the "developed"—are overrated. The real differences are between those whose lives matter and those whose sickness and death are nearly invisible.

For example, I wrote the following field notes in 2000, while working as a short-term consultant on maternal mortality reduction in Ministry of Health hospitals in Upper Egypt—the poorest part of Egypt, which is actually in the southern part of the country, taking its name from the south to north flow of the Nile:

1:00 a.m.: I was walking through the hospital's empty reception-emergency area, and came upon a group of people all yelling at once, half dragging a pregnant woman and being led by the hospital gatekeeper through the darkened first floor of the hospital to the elevator. The elevator doors remained shut, however, despite numerous pressings of buttons, banging and yelling for attention—the elevator operator, peacefully napping in a hidden corner, couldn't hear their clamor. We climbed the two flights to the delivery area, pulling and pushing the laboring woman who paused with each pain, arriving breathless, all calling at once to the lone first-year obstetrical resident, who was meanwhile massaging the fundus of yet another just-delivered woman, in an effort to stanch her bleeding. The only other staff on duty—two nurses, inexperienced and under age twenty, and an elderly cleaning woman—helped the newly-arrived woman onto a delivery table, sternly admonishing her chaotic relatives to wait in the hall. The woman's lips stuck to her teeth, she was so dehydrated. The young female resident turned from the woman whose hemorrhaging had slowed to a trickle and proceeded to deliver the baby of the newly arrived woman. The resident urged the nurses and cleaning woman to push on the woman's abdomen to assist the baby's exit, a potentially dangerous maneuver for the mother, and all murmured "*Al hamdu lellah*" (praises to God), when the baby emerged amidst a gush of brown, meconium-stained amniotic fluid. The resident handed the baby to the nurses and cleaner, who shook and slapped the infant to bring on its first breath. Unaware of meconium's risk, the nurses did not suction the baby's mouth and trachea, so the infant's first breath drew the acid fluid deep into its lungs. When the swaddled babe was presented to the grateful kin, their ululations echoed in the hospital corridor.

Is there any doubt that if men got pregnant and delivered babies the care and resources allocated would be greater? When the worldwide effort to prevent maternal mortality—the so-called "Safe Motherhood Initiative"—began in 1987, one of the key rationales for the focus on preventing the pregnancy-related death of women was stated as, "If a mother dies giving birth, then her baby is more likely to die."[23] The death of the woman herself was viewed as an insufficient reason for action; her role as a mother was the redeeming factor in devoting resources to her health. In fact, more women died from pregnancy and childbirth during the twentieth century in the United States than military personnel during wars.[24] Yet, to my knowledge there is no monument for a woman who died bringing forth life, no scholarship in her name, no prayer or blessing or poem, no public recognition. In Europe, prior to the modern era, women who died in childbirth—and thus died in an impure state, according to the book of Leviticus—could be denied burial in sacred church grounds.[25] Clearly, gender, the differential value and socially-prescribed roles of females and males, influences the quality and quantity of healthcare *and* the many other aspects of life that promote good health, such as food, education, housing, and employment.

Let's look now at race, or more properly, racism in New York State, by asking the question, "If African Americans had the same death rates at each age as white residents of Onondaga County, where Syracuse is located, how many more would be alive?" Using data from the New York State Vital Records and the U.S. Census 2000, I calculated the answer to this question for the year 2000: 126 African Americans—75 males and 51 females—would still be alive on January 1, 2001, if they had the same death rates as their white neighbors. These lives lost are invisible to all but the family members and friends of the deceased. No governmental investigation sought the causes for their untimely deaths; no memorials remind us of their loss. And this was just one year in a pattern that likely repeats every year. In epidemiology, we call such deaths "excess mortality," meaning those fatalities that are over and above what would be expected, which is a way to distance ourselves from the implications of so many lives prematurely ended. Anyone who has lost a loved one knows that every death is a tragedy. The year 2000 was actually a pretty good year in terms of African American deaths, in that fewer babies died that year than in the several previous years. So, the 126 African

Americans who died in 2000 represent a smaller number than many other years. The deaths occurred to African Americans of all ages, and their death certificates recorded a diverse set of causes, from premature birth among the infants to complications of diabetes among the elders. The one factor that they shared was being African American, a category that is largely social and in the United States reflects a history of disadvantage. "Race" is a pre–nineteenth century taxonomic construct used by early European adventurers to explain to themselves differences in physical appearance and to justify the European colonial land grabs.[26] The Human Genome Project failed to find a gene that mapped onto races as sub-groups of our species.[27] The excess mortality of African Americans is not due to race as a biological difference, but to racism as a source of inequality in the raw materials of health, including education, food, employment, safe housing, dignity, and healthcare. The thread that connects a poor, rural Egyptian woman nearly dying during childbirth with urban African Americans' disproportionate mortality is that in both cases the lives of those at risk are devalued, resulting in insufficient effort to promote their health or save their lives.

Disciplinary Discourses: Public Health, Bioethics, and Anthropology

Bourdieu, in *A Theory of Practice,* calls for the analysis of *habitus,* by which he means the enactment of cultural patterns in daily life.[28] Produced by collective history, the *habitus* often reinforces social hierarchies. Both public health and bioethics have been profoundly influenced by the *habitus* of individualism, which is so intrinsic to American culture that it is like the air we breathe. The roots of individualism reach back into the European "enlightenment" tradition, beginning in the seventeenth century, in which philosophers questioned both religious and feudal hegemony.[29] Despite its transatlantic roots, scholars commonly identify the United States as the locus of individualism's full flowering. Alexis de Tocqueville, upon touring America, praised the "individualism" that he saw occurring under democratic equality, where each person gained "sufficient education and fortune to satisfy their needs."[30] Germinal American thinkers—Henry David Thoreau[31] in *Civil Disobedience,* Ralph Waldo

Emerson[32] in *Self-Reliance,* and Elizabeth Cady Stanton[33] in *The Declaration of Sentiments*—argued for the right and responsibility of men, and, in Stanton's case of women, for self-determination. It would not be an exaggeration to say that individualism represents a core element of American national culture.

Public health texts extol the twin trilogies of person-place-time and host-agent-environment to explain the transmission of diseases. Despite public health's stated devotion to these tripartite mantras, place and environment are given short shrift. As a result, public health's predominant focus on individual lifestyle-risk factors in health behavior—biomedical individualism[34]—largely ignores the institutional disadvantages constraining healthy behavior among racial and ethnic groups. Bioethics analyses also privilege such individual-level healthcare concerns as assisted suicide, end-of-life decision making, organ transplantation, and informed consent. A search of the citation database *Bioethics Line,* for articles in which one or more of the four bioethical principles—autonomy, beneficence, non-maleficence, and justice—was coded as a key word found that autonomy—or a concern with *individual* agency—was the focus of more than half of the studies, whereas less than one quarter centered on justice.[35] Bioethicists whose work addressed justice, moreover, tended to focus on access to highly technological medical treatments like in vitro fertilization or liver transplants.

Yet, the roots of both disciplines emerged from social justice struggles. Public health's nineteenth century roots in the sanitary reform movement and control of tuberculosis among tenement dwellers directly linked impoverished living conditions with sickness and resulted in improvements in housing and nutrition for the poor.[36] Bioethics' beginning in the 1947 Nuremberg Code of Bioethics was a response to the Nazi abuses in medical research.[37]

Anthropology's abiding concerns with social structure and the context of power negotiations provides a counterbalance to this individual-level focus and a theoretical framework for understanding both macro-level disadvantages associated with disproportionate infant death, and individual-level parental perceptions about their struggle to nurture their children in unhealthy environments. Several of my colleagues have produced work that integrates the interpretive strength of ethnography with a clear-eyed assessment of inequality in the study of biomedically-defined diseases. Susan Scrimshaw and her colleagues conducted groundbreaking work linking poverty and infant death, and Scrimshaw also did research on biocultural factors in prematurity and low birth weight.[38] Marcia Inhorn's work on infertility and patriarchy integrates Middle Eastern women's narratives of their struggles to conceive with clinical analysis of the causes of their barrenness and a critique of the now-global market in reproductive technologies.[39] Merrill Singer[40] links the lived experience of substance abusers in Hartford, Connecticut—stigmatized and exposed to HIV/AIDS and violence—with clear analyses of how powerlessness increases their risk of infection, while it decreases their abilities to protect themselves. Paul Farmer's[41] body of work on structural violence and infectious disease shows how inequality, institutional discrimination, gender bias, and racism are root causes of HIV/AIDS in Haiti and tuberculosis in Russia. William Dressler[42] ties together political ecology, social stigma, and social structure with an in-depth understanding of the lived experience of hypertension. My work on racial and ethnic disparities in infant death draws on these multi-faceted and multi-leveled methodologies.

Syracuse Healthy Start

In 1985–1987, infant mortality in Syracuse averaged fifteen infant deaths per 1,000 live births, making it the fourth worst of fifty-six small United States cities surveyed by the Children's Defense Fund.[43] African American infant death was higher still; the African American infant mortality rate in Syracuse reached 30.8 per 1,000 live births during 1985–1987, the worst of forty-seven other United States comparably-sized cities. Many intervention programs began or expanded in response to this crisis. The City of Syracuse Commission on Women was the first to publicly address the alarming rates and to call on health and human service leaders to work with them on this critical issue. The county health department conducted an Infant Mortality Review (1991–1993). A state-funded perinatal network—Family Ties Network, Inc.—and three case management agencies began serving impoverished pregnant women and families with infants.[44] By 1997, the Syracuse African American infant mortality had dropped to 22.7 per 1,000 live births, which, although a great improvement over the previous decade, was still higher than

Tonga, Fiji, and Micronesia for that year, according to *The State of the World's Children 1997.*[45] African American infants died nearly three times as often as white infants, a disparity that was larger than any other upstate New York county and the nation as a whole.

I arrived in Syracuse in the fall of 1996 and joined the Onondaga County Health Department to write grants for infant mortality reduction. Two weeks before I visited his office to seek employment, the county-commissioner of health had given a press conference in which he committed his administration to reducing infant mortality. Since I had a wealth of maternal and child health experience, albeit most of it overseas, I was hired on the spot.

I began in the way that anthropologists have long initiated fieldwork in a new community. I started by meeting as many people as possible, including public health and elected officials, community leaders, minority agency staff, home visiting nurses, outreach workers, and adolescent group facilitators. I asked each person why they thought Syracuse had so many babies dying, then listened, took notes, and asked who else they thought I should speak with. I collected available statistics on many aspects of the city, trying to piece together a coherent picture of it. With the county director of statistics and surveillance, Don Cibula, Ph.D., I examined in detail the death-certificate data for the 207 county-wide infant deaths in the preceding twenty-eight months. I requested, and was given permission, to go through the medical examiner's files on infant deaths for 1996, which were only in hard-copy paper archives at that time. The infant mortality review, conducted by the health department from 1991 to 1993, had been only partially analyzed and three boxes of the review's original files remained in storage. I requested these boxes and read through the medical charts of each of those deceased infants. With each new idea, or hunch, about what was going on, I searched through the medical literature and made telephone calls to health researchers around the country to find out, as much as possible, what was known about the issue. Two months after starting this work—on December 20, 1996—I submitted a memo to the commissioner of health detailing the causes of infant death, maternal risk factors, gaps in services, and need for provider education. Among the key findings in the memo were that despite well-intentioned staff in numerous agencies, pregnant women had to find their way through a maze of fragmented programs, many of which gave health advice that contradicted that of other programs.

A second issue was that most of the mothers whose babies had died from Sudden Infant Death Syndrome (SIDS) had not completed high school and more than half smoked cigarettes, two risk factors that we integrated into our subsequent SIDS prevention work. The memo also described my suspicion that something infectious seemed to be happening when women repeatedly miscarried, because so many of the pathology reports in the medical records documented "chorioamnionitis," meaning that the amniotic sac was inflamed and probably infected. These issues formed the basis of much further analysis and subsequently developed interventions, which are described in later chapters.

During this initial phase, I met with several community groups to discuss these preliminary findings and get feedback, a process which I have continued to do on a regular basis ever since. In February 1997, one of the public health nurses with whom I had met gave me a notice issued by the Health Resources and Services Administration of a request for proposals to fund Healthy Start projects. I brought the notice to the commissioner of health, but he and the other county officials were not convinced it would be worth it to devote staff time to writing a proposal for what they considered "a long shot." However, the "bidder's conference" for all potential grantees was to be held in Washington, D.C., on February 28 and the health department allowed me to go. The truth was that no other staff member was willing to pay up front for the trip and wait to be reimbursed, which took many months. Back from the bidder's conference, I was able to convince the county health department administration that we should submit a proposal. I led the team that wrote the proposal, bringing together many of the agencies and people with whom I had been meeting and from whom I had been learning. In September 1997, Onondaga County was awarded a nearly $5 million Healthy Start grant to run for four years, 1997–2001.[46] In 2001, I led the team that wrote a second grant, which was awarded for another four years for $3.8 million.[47] From 1997-2002, I served as Director of Syracuse Healthy Start (SHS); the analyses in this book focus on those years. SHS continues to provide care to pregnant women and their families.

SHS brought together more than thirty agencies to coordinate and enhance the care of pregnant women and families with infants throughout Syracuse. Rather than put in place a new and separate program, we sought to integrate and enhance the many existing, but fragmented, programs. These included four case management services and four obstetrical clinics serving the majority of lower socioeconomic, teen, and minority clients. SHS staff and partners developed a community-based consortium to advise the project and made links where there had been none, for example, between drug and alcohol treatment and obstetrical providers, who should have been coordinating their services all along. We revamped the literacy level, and the clarity, of health education materials[48] across multiple agencies; introduced a coordinated risk screening and referral protocol; trained local hair stylists in infant mortality prevention and domestic violence recognition, so that they could help their clients; and created five television commercials that aired during *Jerry Springer* and *Judge Judy.*

By 2000, the network of SHS partner agencies was reaching half of all pregnant women in the City of Syracuse with enhanced services. By 2000, infant mortality in Syracuse decreased by 25 percent and we celebrated this success, although, since SHS was not a controlled research study, we cannot say what part of the improvement was due to program efforts. By 2001, however, welfare reform had drastically reduced the proportion of pregnant women in Syracuse receiving public assistance.[49] Later that year, the aftermath of the Twin Towers and Pentagon bombings diverted funding from traditional public health efforts to bioterrorism preparedness. Month by month in 2001 we frantically read the mounting death certificates of babies and by the end of the year we realized that infant deaths had again peaked. We realized, with painful clarity, that the prevention of infant death, like many public health achievements, is not a goal that can be reached once and for all. Our society tends to think of progress toward social objectives in terms of military campaigns, or even holy crusades, like the "war on drugs" or the "war on poverty." But babies are conceived and born minute by minute and programs developed and funded to enhance their survival must be guided by a different metaphor than war. Rather than a battle, with an initial confrontation leading sooner or later to a declaration of victory and medals to be displayed under glass, the prevention of infant death is more like housework. It will never finally be achieved, there will always remain more to be done, and many of the people working hardest—the community health workers, the public health nurses, clinic social workers, and labor and delivery staff—will not receive medals.

In one of our first Healthy Start community outreach efforts we plotted the infant deaths from 1995–1997 on a three-foot by five-foot map of the City of Syracuse, which had street names enabling project area residents to locate their homes and neighborhoods. We placed a dot on the map for each dead baby. During 1995 to 1997, four census tracts on the south and southwest part of the city had the highest numbers of infant deaths in the city. We held more than thirty meetings in those four census tracts with clergy and congregants of faith communities, neighborhood action councils, Early Headstart mothers, the Syracuse chapter of the Association for Black Social Workers, and many others. At every meeting women would kneel before the map and gently stroke the areas where the dots clustered; we felt that the map was somewhat like the AIDS quilt, in that it made otherwise dehumanized statistics visible and easily understood.

At these meetings community members would ask me, "Why are our babies dying?" They would sometimes speculate on esoteric causes, asking if there was something in the air or water that put them at risk. All of my subsequent work, the basis of the material presented in this book, has been an effort to answer this question.

Also, during 1997, I joined the county's newly created Child Fatality Review Team, which meets monthly to review all cases of potentially preventable infant and child death (age 0 to 18).[50] In the first two years of this work, I made numerous home visits to bereaved families to find out more about how the deaths occurred and how such tragedies might be prevented in the future. I was initially more comfortable making home visits than many of the other team members, in part due to my training in anthropological fieldwork techniques, which are often carried out though visiting and unstructured conversation. I had also traversed grief's alternating waves of numbness and anguish, because my first baby had been stillborn; mourning the unspeakable loss of a child was sadly familiar, rather than frightening, terrain. Initially, the other team members, who ranged from leading physicians to attorneys in the office of the district attorney, wanted me to have a formal list of questions that I would ask the families. When I said that I would address the key areas that the team thought were relevant, but did not envision my visits as being structured by a formal questionnaire, they asked in puzzlement, "What will you say?" I responded that I would say, "I am so very sorry for your loss," and "Can you tell me how it happened?" This question proved critical in helping us to understand what policy changes or public education needed to be implemented to reduce the potential for similar preventable fatalities. The Onondaga County Child Fatality Review Team thus structured its deliberations on a qualitative approach to death review, which made it different from the quantitative, highly structured models being used by many of the fetal and infant mortality review and child fatality review teams in other localities. The problem with the structured questions, as anthropologists are certainly aware, is that you can answer them all and still not really know what happened. The goal of such fatality review teams is not simply to collect more data on the known variables, but to have a multidisciplinary group review the unique elements of each case, sifting through the often-horrendous details to get insights about prevention.

Health Disparities Research

Since 2001, I have worked with a group of colleagues to address racial and ethnic health disparities spanning five research projects. Many of the research questions addressed in these subsequent studies came from working closely with pregnant women and families of infants as a part of Syracuse Healthy Start. The data analyses that I conducted for the Syracuse Healthy Start assessment of racial disparity in infant death led me to consider the health and survival of other family members in the communities of color. Not surprisingly, disparities in health and survival continue throughout the life span, in ways that appear to influence infant mortality. A striking finding is that many of the individual-level health behaviors of white, African American, and Latino individuals do not differ greatly enough to give rise to such large differences in outcome. This finding has led my colleagues and me to further examine environmental risk, cumulative risk, and intergenerational risk, which are all increased by institutional racism.

The first project, funded by HRSA and partially funded by the Program on the Analysis and Resolution of Conflicts of the Maxwell School of Syracuse University, was titled "Innovative Models to Analyze and Address Racial, Ethnic and Geographic Disparities in Maternal and Child Health Outcomes."[51] The goal of this larger study was to use population-level data and program data to identify areas for further analysis in the area of racial and ethnic health disparities. This work integrates epidemiological, environmental, and ethnographic methods, to examine racial and ethnic inequality in low birth weight, prematurity, and infant death, as well as the risk factors associated with those disparities.

A second project, funded by the Centers for Disease Control and Prevention, is an evaluation of the SHS strategies to reduce premature births.[52] During the first four years of SHS work, there was considerable reduction in preterm births among the highest risk groups in Syracuse, but we were not able to pinpoint precisely what intervention, or set of interventions, may have influenced the improvement. In the first year of SHS activity, we asked a leading obstetrician, Richard Aubry, to help craft and head up our interventions. I put Dr. Aubry in touch with Robert Nugent of the National Institutes of Health, who had generously taken my calls and advised me during the writing of the SHS grant on the issue of infections and premature births. Dr. Nugent and his colleagues were in the midst of ground-breaking studies on the role of bacterial vaginosis (BV), a reproductive tract infection, in precipitating preterm labor. African American women have consistently been found to have higher rates of BV, which is believed to be a factor in their greater numbers of preterm births. Dr. Aubry developed a protocol to screen women in the SHS project for BV at the first prenatal visit and to treat those who were infected, which he recommended and taught to the providers in all four clinics serving the majority of SHS pregnant participants. The CDC-funded evaluation demonstrated that BV screening and treatment of infected women early in the pregnancy reduced premature births by about 50 percent.[53]

A third project is a study of asthma triggers in infancy, funded by the Environmental Protection Agency.[54] Asthma, which has dramatically increased in recent years, affects many more minority children than white children. We enrolled 135 pregnant women and followed them through to their infants' first birthdays. A pediatric nurse practitioner (PNP) made four home visits to each study family, collecting medical and socioeconomic data, as well as interviewing the parents about their perceptions of their health and the health in their communities. The PNP also collected urine samples from the babies at each visit, which we tested for cotinine, a metabolite of cigarette smoke. One of our key findings is just how heavily exposed to environmental tobacco smoke the babies were, even when the mother was not a smoker. Babies of non-smoking mothers inhaled the second-hand smoke of their fathers, grandparents, and sometimes even their baby sitters. Some of the cotinine levels in the babies' urine were as high as adults who were actively smoking cigarettes.

Two additional projects examine in greater depth the struggles of pregnant women and their babies' fathers. One of these studies looks at religious faith, or spirituality, as a source of resilience.[55] We know that even in the most difficult circumstances, some people manage to thrive and to raise healthy children; this research seeks to uncover the source of that coping strength. The second study examines in closer detail how many baby's fathers are incarcerated during pregnancy and what other factors lead them to be less involved, or more involved, with their offspring.[56]

My teaching also takes me into the community and helps me to understand how patients navigate our complex, and sometimes quite unfriendly, medical system. From 2003 to 2005, for example, I co-directed the MIRACLE Continuity Elective, a sixteen-month-long course that links first year medical students with pregnant women, whom they follow until the infant's first birthday. Each year I recruited ten pregnant women from our university prenatal clinics and matched them with twenty medical students. I asked the pregnant women to help teach the first year medical students what it is like to be a patient and what it is like to be pregnant, give birth, and learn to be a parent. The students made home visits, got to know the women and their families, and assisted with the birth, all of which enhanced their ability to understand the social and interpersonal context in which their patients live. The families in the program have been diverse; a small number were highly literate, read all about pregnancy, planned their pregnancies, and were financially and emotionally ready to care for an infant. The majority of the pregnancies, however, were unintended and the mothers' financial resources limited; some mothers had drug abuse histories and many smoked cigarettes.

My colleagues and I also collaborate with several community-based agencies working on issues of racial justice and the elimination of health disparities in Syracuse. This community-based work is not entirely separate from our research, in that we use the findings of our research projects to write grants for these agencies or to help develop their programs. In this way, my academic colleagues and I gain critical "real-world" feedback regarding our research ideas and findings.

Many of the research findings and program evaluations that emerged from Syracuse Healthy Start and our subsequent studies have been published in academic journals.[57] Writing this book allows me to present a more complete picture of infant health and survival in Syracuse in the context of structural violence caused by imbedded racism. It is my hope that this book will be useful to community members, who want to better understand the environmental and social context of health inequalities, as well as to students of anthropology, bioethics, and public health.

Several threads run through each of the chapters. First, discrimination based on poverty, and on gender, race, and ethnicity overlap, but they are not the same. Women and people of color with financial resources can afford better health care, food and homes, but their resources cannot entirely protect them. Second, many health risks—such as childhood lead poisoning or asthma—have roots in infancy or the prenatal period. Some health risks grow cumulatively throughout life, in a manner that simple cross-sectional "slice-in-time" analyses do not capture. A few social and health risks become intergenerational, making children suffer from the health inequalities of their parents' early development. Third, looking only at individual responsibility for health and disease is inadequate. A person's knowledge and ability to protect his or her health, while reducing exposure to disease, does not occur in isolation; unsafe, sickness-inducing environments are hard to overcome. History matters and place matters; the context in which people live—their neighborhoods, as well as their culture and social institutions—shapes their health behavior. Finally, racial and ethnic health disparities emerge from unequal healthcare *and* from patterns of discrimination in housing, education, jobs, incarceration, and exposure to environmental toxins. Efforts to decrease healthcare disparities are important. But even if all healthcare disparities were eliminated, unequal health and survival would remain if we did not address the structural violence and embedded racism in environments, policies, and institutions.

Outline of the Chapters

The outline of the chapters is as follows:

Chapter 2, "Lots of Trouble Out Here": This chapter briefly outlines the history of Syracuse with regard to those aspects of the city's past and present that most affect the health of families of color. The after-effects of urban renewal on housing, the closure of food retail outlets in the central city, and the intertwined increase in neighborhood violence and unemployment form the crucible in which infant death occurs. This chapter also addresses the poles of tension in Syracuse between socially progressive movements and the often-racist backlash.

Chapter 3, "Math and Biology": This short chapter provides the general reader with the background to understand the rates and causes of infant death. I use stories and my own experience as the mother of a stillborn infant to illustrate many of the concepts. This chapter is designed to bring the average reader up to speed in understanding pregnancy, infant death, and how we measure such outcomes.

Chapter 4, "Risk in Social Context": This chapter addresses how risks emerging from or exacerbated by environmental factors impact the gap in infant mortality between African Americans and European Americans. This chapter examines the extent to which poor and low-income mothers in Syracuse control the risks they face in giving birth to healthy babies. In addition to poverty and racism, I examine welfare reform, substance use, depression, domestic violence, and the problem of inadequate medical translation for those with limited English proficiency. By weaving narratives with ethnographic description of neighborhood risks and the actual rates of each factor in Syracuse, I provide a full description of how such risks fit into the lives of women who experience them.

Chapter 5, "Babies Having Babies": Teen pregnancy, which is blamed for so many of our social ills, was actually decreasing in Syracuse and elsewhere until the beginning of "abstinence-only" funding. Virginity pledges and "just saying no" replaced some of the most effective, comprehensive teen pregnancy prevention programs; since then teen pregnancy has again begun to climb. A number of programs serve pregnant and parenting teens in Syracuse, with what appears to be great success. Teen mothers during 2000–2001 had better birth outcomes and lower infant death than adult mothers, whereas in many other U.S. cities teen mothers have much higher rates than adult mothers of infant death. Despite these gains, some pregnant teens—who often give birth to the babies of adult men—have alarming levels of substance use, sexually transmitted diseases, and school failure. Chapter 5 concludes with an analysis of data from Syracuse linking lead poisoning prior to age three with repeat pregnancy and tobacco use in the teen years. Lead poisoning is an environmental injustice affecting African American children at twice the rate of white children in Syracuse.

Chapter 6, "Health Literacy": The Syracuse City School District graduation rates are among the worst in New York State. Half of adults in Syracuse read at or below the eighth and one quarter at or below the fourth grade level. In Syracuse, as elsewhere, mothers with less education have higher infant death. Yet, the written materials produced by federal, state, and private agencies to instruct parents on how to avoid infant death are above the reading level of more than half of the parents. Syracuse Healthy Start focused specifically on reaching low literacy parents with services, support, and information to prevent infant death. Evaluations with mothers who have not graduated from high school indicate that these programmatic efforts worked.

Chapter 7, "Missing Fathers": In nearly half of African American births in Syracuse the baby's father does not sign his child's birth certificate, compared with about a quarter of white births. Faced with an increasing proportion of single African American mothers, social policy discourse has grown more strident in trying to create incentives that will lead these women to wed, as if their single status was a personal preference that could be changed by social policy bringing forth the right combination of carrots and sticks. Yet, the mathematical fact is that in Syracuse there are fewer African American men than African American women. Two factors account for the dearth of men of color: incarceration and death. Babies whose fathers are missing have higher rates of infant death. Women whose male partners are incarcerated face increased risks of HIV transmission when their partners are released, because of the extremely elevated rates of HIV transmission in correctional facilities. An environmental assessment shows that in neighborhoods where fathers are missing, single motherhood, grandparents caring for their grandchildren, and criminal arrests are widespread. Women's narratives, woven throughout the chapter, describe the experience of birth when the baby's father is incarcerated and the struggle to make relationships work when there are too few men.

Chapter 8, "Food Is Just Decoration": To grow a baby you need healthy food. Unfortunately, since the late 1970s most full service retail food markets in the center of Syracuse have closed. Statistical analyses and ethnographic description demonstrate that in the neighborhoods without access to healthy food, low birth weight births are higher. Corner stores, which are licensed to sell food, instead carry on a lively business in lottery tickets, mentholated cigarettes, and 40 oz. malt liquor. In these corner stores a thick patina of dust covers many of the cereal boxes; observing the inside of one of these stores, a member of my research team commented, "The food in there is just decoration, it is not what they are really selling." Neighborhood violence clusters around these corner stores, because drug dealers also ply their wares in and around the small markets. Markets in the poorest neighborhoods in Syracuse sell the most lottery tickets and have the highest numbers of drug arrests in and around their corner stores. The data in this chapter also demonstrate that where lotto sales are high, low birth weight increases as well.

Chapter 9, "Plenty Blame to Go Around": The story of infant mortality in Syracuse resonates with the problems in many other Northeastern cities, and perhaps with others worldwide. This concluding chapter pulls together what worked in Syracuse and what did not work. The analyses in this book demonstrate that infant mortality occurs in unhealthy environments and, for many low-income families, Syracuse is unhealthy.

A note about the statistical analyses and presentation of data: The research presented herein integrates quantitative and qualitative methods to address each issue. The health disparities addressed by this work focus on disadvantages faced by African Americans and Latinos in Syracuse. Where possible, I present data comparing white, African American, and Latino health risks and outcomes. Some analyses, however, only compare African American and white Syracuse residents, because the number of Latino births per year in Syracuse is too small for accurate statistical calculations. To make this book readable to those without statistical training, I have placed most of the quantitative analyses in the footnotes and described the quantitative findings in plain language in the narrative. Multiple births—twins, triplets, and the occasional set of quadruplets—complicate the statistical analysis of pregnancy and births because babies who share space in their mother's womb are very often born earlier and smaller than singletons, who grew inside of their mothers by themselves. To control for this potential source of bias, many analyses presented in this book are based on singleton babies only. In each case, I identify whether the analysis is based on "singletons only" or "all births."

Notes

1. The opening case study and the quote are drawn from our research, 2001–2003, "Innovative Methods for Assessing Racial and Ethnic Disparity in Maternal and Child Health in Onondaga County, New York." Health Department from the federal Health Resources and Services Administration. Approval was awarded by the SUNY Upstate Medical University IRB.

2. Emmanuel J. Carter Jr., Associate Professor, Faculty of Landscape Architecture, "ESF Projects Aim to Revitalize American Cities." http://fla. esf.edu/people/faculty/carter/revitalize.htm.

3. All demographic data are taken from the U.S. Census 2000.

4. Urban renewal was the topic of one of our research projects. The website "Syracuse Then and Now," http://www.syracusethenandnow.net/, also presents a wealth of historic information and photos of Syracuse before and since urban renewal. Data on lead poisoning is from the NYS DOH, "Eliminating Childhood Lead Poisoning in New York State by 2010," New York State Department of Health (June 2004), http://www. health.state. ny.us/nysdoh/environ/lead/finalplantoc.html..

5. This information is from the New York State Lottery, which my colleagues and I received as a result of a freedom of information request. We asked for and received data on every retail location selling any type of lottery ticket, by year and amount, for the years 2000–2002.

6. Syracuse City School District report cards, http://www.emsc.nysed. gov/repcrd2003/links/d_421800.html. Also see Christopher B. Swanson, *Who Graduates? Who Doesn't? A Statistical Portrait of Public High School Graduation, Class of 2001*, http://www.urban.org/publications/410934.html.

7. M. Mauer, *Race to Incarcerate* (New York: The New Press, 1999).

8. Sandra D. Lane, Robert A. Rubinstein, Robert Keefe, Michael Freedman, Brooke Levandowski, Don Cibula, and Maria Czerwinski, "Marriage Promotion and Missing Men: African American Women in a Demographic Double Bind," *Medical Anthropology Quarterly* 18, no. 4 (December 2004): 405–28.

9. I am grateful to my colleagues at the Center for Community Alternatives, Alan Rosenthal and Marsha Weissman, who told me about the concept of prisonization.

10. This information is drawn from focus group interviews conducted

by Maizie Shaw and Tarah Tapley, of the FACES Program of the Syracuse Model Neighborhood Facility.

11. "Convicted felons in NYS cannot vote while serving their sentences," "Felony Disenfranchisement, The Sentencing Project," http://www.sentencingproject.org/issues_03.cfm.

12. Sandra D. Lane, Rob Keefe, Robert A. Rubinstein, Noah Webster, Alan Rosenthal, Don Cibula, and Jesse Dowdell, "Structural Violence and Racial Disparity in Heterosexual HIV Infection," *Journal of Health Care for the Poor and Underserved* 15, vol. 3 (August 2004): 319–35.

13. Infant death data are from the vital records of the NYS Department of Health. Birth data are from the Regional Perinatal Data System, used as a part of research funded by the Health Resources and Services Administration, with approval of the SUNY Upstate Medical University IRB.

14. See also M. C. Lu and N. Halfon, "Racial and Ethnic Disparities in Birth Outcomes: A Life-Course Perspective," *Maternal Child Health* 7, no. 1 (March 2003): 13–30.

15. Commonwealth Fund National Scorecard on U.S. Health System Performance, 2006, http://www.commonwealthfund.org/usr_doc/Schoen_natscorecard_chartpack_955.pdf?section=4039.

16. T. J. Mathews and Marian F. MacDorman, "Infant Mortality Statistics from the 2004 Period Linked Birth/Infant Death Data Set," *National Vital Statistics Report* 55, no. 14.

17. UNICEF, "Child Poverty in Perspective: An Overview of Child Well-Being in Rich Countries," *Innocenti Report Card* 7 (Florence, UNICEF Innocenti Research Centre, 2007): 13.

18. J. Galtung, "Violence, Peace, and Peace Research," *Journal of Peace Research* 6, no. 3 (1969): 167–91.

19. K. M. Weigert, "Structural Violence," in *Encyclopedia of Violence, Peace, and Conflict,* ed. L. Kurtz (New York: Academic Press, 1999), 3:431–40.

20. Steven Steinberg, *Turning Back: The Retreat from Racial Justice in American Thought and Policy* (Boston: Beacon Press, 1995).

21. Board on Health Sciences Policy, Institute of Medicine, *Unequal Treatment: Confronting Racial and Ethnic Disparities in Health Care* (National Academy Press, 2003).

22. M. C. Lu, V. Tache, G. R. Alexander, M. Kotelchuck, and N. Halfon, "Preventing Low Birth Weight: Is Prenatal Care the Answer?" *Journal of Maternal Fetal Neonatal Medicine* 13, no. 6 (June 2003): 362–80. M. C. Lu, Y. G. Lin, N. M. Prietto, and T. J. Garite, "Elimination of Public Funding of Prenatal Care for Undocumented Immigrants in California: A Cost/Benefit Analysis," *American Journal of Obstetric Gynecology* 182, no. 1, pt. 1 (January 2000): 233–39.

23. S. D. Lane and R. A. Rubinstein, "International Health: Problems and

Programs in Anthropological Perspective," in *Medical Anthropology: Contemporary Theory and Method, Second Edition,* eds. Thomas Johnson and Carolyn Sargent (Westport, Connecticut: Praeger, 1996): 396–423.

24. I calculated the maternal deaths during the twentieth century using vital records data on births and the estimates of maternal deaths in: (1) "Achievements in Public Health, 1900–1999: Healthier Mothers and Babies," *MMWR* 48, no. 38 (October 1, 1999): 849–58 and (2) "Maternal Mortality—United States, 1982–1996," *MMWR* 47, no. 34 (September 04, 1998): 705–7. The source for military deaths is "First Measured Century," PBS, http://www.pbs.org/fmc/book/11government8.htm. Based on these sources, my estimates of the two causes of death during the twentieth century are: Maternal deaths = 978,885; Military deaths = 440,000.

25. "There are also records of a debate whether a woman who had died in giving birth should be buried in the church graveyard if she had died unchurched. Popular custom occasionally had another woman undergoing the ceremony for the woman who had died, but such practice was not favored by the church. It was eventually decided that an unchurched woman could be buried, but in a number of cases they were buried in a special part of the graveyard and superstitious belief had it that women between 15 and 45 were not supposed to be going to that particular part of the graveyard (Franz 241)." Adolph Franz, *Die kirchlichen Benediktionen im Mittelalter,* 2 vols. (Freiburg: Herder, 1909). See also William Coster, "Purity, Profanity and Puritanism: The Churching of Women, 1500–1700," in *Women in the Church,* eds. W. J. Sheils and Diana Wood (Oxford: Blackwell, 1990): 377–87.

26. American Anthropological Association Statement on "Race," http://www.aaanet.org/stmts/racepp.htm.

27. C. D. M. Royal and G. M. Dunston, "Changing the Paradigm from 'Race' to Human Genome Variation" (Nature Publishing Group), http://www.nature.com/ng/journal/v36/n11s/pdf/ng1454.pdf.

28. Pierre Bourdieu, *Outline of a Theory of Practice* (New York and Cambridge: University Press, 1977) and Pierre Bourdieu, *The Logic of Practice* (Stanford, California: Stanford University Press, 1990).

29. 27. Edward O. Wilson, *Consilience: The Unity of Knowledge* (New York: Vintage Books, 1998).

30. Alexis DeTocqueville, *Democracy in America* (New York: Penguin Classics, 2003, original publication 1831).

31. Henry David Thoreau, *Civil Disobedience and Other Essays* (New York: Dover Publications, 1849/1993).

32. Ralph Waldo Emerson, *Self-Reliance and Other Essays* (New York: Dover Publications, 1841/1993).

33. Elizabeth Cady Stanton, *The Declaration of Sentiments (Address at the*

First Women's Rights Convention) (1848), http://www.libertynet.org./edcivic/stanton.html (accessed April 9, 2000).

34. I believe that Aral coined this phrase, in S. O. Aral, "Determinants of STD Epidemics: Implications for Phase Appropriate Intervention Strategies, *Sexually Transmitted Infections* 78, supplement 1 (2002): 3–13.

35. S. D. Lane, R. A. Rubinstein, D. Cibula and N. Webster, "Toward a Public Health Approach to Bioethics, Ethics and Anthropology: Facing Future Issues in Human Biology, Globalism, and Cultural Property," *Annals of the New York Academy of Sciences* 925 (2000): 25–36.

36. J. W. Leavitt, "The Wasteland: Garbage and Sanitary Reform in the Nineteenth-Century American City," *Journal of Historical Medical Allied Science* 35, no. 4 (October 1980): 431–52.

37. B. A. Fischer IV, "A Summary of Important Documents in the Field of Research Ethics," *Schizophrenia Bulletin* 32, no. 1 (January 2006): 69–80. E-publication September 28, 2005.

38. S. C. M. Scrimshaw, "Infant Mortality and Behavior in the Regulation of Family Size," *Population and Development Review* 4, no. 3 (September 1978): 383–403; M. Lobel, C. Dunkel-Schetter, and S. C. M. Scrimshaw, "Prenatal Maternal Stress and Prematurity: A Prospective Study of Socio-economically Disadvantaged Women," *Health Psychology* 11, no. 1 (1992): 32–40; R. E. Zambrana, C. Dunkel-Schetter, N. Collins, and S. C. Scrimshaw, "Mediators of Ethnic-Associated Differences in Infant Birth Weight," *Journal of Urban Health* 75, no. 1 (March 1999): 102–116.

39. M. C. Inhorn, *Infertility and Patriarchy: The Cultural Politics of Gender and Family Life in Egypt* (University of Pennsylvania Press, 1996).

40. M. C. Singer, P. I. Erickson, L. Badiane, R. Diaz, D. Ortiz, T. Abraham, and A. M. Nicolaysen, "Syndemics, Sex and the City: Understanding Sexually Transmitted Diseases in Social and Cultural Context, *Social Science and Medicine* (forthcoming); Merrill Singer, ed., *The Political Economy of AIDS* (Amityville, New York: Baywood Publishing Co., 1997); M. Singer, T. Stopka, S. Shaw, C. Santelices, D. Buchanan, W. Teng, K. Khoshnood, and R. Heimer, "Lessons from the Field: From Research to Application in the Fight Against AIDS among Injection Drug Users in Three New England Cities," Human Organization 64, no. 2 (2005): 179–91.

41. Paul Farmer, *Infections and Inequalities: The Modern Plagues* (Berkeley, California: University of California Press, 1999); Paul Farmer "An Anthropology of Structural Violence: Sidney W. Mintz Lecture for 2001," *Current Anthropology* 45, no 3 (2001): 305–25.

42. William W. Dressler, *Stress and Adaptation in the Context of Culture: Depression in a Southern Black Community* (Albany, N.Y.: State University of New York Press, 1991); Clarence C. Gravlee and William W. Dressler, "Skin Pigmentation, Self-Perceived Color, and Arterial Blood Pressure in Puerto

Rico," *American Journal of Human Biology* 17 (2005): 195–206; William W. Dressler and José Ernesto dos Santos, "Social and Cultural Dimensions of Hypertension in Brazil: A Review," *Cadernos de Saúde Pública* 16 (2000): 303–15.

43. S. D. Lane, D. Cibula, L. P. Milano, M. Shaw, B. Bourgeois, F. Schweitzer, C. Steiner, K. Dygert, K. Demott, K. Wilson, R. Gregg, N. Webster, D. Milton, R. Aubry, and L. F. Novick, "Racial and Ethnic Disparities in Infant Mortality: Risk in Social Context," *Journal of Public Health Management and Practice* 7, no. 3 (2001): 30–46.

44. These programs included the Comprehensive Medicaid Case Management program, the Community Health Worker Program, and the Salvation Army Teen Support and Advocacy, which are all coordinated by the ACCESS Center of the Department of Social Services.

45. UNICEF, 1997, http://www.unicef.org/sowc97/.

46. "Syracuse Healthy Start," From the Health Resources and Services Agency to the Onondaga County Health Department, $5 million over four years (1997–2001). I led the team that wrote the grant and served as project director.

47. "Eliminating Racial, Ethnic and Geographic Disparities in Maternal and Child Health," From the Health Resources and Services Agency to the Onondaga County Health Department, $3.8 million over four years (2001–2005). I led the team that wrote the grant and served as project director (2001–2002).

48. B. Levandowski, P. Sharma, S. D. Lane, N. Webster, A. Nestor, D. Cibula, and S. Huntington, "Parental Literacy and Infant Health: An Evidence-Based Healthy Start Intervention," *Health Promotion Practice* 7 no. 1 (2006): 95–102.

49. Data on pregnant women receiving public assistance are drawn from the Regional Perinatal Data System, 1996–2003. Used with approval of the SUNY Upstate Medical University IRB.

50. I also wrote three grants for the activities of this group, two of which were funded by the NYS Office of Child and Family Services.

51. "Innovative Methods for Assessing Racial and Ethnic Disparity in Maternal and Child Health in Onondaga County, New York," to the Onondaga County Health Department from the federal Health Resources and Services Administration, 2001–2003. This project used epidemiological, environmental, and ethnographic data to come up with new hypotheses about why infants of color have higher rates of low birth weight and infant death. The epidemiological analyses use a database on all births in the city of Syracuse (2000–2001), which was drawn from the Central New York Perinatal Data System, a population-based birth registry that captures all birth certificate information and additional quality improvement data items for

use by maternal and child health administrators, planners, and evaluators; and in the Electronic Birth Certificate database. This combined database contains 4,506 birth records (without any personally identifying information) of which 54 percent are white, 35 percent African American, 3.2 percent Latino, 5 percent Asian, and 3 percent Native American. The environmental database was compiled at the level of the census tract, on the fifty-seven city of Syracuse census tracts, using data from 2000–2001. The census tract–level environmental database contains information on health measures (elevated blood lead levels in children, sexually transmitted infections); pregnancy outcome measures (low birth weight, infant mortality, and births to mothers under age eighteen); household composition (single-mother and single-father households, grandparents caring for children); housing, poverty and economic measures; arrests for various crimes; racial/ethnic backgrounds of residents; and educational level of residents by gender and age. All data were calculated in the form of a rate, using variables from the 2000 census as population denominators. Ethnographic data including participant observation were used to identify the research questions and to provide detailed descriptions and context for the quantitative findings. The ethnographic data also included twelve case studies of families with young children who reside in one of the census tracts that the environmental analysis described above, shown to contain the highest level of risk factors. The families, who were identified by community-based agencies, had infants who were born during 2000–2002. In eight families the mother was interviewed and in four families the father was interviewed. Interviews were conducted with eight African American families and four white families, and the interviewers matched the interviewees in racial background and gender. These case studies addressed the social and environmental concerns that emerged from the epidemiological and environmental analyses. The issues included housing, neighborhood safety and violence, father involvement, lead poisoning, vacant housing, drugs, corner stores and grocery markets, schools and education, and access to health care. We also gave more than ten presentations of our findings to community stakeholders, including clergy, agency staff serving the Syracuse area communities of color, neighborhood action committees, and other community coalitions, from which we received extensive feedback. In giving these presentations we were not only able to let the community know about our study's findings, but also gained greater ethnographic understanding of the statistical results. IRB approval was awarded by the SUNY Upstate Medical University IRB.

52. "Program Evaluation of Screening and Treatment for Bacterial Vaginosis to Reduce Prematurity in the Syracuse Healthy Start Program." Funded by the Centers for Disease Control and Prevention (through the NYS DOH) to the Onondaga County Health Department, 2001–2004. This evaluation

sample includes all infants born at the largest birth hospital in Syracuse to mothers who resided in nine zip codes overlapping Syracuse (13202, 13203, 13204, 13205, 13206, 13207, 13208, 13210, and 13224 between January 1, 2000, and March 31, 2002. The sample includes 2,995 births. These data include statistics on: prenatal and birth problems and outcomes, neonatal intensive care unit admissions, case management received, and documentation of infant deaths. No names or other identifying information were collected. IRB approval was awarded by the SUNY Upstate Medical University IRB.

53. Kathy DeMott, "Antenatal Risk Reduction: Effectiveness of a Community Based Public Health Initiative in Syracuse, New York." (doctoral dissertation submitted to the London School of Hygiene and Tropical Medicine, 2006); Emilia Koumans, Sandra Lane, Richard Aubry, Noah Webster, Booke Levandowski, Martha Wojtowycz, Stuart Berman, and Lauri Markowitz, "Bacterial Vaginosis Screening and Treatment in Syracuse" (paper presented at the 12th Annual CDC Maternal and Child Health Conference, section "Infections among Women of Reproductive Age," Atlanta, Ga., December 6, 2006): A2.

54. "Assessing and Mitigating the Impact of Exposure to Multiple Indoor Contaminants on Human Health (AUDIT)," co-investigator, funded by the Environmental Protection Agency to the SUNY/Upstate Medical University, 2000–2003. This study followed 135 pregnant, asthmatic women and their infants from the latter part of pregnancy until the infants' first birthday. The study included four home visits by a nurse practitioner and an assessment of indoor air quality. The goal of the study was to identify triggers for the development of asthma in the infants. The study design and preliminary findings are in Judith A. Crawford, MS; Teresa M. Hargrave, MD; Andrew Hunt, PhD; Chien-Chih Liu, BS; Ran D. Anbar, MD; Geralyn E. Hall, FNP; Deepa Naishadham, MS; Maria H. Czerwinski, MD; Noah Webster, BA; Sandra D. Lane, PhD; and Jerrold L. Abraham, MD, "Issues in Design and Implementation of an Urban Birth Cohort Study: The Syracuse AUDIT Project," *The Journal of Urban Health* (2006).

55. "Childbirth as a Pathway for Spiritual Transformation," Metanexus Program on the Scientific Study of Spiritual Transformation (funded by the John Templeton Foundation) (2004–2006).

56. "Pregnancy Outcomes and Father of Baby Incarceration," SUNY Upstate Intramural Research Grant Program, 2004–2005.

57. Judith A. Crawford, MS; Teresa M. Hargrave, MD; Andrew Hunt, PhD; Chien-Chih Liu, BS; Ran D. Anbar, MD; Geralyn E. Hall, FNP; Deepa Naishadham, MS; Maria H. Czerwinski, MD; Noah Webster, BA; Sandra D. Lane, PhD; and Jerrold L. Abraham, MD, "Issues in Design and Implementation of an Urban Birth Cohort Study: The Syracuse AUDIT Project," *The Journal of Urban Health* (2006); B. Levandowski, P. Sharma, S. D. Lane,

N. Webster, A. Nestor, D. Cibula, and S. Huntington, "Parental Literacy and Infant Health: An Evidence-Based Healthy Start Intervention," *Health Promotion Practice* 7 no. 1 (2004): 95–102; Sandra D. Lane, Robert A. Rubinstein, Robert Keefe, Michael Freedman, Brooke Levandowski, Don Cibula, and Maria Czerwinski, "Marriage Promotion and Missing Men: African American Women in a Demographic Double Bind," *Medical Anthropology Quarterly* 18, no. 4 (December 2004): 405–28; Sandra D. Lane, Rob Keefe, Robert A. Rubinstein, Noah Webster, Alan Rosenthal, Don Cibula, and Jesse Dowdell, "Structural Violence and Racial Disparity in Heterosexual HIV Infection," *Journal of Health Care for the Poor and Underserved* 15, no. 3 (August 2003): 319–35; Maria Czerwinski, Sandra D. Lane, Rob Keefe, Martha Wojtowycz, Carla Liberatore, and Don Cibula, "Missing Fathers and Incarceration: Health Impacts of Structural Violence," *Social Justice: Anthropology and Human Rights* 4, no. 1-2 (Winter/Spring 2003): 147–67; S. D. Lane, S. Teran, C. Morrow, and L. F. Novick, "Racial and Ethnic Disparity in Low Birth Weight in Syracuse, New York." *American Journal of Pediatric Medicine* 24, 4 suppl. (May 2003): 128–32, http://www.curriculum.som.vcu.edu/popmed/; S. D. Lane, D. Cibula, L. P. Milano, M. Shaw, B. Bourgeois, F. Schweitzer, C. Steiner, K. Dygert, K. Demott, K. Wilson, R. Gregg, N. Webster, D. Milton, R. Aubry, and L. F. Novick, "Racial and Ethnic Disparities in Infant Mortality: Risk in Social Context," *Journal of Public Health Management and Practice* 7, no. 3 (2001): 30–46; S. D. Lane, R. A. Rubinstein, D. Cibula, and N. Webster, "Toward a Public Health Approach to Bioethics," in "Ethics and Anthropology: Facing Future Issues in Human Biology, Globalism, and Cultural Property," *Annals of the New York Academy of Sciences* 925 (2000): 25–36; Lilie Welych, Barbara Laws, Amy Fitzgerald, Tracey Durham, Don Cibula, and Sandra Lane, "Formative Research for Public Health Interventions among Adolescents at High Risk for Gonorrhea and other STDs," *Journal of Public Health Management and Practice* 4, no. 6 (1998): 54–61.

Chapter 2

Lots of Trouble Out Here

"Now I have a baby and things getting harder, there's lots of trouble out here."
—African American mother, Syracuse

Syracuse was home to the Haudenosaunee ("people of the long-house"), or Onondaga nation, for centuries prior to European settlement.[1] The Onondaga, together with the Seneca, Cayuga, Oneida, Mohawk, and Tuscarora Nations, are part of the Iroquois confederacy.[2] As in many other parts of North America, early missionaries and traders were followed by settlers pushing west to acquire land. The soil proved too swampy for much farming, but it was so salty that an industry developed to extract the salt—in that pre-refrigeration era a valuable commodity for food preservation—giving rise to Syracuse's moniker: "Salt City."[3] The Erie Canal, built in the 1820s to link the Atlantic Ocean with the Great Lakes, propelled what was then a small collection of eighteenth-century villages into explosive growth based on commerce. Erie Boulevard, now a four-lane thoroughfare running through the center of Syracuse—lined with strip malls, chain restaurants, and the occasional adult bookstore or "gentlemen's club"—sits on top of the former Erie Canal's water highway with its system of locks, through which boats were towed by mules.[4]

One third of Syracuse residents are people of color. Present-day Syracuse, the Onondaga County seat, is the fifth largest city in New

York, with a 2000 population of 147,306, which is composed of 64.3 percent European Americans, 25.3 percent African Americans, 3.4 percent Asian Americans, 1.1 percent Native American, and 3.6 percent of two or more racial ancestries.[5] Among these groups, 5.3 percent are Hispanic. African Americans, who have lived in Syracuse since the early European settlements in the seventeenth century, came north in larger numbers in succeeding waves from the antebellum period to escape slavery, to the twentieth century in search of a better life than the impoverished rural South could provide.[6] Onondaga County's half million residents live for the most part in highly racially segregated areas; outside of the city of Syracuse only 1.3 percent of Onondaga County's residents are African American.

The 1880 census tallied ten Latinos in Syracuse, from Mexico, Cuba, and South America, but the Latino community's greatest increase has occurred since 1960.[7] Latinos in Syracuse are themselves diverse; nearly 5,000 characterize themselves as white, 1,239 as African American, more than 200 as having Native American ancestry, and 57 as Asian. The largest group of Latinos in Syracuse is of Puerto Rican ancestry, with others of Cuban, Mexican, Dominican, Peruvian, and Central American ancestry. The Onondaga Nation Territory is located in Onondaga County and many Syracuse residents are members of the Onondaga Nation; however, Native Americans are seriously under-enumerated in the U.S. Census, which only counted 1.1 percent of Syracuse residents as reporting Native American ancestry.

Syracuse is home to two major refugee resettlement agencies, each with a network of families and faith communities that volunteer to help resettle asylum seekers, who have been through hell and beyond before arriving in central New York. In the 1980s, Vietnamese and Hmong, fleeing civil conflict, arrived in Syracuse, with many going on to become business owners and seeing their children graduate from college. Since 2000, young males from South Sudan, members of the so-called "lost boys of Sudan" contingent, Liberian war orphans, and more than 300 Somali Bantus, among numerous others, are in the process of adjusting to very different conditions than they have previously experienced.[8] Newly arrived individuals from near the equator learn to cope with several yearly months of deep snow and below zero temperatures; Syracuse regularly wins the *Golden Snowball Award* as the New York State City with the "crappiest winter weather."[9] The 2000 census recorded 8 percent of Syracuse residents as foreign-born, having come to the city as refugees, voluntary immigrants, and undocumented labor migrants, of whom 42 percent were from Asia, 32 percent from Europe, 20 percent from the Caribbean and Central/South America, and 5 percent from Africa. Hospitals and other clinical services now serve patients from Liberia, Sudan, Nigeria, Somalia, Vietnam (including those of Hmong and Vietnamese ancestry/language), and individuals from Myanmar (who speak a Thailand/Burmese dialect).

Syracuse and the surrounding areas were proving grounds for key nineteenth-century social reforms. In 1851, Frederick Douglass spoke at a meeting of abolitionists in Syracuse.[10] That same year, federal marshals pursued and handcuffed William Henry, an African American known as "Jerry," with the aim of returning him to his purported "owner" under the Fugitive Slave Law. Alerted by church bells, local abolitionists rushed to his aid, successfully freeing Mr. Henry in an episode commemorated in a downtown sculpture as the "Jerry Rescue."[11] Nearby Seneca Falls was the site of the first Woman's Rights Convention, in 1840. In Auburn, some thirty miles from downtown Syracuse, is the house that was sold to Harriet Tubman in 1857 by an abolitionist New York State Senator, a sale that was legally prohibited in that era.[12]

Urban Renewal

In the second half of the twentieth century, cities all over the United States began to "modernize" and "clean up," by bulldozing older, minority neighborhoods and replacing them with grand plazas and public arenas. Mindy Thompson Fullilove, a Columbia University psychiatrist whose work on how the environment affects health, links urban renewal to health disparities like the HIV epidemic, which is currently ravaging African American and Latino communities in U.S. cities.[13] Similar to Dr. Fullilove's findings in other cities, in Syracuse the unintended consequences of urban renewal and the collapse of local industry have led to profound inequalities in the health and well-being of Syracuse families of color.

Beginning in the late 1950s, Syracuse cleared the former fifteenth ward in the central and near east sectors of Syracuse,[14] a neighborhood that was described by Win Jones, a former resident, as integrated, where people of color and white residents of many ethnicities lived side by side. Each month a famous entertainer played at the Strand

Theater; there were butchers, bakeries, two large grocery markets, and numerous body shops and other small businesses. An African American elder recalled,[15]

> We had a major grocery store called Loblaw's and other corner stores, mostly run by Jewish because we lived in an old Jewish neighborhood. The fifteenth ward was an old Jewish neighborhood, so there were all kinds of corner stores run by Jewish, [who] used to be residents. We also had some Black businesses such as small diners, barbershops, pool halls; we had a pharmacy, delis, several bakeries, and several what you would call night clubs.

Students could find after-school or summer employment to make a little money and gain job skills. Bus routes passed through the fifteenth ward, with stops timed to get employees to and from local factories in other parts of the city. Many families could get by on the pay of the man of the family; most families were two-parent units. A former fifteenth ward resident said of the job situation,

> Everybody worked, most men worked at the steel mill and Crouse Hinds, women did day labor. I was the first full time Black sales clerk at a department store downtown, so we were breaking the color barrier down there, and then that led to other females getting hired there, there were nurses' aid jobs, nursing homes, [and] menial labor. Some men were lucky enough to get on DPW [Department of Public Works] which at that time [was] considered a very good job because of benefits. Once you got in you usually were able to stay in.

Another former resident said,

> Jobs were very plentiful. I have known people who had two full-time jobs. A lot of guys when I was a kid, older men worked for the city during the day 'cause you go to the city, you go three or four o'clock in the morning and get off at ten or eleven o'clock and then would go to the railroad yards in the evening. Or GE or Carrier, and they'd work two full-time jobs. Syracuse was a very industrial city, you had foundries ... factories. The largest employer when I was a kid was GE out on Electronics Parkway in Liverpool and a lot of Blacks worked at GE. General Motors was big. The largest employer in Syracuse now is Syracuse University.... Blacks didn't get the best jobs in the world, but they got good paying jobs. Do you know what I'm saying? They worked, they had an income.

Another African American who grew up in the fifteenth ward reminisced,

> It [the fifteenth ward] was beautiful, that's all I can tell you. Our community was very, very small. The Black neighborhood, basically, Blacks and Jews lived together back in the early 30s, 40s and 50s, and because our neighborhood was so small, everybody knew everybody. You had small families, you had big families—ten, eleven kids—some families had five children. Some families had two kids. I moved into the housing project, which is Pioneer Homes, which was built in 1939. I moved into Pioneer Homes in 1942, from a cold-water flat. Cold water flat you had no hot water, you had to heat the water on the stove. You had to take a bath in a tin tub, yeah, me and my sister shared the same bath water many times prior to moving into Pioneer Homes. When we moved into Pioneer Homes, we had a three-bedroom flat on South Townsend Street and it was like heaven. Because we had a refrigerator, we had a gas stove, and we had a bathtub with hot running water. So, back in the day, everybody knew everyone. The majority of the Blacks at that time, young children, I was a young man then, the boys usually went to the Boys Club and the boys and girls went to Dunbar Center [a community center] ... everybody congregated at the Dunbar, that's where I learned to play basketball.

There were also places for adolescents to gather, as recalled by a former fifteenth ward resident, "You know, we had dances, we had places to go for dances, the Dunbar Center had dances, Cooperative's Hall, Carpenter's Hall, and everything was great." "Although there was poverty," said Jesse Dowdell, now Director of the Syracuse Model Neighborhood Facility, Inc., "folks were poor, but we didn't know it." Youth walked everywhere they needed to go and obesity was rare.

To the city fathers, however, the fifteenth ward looked different than it did to its residents. Whereas the residents saw a warm, vibrant collection of people and places, the all-white city and county officials saw an eyesore of older buildings, inhabited by poor "Negroes." The cleaning up envisioned by the architects of urban renewal meant moving the people of color away from the central city; indeed, calling the process ethnic cleansing might not be too great of an overstatement.[16] Neighborhoods were graded on a color-coded scale, beginning in the late 1930s, from green (the best) to red (the worst) to determine the localities where federally backed home loans would be made.[17] The criteria on which areas were judged included the quality of the buildings and the proportion of "foreign-born" and "Negro" residents. In the red neighborhoods, from which term *redlining* originates, banks refused to extend credit for home mortgages. As an African American elder recalled, "The majority of Blacks that lived in the neighborhood [the fifteenth ward] didn't even own a house because back in the day they 'red lined.'" Another elder remembers, "Back in the [19]40s that's when Blacks started buying property. Starting in the late 40s early 50s, a lot of them still couldn't get loans from the bank [in] the areas [that] were 'red lined.' Our area was red lined and banks didn't want to give out money." The redlined areas circled the center part of Syracuse, surrounding downtown's historic nineteenth- and early twentieth-century buildings, covering a large area in the south and southeast parts of the city. These areas, once called the fifteenth ward, were the sites of urban renewal.

What happened to the folks displaced by urban renewal? Starting in 1961, twenty-seven square blocks were leveled, displacing some 1,300 residents.[18] Homeowners were given lump sum payments and many eventually purchased new homes; others found new apartments to rent. The process of sorting out where to move was fraught with discrimination, which forced people of color into small areas adjacent to the razed fifteenth ward. Mortgage discrimination, if not official redlining, continued throughout the twentieth century; between 1996 and 2000, only 1.3 percent of 2,169 home loans funded housing purchases in predominately minority neighborhoods.[19] One woman whose family was displaced remembered,

> Because of the discrimination in housing ... White people did not want Blacks moving into their neighborhoods, so it was difficult to find places to live. Once one Black got established in a household then things became easier, because Whites in that neighborhood moved out and the houses became available ... [It took my family] a good six months to a year [to find a home]. It was a lengthy process, it was very upsetting, leaving neighbors we've had for years, growing up years, losing friendships, it was like breaking up families. Like a death really.

In place of jumbled, but lively and functionally cohesive neighborhoods, we now have a wind-swept plaza, the Everson Museum of Art, Civic Center, several large parking lots, and an enlarged county jail—known as the Justice Center. SUNY Upstate Medical University,

University Hospital, Syracuse University, and SUNY/Environmental Sciences and Forestry expanded to occupy large parts of the once redlined areas in the near-southeast part of Syracuse. Some of these buildings, it must be said, are beautiful. The Everson shines with carefully selected installations of modern, folk, and fine art; eating lunch at its café, one soaks in the elegant ambiance while tasting contemporary cuisine. Every single one of these institutions, however, was built on appropriated land, for which they pay no property taxes. Property taxes fund schools. Is it just a coincidence that the major daily—the Syracuse *Post-Standard*—changed the reading level of its text from eleventh grade prior to urban renewal (1900 to 1970) to eighth grade after the major changes had taken place (1980 to the present)?[20]

By the mid-1970s, construction was completed on two high-ways—690 and 81—bisecting the city and splitting neighborhoods by socioeconomic status and race, into the "haves" and "have nots." The highways made "white flight" to the suburbs possible, shrinking the population of Syracuse and further depleting the tax base to fund public schools and services. From a 1960 Syracuse population of 216,038, by 1980 there were 170,105 residents, and in 2000 only 147,306.

Fullilove[21] describes how following urban renewal, families of color were pushed to a concentric ring around the edges of their former neighborhood, often increasing already existing racial segregation. In Syracuse, following urban renewal and largely due to housing discrimination, people of color became concentrated in the south and southwest sides of the city. As Map 2.1 shows, in five city of Syracuse census tracts, 80 percent or more of the residents are African Americans. African Americans who live in those five census tracts comprise 26 percent of all African Americans in Syracuse. Three census tracts contain more than 400 Latino residents each; those three census tracts include 21 percent of all Latinos in Syracuse. These census tracts overlap with zip codes 13204—on the southwest—and 13205—in the south parts of the city.

Numerous studies look at the impact of the built environment, such as houses and roads, on health outcomes. Broken windows, litter, and dilapidated housing characterize neighborhoods with high crime (resulting in increased stress levels and associated effects), poverty (lack of funds to buy nutritious foods leading to obesity,

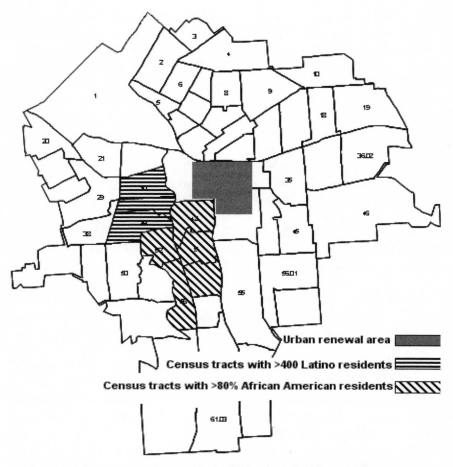

Map 2.1 African American and Latino Residence and Urban Renewal, Syracuse, NY

diabetes, and poor birth outcomes), and residents with inadequate health care.[22] Lead poisoning, for example, disproportionately affects impoverished children living in urban areas, where children of color are documented to have considerably higher levels of this preventable toxic exposure.[23] Five zip codes in the City of Syracuse, Onondaga County's seat, account for 76 percent of the county's total childhood lead poisoning and 7.7 percent of the *entire incidence* of elevated blood lead (EBL) in New York State children for the years 2000–2001.[24] The highest of these five zip codes and the second highest zip code in New York State is 13204, on Syracuse's southwest side, where the EBL exceeds 10 percent of all children tested, compared with an average 1.3 percent of children in Onondaga County, exclusive of the five high-lead zip codes. Lead poisoning injures children's developing brains and stunts their ability to learn. As described in Chapter 5, my research team found childhood lead poisoning to be associated with repeat teen pregnancy and teen smoking.

The neighborhoods with highest lead poisoning, which border the urban renewal area, exhibit what Deborah and Rodrick Wallace call "contagious housing destruction."[25] These neighborhoods have the highest number of vacant houses and empty lots in the city, looking like what Fullilove has likened to missing teeth in a mouth too long without dental care.[26]

Map 2.2 shows the census tracts with the top 20 percent of housing lead violations in Syracuse—houses with peeling or powdery lead paint that have poisoned at least one child.[27] As Map 2.2 illustrates, the highest rates of lead problems occur in the concentric half-circle bordering the urban renewal area. The twelve census tracts with the top quintile of all housing lead violations are all located in the five high-lead zip codes described earlier. Within the twelve high-lead-housing-violation census tracts, 22.3 percent of all houses are vacant, compared with 10.7 percent in the remainder of Syracuse,[28] a difference that is statistically significant.[29]

A report by the Syracuse *Post-Standard,* based on data obtained from the Onondaga County Health Department, indicated that from 1995 to 2000, "20 property owners account[ed] for 175 of the 1,287" rental properties in which unsafe levels of lead had been identified.[30] About two thirds of the landlords of multiple lead-laden rental properties listed in this news report live in the suburbs in Onondaga County where the median household income is $41,904, compared with $18,417 in the census tracts with greatest lead violations in housing.[31]

Many of these 1,287 houses cited for lead violations probably poisoned more than one child each.[32] First, it is common for siblings living in the same dwelling to ingest dangerous amounts of lead. Second, between 1995 and 2000, a total of forty-eight children were lead poisoned in houses that had previously been cited for lead violations.[33] New York State law requires landlords to correct the lead hazards in their rental properties if a child resident in that property

Map 2.2 Top Quintile of Housing Lead Violations and Urban Renewal Area, Syracuse, 2000–2001

has a blood lead level of 20 mcg/dl or above.[34] This remediation generally includes removing chipping or peeling paint and painting over lead-laden surfaces, with paint designed to seal in the lead. On friction surfaces such as windows and doors, however, painting over the surfaces may be insufficient to keep the lead-based undercoats of paint encapsulated.

Babies born to mothers living in devastated neighborhoods have higher rates of low birth weight and infant death. My colleague Don

Cibula and I conducted a mapping analysis to identify the census tracts in Syracuse with the highest proportion of risks for poor birth outcomes.[35] These risks included teen births, low birth weight births, sexually transmitted infections among women, lead poisoning, violent crimes, female-headed households, and poverty. Most of the risk factors for poor birth outcomes are the same risk factors for poor health throughout the lifespan. These six census tracts with the highest level of health and social problems fall in the concentric half circle bordering the urban renewal area, as illustrated by Map 2.3.

Our team conducted a structured observational analysis of thirty randomly selected city blocks in the six census tracts with the highest level of risk for poor birth outcomes. We walked and mapped each block, documenting vacant lots, abandoned houses, broken glass, and other types of neighborhood degradation. Among these thirty blocks, there were fourteen abandoned houses and seventy-six vacant or empty lots where houses once stood. Only four of these thirty blocks had no abandoned houses or vacant lots. In the majority—nineteen of the thirty lots—an average of four houses on each block were either boarded up and abandoned or had been destroyed by fire and demolished, leaving an empty lot on the former site.

Fullilove describes how in the areas bordering urban renewal, property becomes devalued and rental property owners become less likely to keep up the necessary repairs to maintain the property. Eventually, owners who have failed to pay taxes on the properties abandon many properties and these abandoned vacant houses are disproportionately set ablaze by arsonists.[36] Of the thirty-six fires in vacant houses reported by the Syracuse *Post-Standard* from 1995 to 2000, 69 percent were in zip codes 13204 and 13205, in the near-south and southwest parts of the city, the bottom portion of the concentric half circle where lead poisoning is greatest.[37] The vacant houses are thus not only neighborhood problems, but are also markers for the location of lead poisoning. Where a substantial proportion of the neighborhood buildings have been abandoned, boarded up, or torched, the remaining homes probably contain peeling and powdery lead-based paint.

Syracuse's rate of sexually transmitted infections tops New York City's.[38] Among women delivering at the largest birth hospital from 2000 to 2002, 2 percent became infected with gonorrhea and 8.5 percent with Chlamydia during their pregnancies. Sexually transmitted diseases (STDs) peak among teen women of color between the

Map 2.3 Aggregate Risks for Poor Birth Outcomes and Urban Renewal

ages of fifteen and nineteen. Chlamydia is 15.6 times more prevalent among African Americans in Onondaga County compared with white residents, and gonorrhea is 40.8 times higher.[39] Since 1996, cumulative AIDS cases in Onondaga County have risen by 51 percent among African Americans and Latinos, compared with a 30 percent increase for whites. The most dramatic rise in new infections among women of color results from heterosexual transmission. STD rates provide insight into the potential future trends of the HIV epidemic, because both infections share the same transmission risk of unprotected sexual exposure with an infected partner. The alarming pattern of high STDs among female teens of color indicates that heterosexual HIV transmission among women of color will probably continue to rise and will likely affect much younger women. From 2000 and 2001, there was a 142-percent increase in AIDS cases in Onondaga County (20-percent increase in Syracuse) and nearly 100-percent increase in gonorrhea diagnoses in both the county and city. In 2001 the Syracuse metropolitan area was thirty-second of 104 metropolitan areas nationwide in new AIDS diagnoses, with the highest New York State rate outside of New York City.[40] Among youth ages thirteen to twenty-five, those living in zip code 13204 have more HIV infections than same-age residents of any other Syracuse zip code; zip code 13205 is the second highest. Zip codes 13204 and 13205 also have the highest and second highest numbers of women living with HIV/AIDS in the county and are tied for the highest number of heterosexually transmitted HIV infections.[41] According to the 2000 *Community Needs Index for the Central New York Region*, zip code 13204 has the second-highest rate of pregnant HIV-positive women in Onondaga County.[42] Fortunately, we can now prevent most cases of HIV transmission from mother to baby by giving the mother medications during the pregnancy and birth, so these HIV positive women probably did not infect their infants.

Residents living in neighborhoods with boarded-up vacant buildings with broken windows have high rates of sexually transmitted infections. Syracuse census tracts that have 20 percent or higher abandoned houses have nearly twenty-four times more gonorrhea infections among residents than those with fewer than 20 percent of their houses vacant.[43] Since people of color in Syracuse have higher rates of sexually transmitted infections, it is possible that the link between vacant houses and gonorrhea is mistaken. Maybe the real issue is that more people of color live in impoverished communities where there are higher numbers of vacant houses. A statistical procedure called *logistic regression* controls for this possible source of bias by considering more than one risk factor in the formula at the same time. So, I added the proportion of people of color living in each census tract to the test for the association between vacant houses and gonorrhea diagnoses. Census tracts with vacant houses, in this more careful analysis, were nearly twelve times more likely to have residents with higher numbers of gonorrhea infections, a result that was statistically significant.[44]

So, what is going on? How can a vacant house contribute to sexually transmitted infections? We conducted focus group interviews to find out. Two of our African American colleagues[45] with long experience in HIV/AIDS work led four focus groups with African American and Latino participants over age eighteen. They asked, "There seems to be a correlation between abandoned housing and the high rates of gonorrhea in this community. What are your thoughts on all of that?" The responses, drawn from the focus groups, were in general agreement with the participants who are quoted below:

Person #1: But as far as abandoned houses it's easy access to—and it's probably where some of this rough sex is taking place, you know, like a gang will get a girl or two in there and force them or something like that or people who are on drugs will be lured into places or just go on their own.

Person #2: That's a definite because I actually have one right next door to me that almost got burnt down a couple of days ago because somebody in there doing stuff they got no business doing and there's one across street that we look at every day. That's a definite.

Person #3: They figure that it's abandoned they could be in there doing whatever they want and no one is going to stop or interrupt them or anything like that.

Person #4: Drugs, sex, drinking, you name it; they have no rules there. There's no boundaries because first of all these buildings are not secure enough. You can take and pop the wood right off of that [boarded up door or window], walk in there and throw a little sofa in there and use it as a social lounge.

Person #5: I think sexual activity is going on in the abandoned houses if there is a lot of gonorrhea and stuff going on in the area. Oh, yeah, because some people they're not able to bring the opposite sex over to their house, you know what I'm saying. [They find] a house and they sell drugs there and they bring home whatever.

Person #6: My opinion on abandoned houses, as far as any other activities, it's a safe haven. Criminals, crooks, shady life like dark, hide and being in holes ... trying to smoke weed or get laid back there, whatever, [to find] any privacy.

The narratives from these focus groups echo an earlier study conducted by my colleagues and me at the Onondaga County Health Department.[46] Syracuse youth at high risk for STDs described a behavior called "running a lab" or "running a train" in which one adolescent female has sex with multiple males in abandoned housing. The young women claimed that this activity was consensual, and not rape, a claim that many of us found difficult to believe. My colleagues in a non-profit program addressing HIV/AIDS prevention among people of color subsequently conducted focus groups with youth about sexual violence and HIV risk. A young African American woman reported engaging in sex with multiple gang members in a vacant house. She lived in a gang turf area—gangs in Syracuse define their sphere of influence by geography—and she was coerced into servicing the gang males. She did not report this incident to the police and did not characterize it as rape. Other young women present at the focus group stated, "Girls have sex with multiple gang members to be a part of the gang, for trade, and sometimes they are forced to."

Of course vacant houses are not the sole environmental factor contributing to elevated rates of STDs. The fiscal constraint on sexually transmitted disease (STD) services increases the length of time between infection and effective treatment for individuals who lack health insurance. There is only one public STD clinic providing free treatment, which is open only eleven hours per week.[47] A survey conducted by this STD clinic found that patients often had to wait seven to ten days from the onset of symptoms until effective treatment; many continued to have unprotected sex while waiting to be treated, thus exposing other partners to STDs.[48] Many of the patients reported that they went to local emergency departments seeking treatment and were given written prescriptions but could not afford the price of the medication. Barriers to access for STD treatment greatly increase the likelihood of further STD transmission in the community.

When a woman with an untreated STD has unprotected intercourse with an HIV-infected man, her risk of becoming infected with HIV is increased by two- to fivefold. The reason for this increased risk of HIV transmission is that when infected with an STD, a woman's vagina becomes inflamed, sometimes with tiny erosions, and teems with white blood cells. HIV infects white blood cells and the HIV virus can pass more easily into a woman's body because the erosions provide openings into her blood vessels. In communities where STD services were initially inadequate and were subsequently enhanced to the extent that infected individuals could be screened and treated quickly, the result was fewer new heterosexual HIV infections.[49] Under-funding of STD services not only has a human cost—in more HIV infections and other health consequences of under-treated STDs—but also a potential fiscal cost. The New York State Department of Health estimated in 2002 that the average medical cost per person infected with HIV/AIDS was $30,482 per year, most of which is paid by Medicaid.[50] So, by scrimping on the bill for adequate STD screening and treatment, we may not be saving any tax dollars; instead, we are shifting the cost to more expensive treatment for those with HIV/AIDS.

The summer of 2002 shocked Syracuse citizens with public gun battles between rival gangs, culminating in an all-time high of twenty-five murders for the year. In response to the violence, parents kept their children indoors, seniors curtailed walking outside, and residents of the hardest-hit neighborhoods on the city's near-southwest and south sides hunkered down. Parents whom we interviewed expressed fear for their children and themselves. Fathers of color, especially, worried about being caught up in the mayhem or arrested by police who may not distinguish them from the perpetrators of the violence. One father said, "Well, of course, where there are gangs there will be some sort of illegal activity, usually drugs, and it is making the community unsafe for those that are longtime residents like my mother." When asked, "Do you hear gunshots in your neighborhood?" This father replied, "Sometimes, from time to time ... it's all over turf." Below are excerpts from interviews conducted by an African American male research assistant with fathers of young children who live on the city's southwest side:

How safe is your neighborhood to violence?

Person #1: "From when I was young to now it is very serious. It is a chess game ... [they're] only hurting themselves and the people that love them."

Is it dangerous on a daily basis?

"Mostly on the weekend, something is going to go down. There can be thirty people on the corner all trying to buy something [i.e., illicit drugs], radios blasting through the whole week. It is not safe for your child or anyone to be outside. A lot of times you are guilty by association."

Can you estimate the age group that is perpetuating most of the violence?

Person #2: "The age limit right now between the shootings and the people getting killed is between the age of fourteen to the age of twenty-two (my age right now)."

How many of your people got killed in the last five years, who you knew personally?

"R, my buddy CC, my boy Junior, these are my boys, I was the peacemaker … RR, F, EC, my boy GF, God bless the dead, my cousin SR, my cousin FL, it's a lot of them, and now my home-grown little brother, his funeral is today, God bless the dead. A lot of people I know … my cousin J."

So you just named me about 10 people right off the muscle that they murdered within the last five years that you've known personally.

"It's just not safe to let your child [go outside]. It hurts me more because, I'm like, all these people are dying. One wish, I would wish for there to be less negativity and violence. For people to unite and have an understanding. With the violence out of the way a lot will come."[51]

Beginning in the 1960s, and following changes brought about in part by urban renewal, supermarket chains left inner cities.[52] This shift left smaller, corner markets to serve as the primary food sources for many inner-city residents. By the late 1970s, four of the major supermarkets in Syracuse had closed. As described in Chapter 8, the closing of these sources of healthy food makes it much more difficult for pregnant women and families with small children to eat a healthy diet. Those without cars must take taxies, get rides from others, or take on average two buses each way to a full service grocery, often accompanied by small children. The urban retail food sources left in Syracuse, mostly small corner or convenience stores, not only feature very limited choices of healthy food, but also charge more for such items than suburban supermarkets. To serve healthy food to their families, parents need both sufficient money and access to reasonably priced food.[53] Compared to people living in higher-income areas, residents of low-income, urban neighborhoods have very limited access to high quality food, enjoy fewer options in the variety of foods available to them, and pay higher prices for groceries.[54] The Syracuse Hunger Project has documented that an alarming number of city residents require emergency food assistance from charitable food pantries run by faith communities and other non-profit agencies, without which they would go hungry.[55] In part due to poor nutrition, the rates of obesity, heart disease, and diabetes are growing rapidly, particularly among African American and other inner-city residents, often leading to disproportionate rates of premature death.[56]

The lack of healthy food and the fear of letting children exercise vigorously outdoors both contribute to dramatic increases in obesity. I analyzed the pre-pregnancy weights of women who gave birth in Syracuse between 1996 and 2002 by calculating their body mass index (BMI) from their heights and weights from just before they became pregnant. Pre-pregnancy BMIs give us a picture of average women in the community, between the usual childbearing ages of fifteen to forty-five. Between 1996 and 2002, the pre-pregnancy BMIs of Syracuse residents increased by 2.8 percent. The largest increase in BMI (3.4 percent) was among women twenty to twenty-nine years who were covered by Medicaid insurance, which in Syracuse funds the medical care of the poorer half of the population of pregnant women.[57] African American women started out a bit heavier than white women, but the white women gained almost 30 percent more than the African American women during this six-year period. Researchers split BMI into categories that reflect the seriousness of obesity: Underweight or normal weight is less than twenty-five, more than twenty-five and less than thirty is overweight, and more than thirty is obese. The greatest gain is in the heaviest category, those with BMIs of thirty-five or higher.[58]

Nearly 2 percent of the 2,955 Syracuse women who gave birth at the largest birth hospital in 2000–2002 had pre-existing diabetes. Among those women who had been diagnosed with diabetes prior to the pregnancy, their average BMI was thirty-four, compared to the average BMI of twenty-six among the women who did not have pre-existing diabetes. Women with BMIs over thirty, compared to those less than thirty, were 47 percent more likely to give birth prematurely.[59] Obstetricians often induce the labors of diabetic patients a week or so before the official due date, in order to reduce potential complications. So I decided to look at pregnant women without pre-existing diabetes whose BMI was either less than thirty or thirty and higher. This analysis yielded similar results; among pregnant women without pre-existing diabetes, 44 percent more of those with BMIs of thirty and higher, compared with those less than thirty, delivered premature infants.[60]

Why would obesity make women deliver prematurely? While numerous researchers have found this same increase in premature delivery among obese women, none have yet convincingly worked out why it occurs.[61] A likely explanation is that the women who became heavier are among the poorest city residents, who have numerous other risk factors for premature birth. A second possible explanation is that the increasing obesity itself heightened the women's risk of delivering early. I have a hypothesis about the potential link between obesity and premature birth, but my hypothesis has not yet been tested. My hunch is that the kind of metabolic changes that occur with obesity—alterations in how the body handles sugars in the blood—may make women more vulnerable to infections beginning in about the fifth month of pregnancy. Obese individuals, even those without diabetes, have blood sugars that rise considerably after meals.[62] Since many microorganisms grow prodigiously in the presence of sugar, this transient peak in blood sugar might increase the risk of infection. Prenatal infections are described more fully in Chapter 3.

Obesity leading to hypertension and diabetes is a risk factor for kidney failure and heart disease. Nationwide in 2003, 44 percent of the incident cases of end-stage renal disease were caused by diabetes, and 28 percent by hypertension.[63] Per capita in Onondaga County, African Americans have more than seven times and Latinos more than six times the rate of kidney failure compared with white residents.[64] An Onondaga County resident interviewed by the National Kidney Foundation provides an important example of the danger of unrecognized and untreated hypertension.[65] He is a forty-five-year-old African American college graduate, who said: "I felt nauseous and weak for a couple of weeks and asked my wife to drive me to the hospital. When I got there my blood pressure was 269/189 ... I saw the doctors conferring in a tight circle and knew something was bad. They told me that both my kidneys were gone and I needed dialysis ... My last checkup by a physician was four years before, for a job physical, and the doctor had told me that my blood pressure was a little high, but he said it was nothing to worry about. Since I did not smoke or drink and I am a runner I did not realize that I was at risk for kidney disease."

I created Figure 2.1 for the National Kidney Foundation of Central New York, to illustrate the link between neighborhood factors and subsequent poor health. Several of these neighborhood risk factors—lack of fresh food, violence, vacant housing—predominate in the parts of the city where people of color were pushed into after urban renewal. These risk factors are forms of environmental injustice that disproportionately affect the poor. In addition to diabetes, hypertension, and kidney disease, they increase the risks for infant mortality.

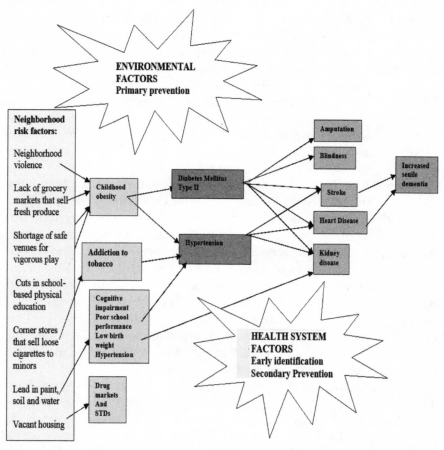

Figure 2.1 From Neighborhood Roots to Preventable Debility and Death

Poverty, Unemployment, and Inadequate Education

The per capita income in the 2000 census for Syracuse was $15,168, compared with the per capita income in the United States of $29,468. The 2000 Syracuse median family income was $33,026, compared with the median United States family income of $50,890. Table 2.1 presents data from U.S. Census 2000 on income, poverty, and education for the total population of Syracuse and for white, African American, and Latino residents.

A problem with assessing inequality in Syracuse is that the white population is impoverished compared with their counterparts in other parts of the United States. African Americans, on many indicators, fare about twice as badly as white Syracuse residents, and Latino rates of poverty and inadequate education are substantially worse than the

Table 2.1 Syracuse: Poverty, Income, Employment, and Education

	Syracuse Total Population 147,306	Syracuse White 94,663	Syracuse African American 37,336	Syracuse Latino 7,768
Children under age 5 living below federal poverty level	43%	27%	57.3%	59%
Residents of all ages living below federal poverty level	27.3%	26.8%	39.2%	49.7%
Median family income	$33,026	$40,254	$21,265	$15,899
Per capita income	$15,168	$17,948	$10,642	$7,088
Unemployed males age 20–54*	10.2%	5.6%	12.6%	14.6%
Unemployed females age 20–54*	8.4%	4.2%	8%	6.9%
Less than high school education, males age 25 and older	22.9%	18.2%	35.5%	45.3%
Less than high school education, females age 25 and older	24.6%	20.9%	32.7%	45.4%

African American rates. White Syracuse residents who see themselves as struggling often find it difficult to perceive how much worse off are their neighbors of color. This poverty disproportionately affects children; Syracuse has New York State's third-highest child poverty level, following Buffalo and Rochester, and the second-highest Latino child poverty rate in the United States, according to the Children's Defense Fund.[66]

Overt Discrimination in Health Care Settings

Syracuse, paradoxically, contains both liberal, even utopian movements and extremely conservative, sometimes racist groups.[67] This tension between those who promote diversity and those who are threatened by difference began in the nineteenth century, or perhaps earlier, but the late twentieth-century loss of industry and economic downturn intensified the clash. Syracuse-based progressive idealists are at times directly opposed by a racist and xenophobic backlash. The Syracuse Peace Council, for example, in 1997 identified "white power" and other hate groups operating in the predominantly segregated rural areas near Syracuse.

Many of my health provider colleagues not only give compassionate care to patients of all backgrounds during their paid shifts, but also attend community meetings and spend their "off time" dreaming up better ways to improve the health of the poor in Syracuse. Despite these examples of physicians, nurses, social workers, and others going well beyond their official duties in their devotion to equity, instances of egregious discrimination occur. In order to understand and stop these wrongs, my colleagues and I have compiled instances of overt discriminatory behavior in health and human service agencies in Syracuse. The following are a few examples from the years 1999 to 2004:

I. A newly hired African American male health employee found a David Duke flyer on his desk (David Duke is an infamous white supremacist from Louisiana.) His supervisor alerted senior management about the incident, but no follow-up investigation was conducted. When the man's supervisor and other staff members continued to press for an appropriate response to this and other racist incidents, they were themselves labeled troublemakers and malcontents.

II. In a heated discussion about extending the hours of operation of a key clinical service, a senior management staff member said, "If those people want to get treated, they can learn to come to the clinic when it is open."

III. A Latina obstetrical nurse was called a "spic" by her nursing supervisor. In this instance, thankfully, the Latina nurse's union stood behind her and there were both consequences to the supervisor as a result of her racist speech and diversity training programs for all staff.

IV. Two Latinas, hired to translate and facilitate services for a company's Spanish-speaking clients, were told by their supervisor that they were not allowed to speak Spanish with each other during their lunch breaks; the supervisor advised them that they were only allowed to speak Spanish with the clients for translation. Otherwise they were required to speak English.

In all of these cases, one individual acted upon his or her prejudice to violate the civil rights of others; some of these incidents may also be illegal according to Title VI of the Civil Rights Act of 1964, which prohibits discrimination based on race or national origin in all agencies receiving federal funds. In only one of the cases was an appropriate response undertaken by senior management, despite the fact that the management was informed in each of these instances. The prejudicial staff members who acted upon their biased beliefs depended upon the silence of a majority of other staff, who feared losing their jobs or feared social ostracism if they reported or even spoke out against the racist acts. I have known many of the individuals who were silent and have spoken with them at length about these and other incidents. Through these discussions I have come to the conclusion that their silent assent to what can only be understood as egregious bias is predominantly based on fear. It is much more difficult, however, to understand the reluctance of senior administration to respond appropriately. Syracuse is a small city and many people in positions of authority—from senior staff at local institutions to elected officials—were born here, went to school together, and may even have family members in common with the racist actors. For the most part, when speaking privately, they do not approve of the actions of their biased colleagues. But they believe that the costs to them of protesting too vehemently might be life-long ostracism, which they are unwilling to risk.

Notes

1. http://www.onondaganation.org/history.html.

2. http://tuscaroras.com/pages/six_nations_ex.html.

3. H. P. Smith and Robert Joki, *Syracuse and Its Surroundings: A Victorian Photo Tour of New York's Salt City* (Black Dome Press, September 10, 2002).

4. Dennis J. Connors's photo-book *Syracuse, NY (Images of America)* (Arcadia Publishing, 1997) compiles historical images of the Erie Canal running through downtown Syracuse.

5. U.S. Census 2000.

6. Barbara Sheklin Davis, *Syracuse African Americans (Black America)*, First Edition (Arcadia Publishing, January 18, 2006).

7. "Latinos in Syracuse," http://www.archives.nysed.gov/projects/legacies/Syracuse/S_Latino/histories/.

8. "A Closer Look at Sudanese Refugee Resettlement," *UMNCOR Update* 9, no. 1 (Spring 2001), http://gbgm-umc.org/UMCOR/update/lostboys.stm.

9. "The Great State of New York Golden Snowball Contest Weather Website," 2005, http://www.goldensnowball.com/.

10. Frederick Douglass, John W. Blassingame, John R. McKivigan, and Peter P. Hinks, *Narrative of the Life of Frederick Douglass, An American Slave: Written by Himself, New Edition* (Yale University Press, March 1, 2001).

11. "The Jerry Rescue," New York History Net, http://www.nyhistory.com/gerritsmith/jerry.htm.

12. "The Harriet Tubman Home," New York History Net, http://www.nyhistory.com/harriettubman/.

13. M. T. Fullilove, *Root Shock: How Tearing Up City Neighborhoods Hurts America, and What We Can Do About It* (New York: Ballantine, 2004); R. Wallace and M. T. Fullilove, "AIDS Deaths in the Bronx 1983–1988: Spatiotemporal Analysis from a Sociogeographic Perspective," *Environmental Planning* 23, no 12 (1991): 1701–23.

14. Maureen Sieh, "Urban Renewal, Syracuse Then and Now, Fifteenth Ward Stood Tall, Fell," *Syracuse Post-Standard,* September 21, 2003, http://www.syracusethenandnow.net/UrbanRenewal/Urban_Renewal.htm.

15. I am grateful to Takika Jones, who conducted interviews with elders in the communities of color in Syracuse on urban renewal. IRB approval was granted by the Syracuse University IRB.

16. E. Michael Jones, "The Slaughter of Cities: Urban Renewal As Ethnic Cleansing" (St. Augustine's Press, December 2003).

17. "Redlining in the Past, Syracuse Then and Now," http://www.syracusethenandnow.net/Redlining/Redlining.htm.

18. J. A. Williams, "Portrait of a City: Syracuse, the Old Home Town, 1994" (Syracuse, N.Y.: Syracuse University Library Associates, 1994).

19. M. Sieh, "Few FHA Loans Go to Minorities, Study Says: Over Four Years, 78.1 Percent Went to City's White Neighborhoods, Group Finds," *Syracuse Post-Standard,* May 21, 2002.

20. I am grateful to my student intern, Johanna Kingson, who conducted the following analysis. She chose two articles from the Syracuse *Post-Standard,* one in January and one in June, for every ten years from 1900 to 2000. Then she conducted a Fry readability analysis, to assess the grade level difficulty of the text on each sample.

21. M. T. Fullilove, "Root Shock.

22. H. Fumkin, "Health, Equity, and the Built Environment," *Environmental Health Perspectives* 113 no. 50 (2005): A290–91; S. Bashir, "Home Is Where the Harm Is: Inadequate Housing as a Public Health Crisis." *American Journal of Public Health* 92, no. 5 (2002): 733–38; J. Kreiger and D. Higgins, "Housing and Health: Time Again for Public Health Action." *American Journal of Public Health* 92, no. 5 (2002): 758–68; D. Cohen, S. Spear, R. Scribner, et al., "Broken Windows and the Risk of Gonorrhea," *American Journal of Public Health* 90, no. 2 (2000): 230–36.

23. H. L. Needleman, "Childhood Lead Poisoning: The Promise and Abandonment of Primary Prevention," *American Journal of Public Health* 88, no. 12 (1998): 1871–77; V. B. Haley, T. O. Talbot, "Geographic Analysis of Blood Lead Levels in New York State Children Born 1994–1997," *Environmental Health Perspectives* 112, no. 15 (2004): 1577–82.

24. The data are drawn from New York State Department of Health, "Eliminating Childhood Lead Poisoning in New York State by 2010," (Albany: New York State Department of Health, 2004). All analyses by the author.

25. D. Wallace and R. Wallace, *A Plague on Your Houses: How New York Was Burned Down and National Public Health Crumbled,* (New York: Verso Press, 1998).

26. Mindy Thompson Fullilove, personal communication, September 2005.

27. Data provided by the Onondaga County Department of Health, analysis done by the author.

28. Vacant housing data are from the 2000 U.S. Census.

29. (Odds ratio 2.06, 95 percent CI, $p<0.0001$).

30. L. Perez, "Owners Slow Getting the Lead Out: Painting over Danger," *Syracuse Post-Standard,* sec. A, July 24, 2001.

31. Analysis based on the Syracuse *Post-Standard* report of the suburbs where the owners lived and household income data from the 2000 census.

32. L. Perez, "System Fails Kids: Hundreds of CNY Children Afflicted by Lead Poisoning Every Year," *Syracuse Post-Standard,* sec. A, July 22, 2001.

33. L. Perez, "Grace Street's Children Have Poison in Blood: Homes There Have One of the Highest Concentrations of Lead-Poisoned Children," *Syracuse Post-Standard,* July 22, 2001.

34. New York State Rules and Regulations, "Title 10: Public Health Law," Section 206(1)(n) and 1370-a Subpart 67-2, "Environmental Assessment and Abatement," http://www.health.state.ny.us/nysdoh/phforum/nycrr10.htm.

35. This study is fully described in note 45.

36. See note 82.

37. Based on a content analysis of the Syracuse *Post-Standard* for the years 1995–2000. The newspaper was searched using the Nexus/Lexus search engine for the terms "vacant house" and "fire." In each article, the authors looked up the zip code, using Mapquest and then tallied the results per zip code. J. Jacobs, "Tipp Hill House Fire Called Suspicious: The House at Willis Avenue and Cayuga Street Was Vacant and Had No Power," *Syracuse Post-Standard,* sec. B, December 7, 2000; S. Errington, "City Fire Leaves Family Homeless: Syracuse Firefighters Face Fire on All Three Floors of Merriman Avenue House," *Syracuse Post-Standard,* sec. B, November 24, 2000; J. S. Merculief, "Vacant House Gutted by Fire: Firefighters Search Flaming Building after Being Told Children Had Been Inside," *Syracuse Post-Standard,* sec. B, November 22, 2000; "Today in History," *Syracuse Post-Standard,* sec. C, November 17 2000; "Cause of Merriman Fire Still Being Investigated, *Syracuse Post-Standard,* sec. B, October 29, 2000; J. Jacobs, "Fire Damages Merriman Ave. Vacant House," *Syracuse Post-Standard,* sec. B, October 28, 2000; M. Sieh, "Tire Dumpers Wear on City: Thousands of Tires Left on Vacant Properties Pose Fire Threat, Syracuse Officials Say," *Syracuse Post-Standard,* sec. B, June 9, 2000; S. Weibezahl, "Fire Damages Salina St. House: Officials Are Still Searching for Cause in Blaze That Ruined the South Side Building," *Syracuse Post-Standard,* sec. B, June 1, 2000; S. Weibezahl, "Morning Fire Destroys Vacant House on South Side: More Than 30 Firefighters Battled the 8:30 A.M. Blaze," *Syracuse Post-Standard,* sec. B, May 31, 2000; " Police: Three Youths Tried to Set Fire in Empty House," *Syracuse Post-Standard,* sec. B, May 26, 2000; "Arson Fire Damages Vacant South Side House," *Syracuse Post-Standard,* sec. B, May 15, 2000; "West Kennedy Street Fire Determined to Be Arson," *Syracuse Post-Standard,* sec. B, April 7, 2000; "Teen Charged with Arson after Tuesday Night Fire," *Syracuse Post-Standard,* sec. B, March 29, 2000; S. Weibezahl, "City Fire Appears Arson: Two Houses Burn on the South Side," *Syracuse Post-Standard,* sec. B, November 17, 1999; S. Weibezahl, "Fire Destroys Abandoned House," *Syracuse Post-Standard,* sec. C, November 16, 1999; "Firefighters Douse Blaze at Vacant Syracuse House," *Syracuse Post-Standard,* sec. B, August 4, 1999; "Firefighters Put out Fire at Vacant Syracuse Home," *Syracuse Post-Standard,* sec. A, July 31, 1999; "Three Children Charged with Setting House Fire," *Syracuse Post-Standard,* sec. B, July 14, 1999; J. S. Merculief, "Vacant City House Damaged by Flames," *Syracuse Post-Standard,* sec. B, July 11, 1999; "Fire at Valley Home Was Set, Firefighters Say," *Syracuse Post-Standard,* sec.

B, October 15, 1998; "Varnished-Soaked Rags Blamed for Apartment Fire," *Syracuse Post-Standard*, sec. B, May 18, 1999; V. Jackson, "Arson Linked to Blaze in Vacant East Side House," *Syracuse Post-Standard*, sec. B, September 13, 1998; P. Ortiz, "Fire Damages House in City's South Side," *Syracuse Post-Standard*, sec. B, September 8, 1998; F. Pierce, "Arson Is Suspected in Vacant House Fire," *Syracuse Post-Standard*, sec. B, August 3, 1998; E. Duggan, "Fire in Vacant House Started by Arson," *Syracuse Post-Standard*, sec. B, July 27, 1998; V. Jackson and P. Ortiz, "Man Charged in Court Street Arson: Police Say Ernest B. Mosier Jr., 36, Set a Couch on Fire in a Building at 312 Court St. (13208) That Damaged Two Adjacent Houses," *Syracuse Post-Standard*, sec. B, July 15, 1998; V. Jackson, "Arson Charged in North Side Fire," *Syracuse Post-Standard*, sec. C, July 14, 1998; M. Weiner, "Arson Suspected in Fire That Damaged Vacant City Row House," *Syracuse Post-Standard*, sec. B, July 4, 1998; E. M. Duggan, "City Firefighters Battle Blaze in Office Building: Authorities Say a Faulty Electrical Box in the Basement of 400 Montgomery St. Is to Blame for the Smoky Fire Sunday," *Syracuse Post-Standard*, sec. B, March 16, 1998; F. Pierce, "Blaze Damages Two-Story House: Arson Suspected," *Syracuse Post-Standard*, sec. B, January 12, 1998; P. Ortiz, "Arson Suspected in Early Morning Fire at Vacant City Home," *Syracuse Post-Standard*, sec. B, January 8, 1998; F. Pierce, "Vacant House in City Damaged by Suspicious Fire," *Syracuse Post-Standard*, sec. B, December 29, 1997; K. Terrell, "Gasoline Used to Start Blaze That Destroyed House," *Syracuse Post-Standard*, sec. B, September 19, 1997; L. Champion, "Two Firefighters Injured in Early-Morning City Blaze: Arson Suspected as Fire Spreads from Vacant House to Home Next Door," *Syracuse Post-Standard*, sec. A, May 28, 1997; P. Ortiz, "Garfield Ave. Fire Is Called Arson," *Syracuse Post-Standard*, sec. C, April 9, 1997; P. Ortiz, "Arson Suspected in Fire That Burned Porch of City Home," *Syracuse Post-Standard*, sec. B, April 9, 1997; "South-Siders Fearful; Need Help; Nobody Listens to Longtime Residents' Concerns," *Syracuse Post-Standard*, sec. A, October 7, 1996; G. Coin, "Man Warned Someone Would Start House Fire Early Morning: Fire Damages Vacant House and Home Next Door," *Syracuse Post-Standard*, sec. C, September 15, 1996; L. Champion, "Vacant City Home Damaged by Arson," *Syracuse Post-Standard*, sec. D, July 25, 1996; J. Theodore, "City Firefighters Put out Blaze at Vacant House," *Syracuse Post-Standard*, sec. B, May 18,1995; L. Rogers, "Firefighters Try to Stop Fires by Children: Vacant Houses Are Favorite Targets for Teen-Agers and Children," *Syracuse Post-Standard*, sec. B, April 28, 1995; L. Duffy, "City Firefighter Injures Back While Battling Blaze," *Syracuse Post-Standard*, sec. C, April 14, 1995.

38. The gonorrhea rates below are from the New York State Department of Health. From 2003–2004 Onondaga County's gonorrhea rate was 23 percent higher than New York City's. The majority of Onondaga County STD diagnoses are among City of Syracuse residents. In 2000–2001, for

example, only 9.3 percent of gonorrhea infections occurred to residents of Onondaga County who lived outside of the City of Syracuse. (Data from Onondaga County Health Department.)

39. Data are from the year 2000, from the Onondaga County Health Department. Analysis by the author.

40. http://encarta.msn.com/media_701500845_761554539_1_1/AIDS_Cases_and_Annual_Rates_per_100_000_Population_by_Metropolitan_Area_and_Age_Group_in_the_United_States.html.

41. Data are from the New York State AIDS Institute.

42. The data are from the Community Needs Index 2000, New York State Department of Health, Albany, N.Y.

43. This analysis is conducted on fifty-five of the fifty-seven City of Syracuse census tracts. The remaining two census tracts are the downtown and the mall.

44. The logistic regression looked at gonorrhea diagnoses in a census tract, with 20 percent or more vacant houses in that census tract as a risk factor and controlling for the proportion of minority residence. Census tracts with 20 percent or more vacant houses had 12.6 times the risk of elevated gonorrhea infections among residents (OR 12.6, 95 percent CI2.415-65.831).

45. I am very grateful to Maizie Shaw and Tarah Tapley for conducting these interviews. IRB approval was granted by the Syracuse University IRB.

46. Lilie Welych, Barbara Laws, Amy Fitzgerald, Tracey Durham, Don Cibula, and Sandra Lane, "Formative Research for Public Health Interventions among Adolescents at High Risk for Gonorrhea and other STDs," *Journal of Public Health Management and Practice,* 4 no. 6 (1998): 54–61.

47. As shown below from the Clinic Website:

Onondaga County STD CLINIC SCHEDULE:
Mondays: 9:00 a.m.–10:30 a.m. and 1:00 p.m.–3:00 p.m.
Tuesdays: 1:00 p.m.–3:00 p.m.
Wednesdays: Closed
Thursdays: 12:30 p.m.–4:30 p.m.
Friday: 9:00 a.m.–10:30 a.m.

48. Sandra D. Lane, Rob Keefe, Robert A. Rubinstein, Noah Webster, Alan Rosenthal, Don Cibula, and Jesse Dowdell, "Structural Violence and Racial Disparity in Heterosexual HIV Infection," *Journal of Health Care for the Poor and Underserved,* 15 no. 3 (August 2004): 319–35.

49. A. M. Renton, L. Whitaker, and M. Riddlesdell, "Heterosexual HIV Transmission and STD Prevalence: Predictions of a Theoretical Model," *Sexually Transmitted Infections* 74, no. 5 (1998): 339–44; D. T. Fleming and J. N. Wasserheit, "From Epidemiological Synergy to Public Health Policy

and Practice: The Contribution of Other Sexually Transmitted Diseases to Sexual Transmission of HIV Infection," *Sexually Transmitted Infections* 75 no. 1 (1999): 3–17; P. Sangani, G. Rutherford, and D. Wilkinson, "Population-Based Interventions for Reducing Sexually Transmitted Infections, Including HIV Infection," *Cochrane Database of Systematic Reviews* 2 (2004).

50. "HIV/AIDS Related Costs and Expenditures in New York State," and "Annual Medicaid Expenditures for People with HIV/AIDS, New York State, Federal Fiscal Years 1986–2002," http://www.health.state.ny.us/diseases/aids/reports/2001/docs/section20.pdf.

51. All initials have been changed. I am grateful to Steve Marston who conducted these interviews. IRB approval was granted by the SUNY Upstate IRB. These interviews were part of the HRSA funded study "Innovative Approaches ..." fully described in note 48.

52. Dana Brunett, "Supermarket Access in Low Income Communities," Prevention Institute for the Center for Health Improvement (CHI), Oakland, California, 2002, http://www.preventioninstitute.org/CHI_supermarkets.html.

53. Monique R. Brown, "Supermarket Blackout—Lack of Quality Grocery Stores in Black Communities," *Black Enterprise,* July 1999; Tom Larson, "Why There Will Be No Chain Supermarkets in Inner City Neighborhoods," *California Politics and Policy* 7, no. 1 (June 2003).

54. J. Putnam, J. Allshouse, and L. S. Kantor, "US Per Capita Food Supply Trends: More Calories, Refined Carbohydrates, and Fats," *Food Review* 25 (2002): 2–15; K. Morland, S. Wing, and A. D. Roux, "The Contextual Effect of the Local Food Environment on Residents' Diets: The Atherosclerosis Risk in Communities Study," *American Journal of Public Health* 92, no. 11 (1992): 1761–67; E. Bolen and K. Hecht, "Neighborhood Groceries: New Access to Healthy Food in Low-Income Communities" (San Francisco: California Food Policy Advocates, 2003).

55. Dale Johnson, Executive Director, Samaritan Center, and Don Mitchell, Chair, Department of Geography, Syracuse University. Maps prepared under the direction of Jane Read, Assistant Professor, Department of Geography, Syracuse University.

56. K. H. Johnson, M. Bazargan, and C. J. Cherpitel, "Alcohol, Tobacco, and Drug Use and the Onset of Type 2 Diabetes among Inner-City Minority Patients," *The Journal of the American Board of Family Practice* 14, no. 6 (2001): 430–36; R. S. Kieffer, S. K. Willis, A. M. Odoms-Young, J. Two Feathers, and J. Loveluck, "Reducing Disparities in Diabetes among African-American and Latino Residents of Detroit: The Essential Role of Community Planning Focus Groups," *Ethnicity and Disease* 14, no. 3, supp. 1 (2004): S27–37; K. M. Flagel, M. Carroll, R. J. Kuczmarski, et al., "Overweight and Obesity in the United States: Prevalence and Trends, 1960–1994," *International Journal*

of Obstetrics 22 (1998): 39–47; P. M. Barnes and C. A. Schoeborn, "Physical Activity among Adults: United States, 2000: Advance Data from Vital and Health Statistics" (Hyattsville, MD: National Center for Health Statistics, 2003); V. A. Diaz, A. G. Mainous, F. J. Koopman, et al., "Race and Diet in the Overweight: Association with Cardiovascular Risk in a Nationally Representative Sample," *Nutrition* 21, no. 6 (2005): 718–25; The Lower Mississippi Delta Nutrition Research Consortium. "Self-Reported Health of Residents of the Mississippi Delta," *Journal of Health Care for the Poor and Underserved* 15, no. 4 (2004): 645–62; I. S. Okosun, M. Glodener, and G. E. Dever, "Diagnosed Diabetes and Ethnic Disparities in Adverse Health Behaviors of American Women," *Journal of the National Medical Association* 95, no. 7 (2003): 523–32; D. N. Cox, A. S. Anderson, M. D. Lean, et al., "UK Consumer Attitudes, Beliefs and Barriers to Increasing Fruit and Vegetable Consumption," *Public Health and Nutrition* 1 (1998): 61–68; J. L. Dannelly, J. R. Kicklighter, B. L. Hopkins, et al., "Recommendations for Nutrition Interventions with Overweight African-American Adolescents and Young Adults at The Atlanta Jobs Corps Center," *Journal of Health Care for the Poor and Underserved* 16, no. 1 (2005): 111–26; A. Drewnowski and S. E. Specter, "Poverty and Obesity: The Role of Energy Density and Energy Costs," *American Journal of Clinical Nutrition* 79 (2004): 6–16; C. S. Hann, C. L. Rock, I. King, et al., "Validation of the Health Eating Index Using Plasma Biomarkers in a Clinical Sample of Adult Females," *American Journal of Clinical Nutrition* 74 (2001): 479–86; R. L. Johnson, "Gender Differences in Health-Promoting Lifestyles of African Americans," *Public Health Nursing* 22, no. 2 (2005): 130–37; R. S. Kington and J. P. Smith, "Socioeconomic Status and Racial and Ethnic Differences in Functional Status Associated with Chronic Diseases," *American Journal of Public Health* 87, no 5 (1997): 805–10; D. Neumark-Sztainer, M. Storey, P. J. Hannan, et al., "Overweight Status and Eating Patterns among Adolescents: Where Do Youths Stand in Comparison with the Healthy People 2010 Objectives?" *American Journal of Public Health* 92, no. 5 (2002): 844–51; C. M. Olson, "Nutrition and Health Outcomes Associated with Food Insecurity and Hunger," *Journal of Nutrition* 129 (1999): 521–24; S. Paeratakul, J. C. Loverjoy, D. H. Ryan, et al., "The Relation of Gender, Race and Socioeconomic Status to Obesity and Obesity Comorbidities in a Sample of U.S. Adults," *International Journal of Obstetric Related Metabolic Disorders*, 26 (2002): 1205–10; P. S. Gardiner, "The African Americanization of Menthol Cigarette Use in the United States," *Nicotine and Tobacco Research* 6, supp. 1 (2004): S55–65.

57. These increases, as measured by students T-test comparing the mean BMIs, were all significant, p<0.01.

58. This analysis was significant; relative risk = 1.26, 95 percent CI 1.08 to 1.48.

59. Odds ratio, 1.47, 95 percent CI 1.08–2.0.

60. Odds ratio, 1.44, 95 percent CI 1.04 to 1.98.

61. K. Panaretto, H. Lee, M. Mitchell, S. Larkins, V. Manessis, P. Buettner, and D. Watson, "Risk Factors for Preterm, Low Birth Weight and Small for Gestational Age Birth in Urban Aboriginal and Torres Strait Islander Women in Townsville," *Australia, New Zealand Journal of Public Health* 30, no. 2 (April 2006): 163–70; B. Reime, P. A. Ratner, S. N. Tomaselli-Reime, A. Kelly, B. A. Schuecking, and P. Wenzlaff, "The Role of Mediating Factors in the Association Between Social Deprivation and Low Birth Weight in Germany," *Social Science Medicine* 62, no. 7 (April 2006): 1731–44. Published online October 17, 2005; T. J. Rosenberg, S. Garbers, H. Lipkind, and M. A. Chiasson, "Maternal Obesity and Diabetes as Risk Factors for Adverse Pregnancy Outcomes: Differences among 4 Racial/Ethnic Groups," *American Journal of Public Health* 95, no. 9 (2005): 1545–51; I. Hendler, R. L. Goldenberg, B. M. Mercer, J. D. Iams, P. J. Meis, A. H. Moawad, C.A. MacPherson, S. N. Caritis, M. Miodovnik, K. M. Menard, G. R. Thurnau, and Y. Sorokin, "The Preterm Prediction Study: Association Between Maternal Body Mass Index and Spontaneous and Indicated Preterm Birth," *American Journal of Obstetric Gynecology* 192, no. 3 (March 2005): 882–86.

62. The type of sugar in the blood is glucose. I am using the more colloquial term "sugar" in this section to make the passage more easily understood by the non-specialist reader.

63. Kidney and Urologic Diseases Statistics from the National Kidney and Urologic Diseases Clearinghouse, 2003, United States, http://kidney.niddk.nih.gov/kudiseases/pubs/kustats/index.htm.

64. Data on end stage renal disease from the National Kidney Foundation.

65. I wrote two grants pro bono for the National Kidney Association of Central New York, one of which was funded, the 2003–2006 National Kidney Foundation of CNY, Minority Health Community Partnership grant, from the New York State Office of Minority Health. The man whose narrative is quoted here generously allowed the NKF to use his story in their public documents. He subsequently appeared on WCNY television to tell his story to the public, to alert the community to kidney disease.

66. Children's Defense Fund, "More than 1 out of 3 Syracuse Children Live in Poverty—Nearly Twice the Rate in New York," press release, June 11, 2004, www.cdfny.org/News/PressReleases.

67. Elise Boulding, "Cultures of Peace: The Hidden Side of History," *Syracuse Studies on Peace and Conflict Resolution* (Syracuse University Press, May 2000).

Chapter 3

Math and Biology

When I was directing Syracuse Healthy Start, my then-seven-year-old daughter visited my office during a "take-your-daughter-to-work" day. I settled her into my office with crayons and paper, and then turned to a spreadsheet on my computer to calculate rates of low birth weight and infant death for that quarterly period. With profound disappointment in her voice, she asked, "Mommy, I know that your work is to help keep the babies from dying, but how can you do that by just doing math on your computer?"

Connecting the stories to the statistics and to the biology is essential to understanding racial and ethnic inequality in infant death. This chapter presents the "math" of pregnancy, birth, and infant death in Syracuse and the "biology" of normal pregnancy and what happens when things go wrong. *Williams Obstetrics,* the bible of clinical wisdom about pregnancy and birth, fills more than 1,400 pages of small print, including complex descriptions of the many potential complications afflicting mother and baby in their journey from conception to birth.[1]

Very broadly—and I can see in my mind my obstetrical colleagues wincing at my oversimplification—in the majority of cases when pregnancy goes wrong, it is either because the baby is born too soon or too small. Although we speak of pregnancy as lasting nine months, new mothers are usually dismayed to realize that the length of gestation, the obstetrical term for the pregnancy period, exceeds nine months. We count the gestational period as forty weeks from the last menstrual period, which is usually two weeks before a lucky sperm successfully merges with an egg in the mother's fallopian tube, resulting in conception. A pregnancy that lasts until the end of the thirty-seventh week is said to be "full term" and a baby that emerges prior to thirty-seven weeks is called "premature."

The rate at which a fetus grows inside the mother has lifelong consequences. Many a new mother will remember a sonographer spreading cold gel on her rounded belly and using a transducer to "look" with sound waves inside her uterus at the developing fetus. In addition to pointing out the baby's features—to parents who are trying to make out the head, or hand, or leg among the mass of indistinct gray—the sonographer measures the length of the thigh, the circumference of the head and abdomen, and other key parts of the baby's anatomy. Immediately after the birth, the infant is weighed and its head circumference and length are also assessed. A baby who weighs less than 2,500 grams (about 5.5 pounds) at birth is considered "low birth weight." Babies weighing less than 1,500 grams (about 3.3 pounds) are "very low birth weight." An infant who is born too soon, but is the right weight for its gestational age, has a much better chance for good health than one who is too "small for its dates." Less than expected fetal growth in a baby whose weight falls below the tenth percentile for its gestational age results from "intrauterine growth restriction," a term nearly always shorted to its acronym, IUGR.

IUGR is associated with future learning problems if the growth of the fetal brain is restricted.[2] A growing body of literature suggests

Table 3.1 Syracuse Birth Outcomes, 2000–2001, by Mother's Race/Ethnicity

	White** (n=2443)	African American** (n=1570)	Latino** (n=142)
Low birth weight* (singletons only)	6.8%	11.2%	14.5%
Premature* (singletons only)	9.0%	12.1%	17.4%
IUGR* (of full term singletons)	2.1%	3.5%	4.4%

*percentages

**Latino births are separated from white and African American births in this analysis.

that IUGR may lead to heart disease, high blood pressure, and type II diabetes in adulthood because the internal organs and blood vessels also grow less robustly than they should.[3] Among the known etiological factors for IUGR are pregnancy-related high blood pressure (preeclampsia), maternal substance use (tobacco, alcohol, cocaine), and multiple births (twins, triplets).[4] Two additional factors have been found in human and animal studies to impede fetal growth: (1) maternal malnutrition, particularly inadequate intake of micronutrients[5] and (2) maternal exposure to stressors.[6]

We divide pregnancy into trimesters, each twelve weeks long. Prenatal care and the experiences of the expectant mother are different in each trimester. I remember testing my urine with a home pregnancy test; my husband and I held our breath for nearly the entire two minutes before the test strip turned blue, showing that "we" were pregnant. At that moment I was already five weeks pregnant and just beginning to feel the breast tenderness and nausea that are the hallmarks of early pregnancy. By the time most women recognize that they are pregnant, the newly joined egg and sperm have traversed the fallopian tube and nestled into the lush blood and nutrient-rich cushion of the uterine lining, where the cells of the developing embryo sort themselves into what will become heart, lungs, kidneys, nerves, and the like. At the completion of the first trimester the embryo has graduated to being a fetus, with the internal structure of its organs largely in place.[7] Most pregnancy losses, or miscarriages, happen in these first three months and are usually due to defects in fetal development. About a third of all conceptions end in miscarriage, but about half of these losses go unnoticed.[8] Women may just experience heavier than usual menstruation. Once a woman realizes that she is pregnant and has begun to feel the signs of pregnancy she has about a 15 percent risk of miscarriage. Even early miscarriages, however, can be traumatic losses that women, and some men, remember lifelong.

By the end of the second three months—the second trimester—the fetus is almost twelve inches in length and weighs about a pound.[9] The mother begins to feel her baby move between the sixteenth and twentieth weeks; usually first-time mothers feel their babies later than those who have given birth before. Historically, in English Common Law, the first time a mother felt her baby move was called "quickening" and was considered to be the moment that the developing organism was formed and, by some, endowed with a soul. According to Common Law as interpreted before the twentieth century, abortion before quickening was not illegal.[10] Currently, twenty-three weeks is the age of "viability," when a baby can first live outside its mother's womb if born prematurely. Advances in neonatal intensive care make the survival of younger babies an ever-greater possibility. Only twenty years ago babies under 750 grams—less than two pounds—rarely survived. In Syracuse during 2000–2001, among babies of twenty-three weeks or greater gestation and less than 750 grams, nearly three quarters left the NICU (neonatal intensive care unit) and returned home with their parents. Among the tiny survivors, however, are many who suffer life-long disabilities in learning, vision, and hearing, as well as those with cerebral palsy.[11]

Pregnancy losses that occur in the second trimester are often caused by problems with the mother's health. Pregnancy can cause a woman to develop high blood pressure, a condition once labeled toxemia and now commonly called preeclampsia. If untreated, the blood pressure can cause seizures and even death in the mother; despite treatment the fetal growth is often compromised, leading to fetal growth restriction. If the mother's blood pressure becomes too high and cannot be controlled with magnesium sulfate or other powerful intravenous drugs, obstetricians must induce the labor to save the mother's life, regardless of how premature the birth may be. Even with less severe increases in a mother's blood pressure, the placenta—the blood-rich maze of intersecting fetal and maternal capillaries delivering oxygen and nutrition to the fetus and removing its waste—can peel away from the uterine wall. This peeling away—called "placental abruption"—is a medical emergency which, if untreated, leads to maternal death through hemorrhage and fetal death by oxygen deprivation. The mother's blood pressure can also become elevated by cocaine use, which clamps down the maternal blood vessels and can induce the separation of the placenta from the womb.

By the middle of pregnancy, women are more vulnerable to infection. Scientists don't completely agree on why pregnancy decreases the body's natural defenses against microorganisms, but the most compelling theory is that when the fetal immune system begins functioning, around the eighteenth week of pregnancy, the mother's immune system gets ratcheted down so that her system will not attack the fetus.[12] The mother's resulting immunologic weakness can produce disastrous consequences for her baby and for her own life, if she is exposed to infection. Group B streptococcus, rubella (German measles), and toxoplasmosis (often from exposure to undercooked meat or to kitty litter), for example, can lead to meningitis, blindness, or death of the fetus. In the developing world, malaria causes a great deal of pregnancy loss and maternal death because the malarial parasite specifically attacks the placenta.[13] Brucellosis and listeriosis both infect the amniotic sac, an organ that one obstetrical resident whom I interviewed, poetically referred to as the "protective snow globe" of translucent tissue that encapsulates the developing fetus. My son Adam died before he was born because I was infected with listeriosis, probably from eating Camembert cheese in 1989 before we understood the risk. The CDC estimates that pregnant women are twenty times more likely to become infected with listeria than non-pregnant adults, and warns them not to eat soft aged cheeses, raw hot dogs, or cold cuts, all of which may harbor the bacterium.[14]

Within the past decade a growing number of studies have looked at the potential for vaginal bacterial infections, associated with a variety of anaerobic bacteria, to cause harm to a pregnancy.[15] Microbiologists who specialize in bacterial vaginosis (BV) speculate that early in pregnancy, BV ascends upwards from the vaginal canal through the cervix, where it reaches the surface of the amniotic sac. As the mother's immune system gets turned down, some microbiologists theorize, the quiescent BV blooms. The mother's body releases a cascade of chemical reactions that retaliate against the threatening bacteria.[16] Unfortunately, this chemical cascade can also stimulate labor, by causing the uterine muscles to contract. This protective response may lead in some cases to premature labor and far-too-early birth.

BV occurs much more commonly in women of color than in white women, for reasons that are not completely understood. In Syracuse, among women delivering at our largest birth hospital (2000–2002), about 49 percent of African American and 44 percent of Latin American women, compared with 19 percent of European American women, were infected during their pregnancies with BV. While we don't yet fully understand the cause of this racial/ethnic difference, we suspect that BV may precipitate many of the otherwise unexplained premature births among women of color. BV may, therefore, be a root cause of at least part of the racial/ethnic disparity in premature birth.[17]

The source of some, but not all, of the racial gap in BV incidence may be vaginal douching. African American women report to researchers that they douche more frequently than European American women.[18] The sale of douche products is also big business—totaling about $144 million per year.[19] Douching can upset the normal balance of bacteria in the vagina, by killing off the beneficial *Lactobacillus*. *Lactobacillus* makes lactic acid and hydrogen peroxide, which inhibit the overgrowth of harmful bacteria. Nine recent studies have found that women who douche are more likely to have BV, although these studies do not prove that douching causes BV.[20] I once jokingly suggested to my colleagues that we conduct civil disobedience in the douche products aisle of our local pharmacy to alert the community to the potential dangers of douching. They were amused and a bit shocked; while refusing to be involved in civil disobedience, several replied that douche preparations could be compared to cigarettes, in that they are unnecessary, sold to make money, and may be harmful.

A second potential cause of BV is sexual transmission. Until recently, BV was not believed to be sexually transmitted, but was thought to be simply an overgrowth of bacteria that are usually held in check, a condition that researcher Sharon Hillier refers to as a disturbance of the "vaginal ecology."[21] Treated women, however, frequently become re-infected with BV. Monogamous lesbians either both have BV, or both remain free of the infection. It is very rare for one lesbian in a monogamous couple to have BV and the partner to be BV free.[22] These factors led researchers to suspect that BV may be shared between partners.

Research by Sharon Hillier, Robert Nugent, and others demonstrated that in many premature births, bacterial vaginosis precedes the onset of labor, and likely precipitates the unexpectedly early delivery.[23] As mentioned in the first chapter, Syracuse Healthy Start's obstetrical consultant, Richard Aubry, MD, MPH, recommended that local prenatal providers screen all Syracuse residents in the first trimester and treat all women with evidence of infection.[24] The obstetricians and nurse midwives who followed Dr. Aubry's recommendations tended to work in the two clinical sites that served the majority of impoverished women, many of whom were women of color. Private providers, for the most part, did not take up Dr. Aubry's recommendations. Syracuse Healthy Start did not undertake this protocol as a research study; indeed, we simply believed that we were following the most up-to-date information. However, it turned out that we were one of the first community-wide demonstrations for BV screening and treatment. Within the first two years of the protocol—1999 and 2000—there was a striking decrease in very premature births (less than 32 weeks gestation) born to mothers receiving care from the two clinical sites following the protocol. Based on this finding, the Centers for Disease Control and Prevention funded us to evaluate our results by reviewing the prenatal and hospital delivery charts of 3,140 babies born to Syracuse residents at the largest birth hospital from January 1, 2000 to March 31, 2002.

Our Syracuse Healthy Start nurse midwife, Kathy DeMott, became a co-principal investigator on our evaluation team, with Dr. Aubry, me, and Emily Koumans, MD, of the CDC's Division of STD Prevention. We compared three groups of women who gave birth: (1) women who were screened for BV but were negative, (2) women who were screened, were positive, and received treatment, and (3) women who were positive but were not treated. We did not withhold treatment from anyone, but some women were untreated because they did not return to the clinic for treatment. Our evaluation demonstrated that the BV screening and treatment worked to reduce premature delivery. Women who were screened and positive had nearly half as many very premature births (less than 32 weeks gestation), compared with women who were positive and untreated. Since our evaluation was not a controlled experimental design—the gold standard to evaluate drug therapy—BV screening and treatment must be further studied in rigorously designed research.

New York State vital records document three possible outcomes of pregnancy: live birth, termination, or fetal death. Just over 2,200 babies are born each year to Syracuse mothers. In Syracuse about a third of all pregnancies are terminated, a rate that is lower than many other cities in New York State. More than 90 percent of abortions in Onondaga County and elsewhere occur in the first twelve weeks of pregnancy; the remaining abortions that take place in the second trimester are most often performed because amniocentesis has detected a serious fetal abnormality, or birth defect.[25] An "infant death" occurs when a baby is born with any signs of life and subsequently dies; if a baby dies before emerging from its mother's body, it is classified as a "fetal death." An infant death that occurs within the first four weeks of life is classified as a "neonatal death." After the first month, but before the first birthday, an infant death is termed a "postneonatal death."

At one minute and five minutes after the birth, labor and delivery nurses assess an aggregate measure known as the Apgar score, which grades the infant's cry, movement, color, heartbeat, and breathing to arrive at a number between zero and ten.[26] Apgars of eight or higher at one minute indicate vigorous health; a perfect score of ten is exceedingly rare. Babies whose Apgars fall below seven may have suffered harm during the pregnancy or birth. The idiosyncrasy in the protocol, as it is currently followed, is that an infant born at fifteen weeks gestation, nearly eight weeks before it could live outside its mother's protective womb, can be termed an infant death if it has an Apgar of one at one minute. A baby born this early will die in the first minutes, resulting in a five minute Apgar of zero. In contrast, a full term fetus that dies during its exit from the birth canal will be termed a fetal death.

In recent years, with great strides in saving the very youngest babies, delivery nurses have gotten more precise in evaluating the slightest signs of life in pre-viable babies. Sometimes this sign of life amounts to a slight and transient pulsation of the umbilical cord in an otherwise blue, tiny, and lifeless body. As a mother of a pre-viable stillborn infant I understand in my bones what a tragedy this death is to the family. But as an epidemiologist it frustrates me that these second trimester pregnancy losses are counted as infant deaths, whereas fetal deaths, being rarely reported, are nearly invisible in the public statistics. Our experience in Central New York is that pre-viable fetuses born in teaching hospitals with Neonatal Intensive Care Units are more likely to be categorized as live births than those born in non-teaching facilities. Nurses who are experienced at highly technological procedures that save the smallest viable babies are more likely to notice and record even slight and transient signs of life in pre-viable births.

There are three problems with this situation. First, since different localities categorize fetal and infant death differently, it makes precise comparisons impossible. Second, in my international experience I have found that other countries do not include the losses of pre-viable fetuses in their infant mortality calculations. Including these fetal losses in our infant death data inflates our infant mortality statistics. Third, since women of color are more likely to deliver in large, urban teaching hospitals—both because they more often live in cities where such facilities are located and are more often covered by Medicaid—this situation inflates African American infant mortality rates.

Tables 3.2 and 3.3 illustrate the magnitude of the difference. Table 3.2 presents the neonatal deaths of babies who were categorized as live born and who died in the first twenty-eight days. During 2000–2001, eleven Syracuse neonatal deaths occurred to infants whose gestational ages were fifteen to nineteen weeks, most of whom had one minute Apgar scores of one and were pronounced dead in the first minutes after birth. Calculating neonatal infant deaths in this way inflates the racial disparity. A way to partially correct for the bias of fetal and neonatal deaths being categorized differently in teaching and non-teaching hospitals is to include both fetal deaths (more than twenty weeks gestation) with neonatal deaths in the analysis.[27]

Table 3.3 presents the rates of fetal/neonatal deaths grouped this way, which shows that the African American/white difference is smaller than we realized when we looked at the neonatal deaths alone.

What Do Babies Die From?

In Syracuse from 1999–2001, about two thirds of infant deaths occurred during the neonatal period, with the remaining one third being postneonatal deaths. Deaths in these two time periods usually resulted from different causes.

About a quarter of neonatal deaths in Syracuse from 2000 to 2001 resulted from congenital anomalies, including malformations of the

Table 3.2 Neonatal Deaths, per 1,000 Live Births, Syracuse*

	White	African American	Racial disparity (African American/White)
1997	1.5	10.2	6.7
1998	3.0	7.4	2.5
1999	4.0	13.7	3.4
2000	4.6	7.7	1.7
2001	3.2	20.7	6.4
2002	9.1	15.5	1.7

Source data: New York State Department of Health, analysis by the author.
*All births (includes multiples).

**Table 3.3. Fetal (over 20 weeks) and Neonatal Deaths*,
per 1,000 Live Births plus Fetal Deaths**

	White	African American	Racial disparity (African American/White)
1997	11.2	25.6	2.3
1998	7.5	19.4	2.6
1999	10.4	22.5	2.2
2000	12.9	16.4	1.3
2001	17.6	29.0	1.6
2002	22.1	23.6	1.1

Source data: New York State Department of Health, analysis by the author.
* All births (includes multiples).

heart, central nervous system, chromosomal defects, and a few babies with widespread abnormalities in many of their organs. Three quarters of neonatal deaths resulted from premature births. Typically in a neonatal death due to premature birth, the baby emerges from the birth canal at the cusp of viability; the mean gestational age of such babies was twenty-two weeks, and the mode was twenty-three weeks during 2000–2001 in Syracuse. Neonatal deaths disproportionately occur to African American babies in Syracuse. In the majority of births in which the baby is just too tiny and too early to survive, until recently obstetricians could not pinpoint a precise cause. The usual risk factors (e.g., tobacco, cocaine, marijuana, or alcohol) do not fully explain the majority of such extremely premature births. *Placenta abruption,* the placenta peeling away from the lining of the uterus, accounts for a small number of neonatal deaths among very premature babies. Researchers now suspect, as explained earlier, that a large proportion of these preterm births result from sub-clinical infections, such as bacterial vaginosis.

As elsewhere, in Syracuse assisted reproduction has dramatically increased the number of multiple births; unfortunately, some of these high-risk pregnancies end tragically. About one fifth of the preterm births happen to twins, triplets, and quadruplets, and about one third of those multiple pregnancies were conceived with the help of in vitro fertilization or fertility medications. Among babies born in the largest birth hospital in Syracuse (2000–2002), 1.7 percent of them were conceived with the assistance of reproductive medicine. More than half of those pregnancies were the products of in vitro fertilization and the others of fertility stimulating medications. Although these miracle babies represented fewer than 2 percent of all Syracuse births during 2000–2001, they account for 7 percent of all neonatal deaths. More than one third (36.7 percent) of the infants who were conceived with medical intervention required NICU (neonatal intensive unit) care; they stayed for an average of twenty days each.[28]

Whereas the causes of neonatal deaths usually originate in fetal anomalies or problems during pregnancy, postneonatal deaths frequently arise from problems in parenting. Some babies die accidentally, such as drowning in bathwater while a parent leaves the infant to answer the door. Nearly every year in Onondaga County a baby is murdered by a caretaker, sometimes shaken by the mother's male partner in blind frustration at the baby's cry. Rarely, a baby succumbs to dehydration from repeated bouts of diarrhea; as in the developing world, sometimes mothers withhold fluids in a misguided attempt to stop the diarrhea. Table 3.4 presents postneonatal deaths by mothers' racial identity, for all Syracuse births during 2000–2001.

The largest single cause of postneonatal deaths, including more than half of such deaths in Syracuse during 1999–2001, was "Sudden Infant Death Syndrome" (SIDS). Almost three quarters of these SIDS deaths occurred to African American and Latino infants. Medical examiners describe SIDS as a "diagnosis of exclusion," meaning that since there are no absolutely characteristic signs of the cause of death on the deceased baby's body, they must exclude all other

Table 3.4 Post Neonatal Mortality, by Mother's Race, per 1,000 Live Births*

	White	African American	Racial disparity (African American/White)
1997	1.5	6.8	4.5
1998	1.5	4.9	3.3
1999	4.0	3.4	0.8
2000	0.8	4.4	5.7
2001	4.9	11.0	2.3
2002	1.7	3.6	2.2

Source data: New York State Department of Health, analysis by author.
*This analysis includes multiple births

causes.[29] Typically, SIDS strikes infants between one and six months of age. Since the early 1990s, pediatricians have advised parents to place infants face up to sleep, because SIDS occurs more often when babies sleep on their abdomens. Infants whose mothers smoke during pregnancy and whose caretakers smoke around them have two to four times the risk of dying of SIDS, a risk factor that is described in more detail in Chapter 4. Some researchers claim that overheating babies by bundling extra layers of clothes or turning the heat up increases the risk for SIDS. Many babies whose deaths are labeled SIDS have actually suffocated. Over the past several years the Onondaga County Child Fatality Review Team has assessed the deaths of babies who got trapped in sofa cushions, between a wall and mattress, or those whose older siblings rolled on top of them during sleep. Such deaths should now be classified as due to positional asphyxia, rather than SIDS, but making such a precise distinction is not yet the norm nationwide.

Babies who share a bed with parents or siblings may succumb to SIDS or positional asphyxia.[30] Responding to this finding, in 1999 the Consumer Product Safety Commission recommended against parents or siblings sleeping with a child under age two.[31] When I first heard researchers speak about co-sleeping as a risk factor for SIDS I scoffed at the notion; as an anthropologist I realized that babies and parents have shared sleeping space for millennia. In the developing world, fellow anthropologist James McKenna documented that sleeping next to their mothers helps regulate babies' breathing.[32] But, as I reviewed cases in which babies died while sharing beds or couches with caretakers, I became convinced that co-sleeping can be dangerous.

Two factors make sleep conditions more dangerous for infants in the United States. First, some babies who died of SIDS or asphyxia were sleeping with intoxicated adults. Second, contemporary bedding fashions feature an elaboration of plush material in mattresses, quilts, pillows, and the like. These cushiony surfaces allow babies to sink down into a depression; in such a depression, especially if they turn to the side or onto the abdomen, they may re-breathe their expired air and suffocate. When a friend gave birth and wanted to breastfeed, I searched for a solution that would allow her to remain very close to her new baby, but would reduce the risk of suffocation. On the Internet I found the Arms Reach Co-Sleeper, a type of three-sided infant sleeping platform, which hooks onto the parent's bed, allowing the mother to reach her infant.[33] James McKenna, the anthropological proponent of co-sleeping, provided a testimonial on the Arms Reach Co-Sleeper website:

> The practice of infants and children sleeping beside their parents is found in the great majority of contemporary world cultures. In fact, parents and children sharing the same sleeping place was common for all peoples, including all industrialized countries up until about 200 years ago. The question should not be: should I sleep or not sleep with the baby? A better question is: how can parents and infants safely and comfortably benefit from sleep proximity with one another? From the standpoint of the infant, any form of sensory contact, however limited, is better than none. Research suggests that infants should sleep in the context of family activities and not in an isolated room.[34]

So, at a cost of nearly $170, middle class parents can purchase a safer way to sleep next to their infant. Additional, somewhat less costly, infant sleeping platforms, shaped like small bassinettes with mesh sides for air circulation, are designed to sit on top of the parent's bed. Many low-income parents, however, would not be able to afford these protective devices.

Just recently, scientists have found that in a few deaths attributed to SIDS, the electrical conduction in the baby's hearts seems to have been wired in a way that tripped up the smooth flow of the chemical impulse through the muscle. This alteration—known as a prolonged Q-T interval—also results in the occasional sudden death of adults with the defect.[35] With each beat, our cardiac muscles squeeze blood through the chambers of our hearts in a rhythmic pattern triggered by the heart's own electrical conduction system. In this system an electric impulse runs from the top of the small, upper heart chambers and on through the larger, lower heart chambers, upon which a resting or repolarization wave resets the system for the next impulse. We can read these waves with an electrocardiograph machine, or EKG. Cardiologists label waves in normal rhythm with letters to indicate which part of the heart has contracted, "P" for the atria or small upper chambers, "QRS" for the lower, larger ventricles, and "T" for the repolarization wave. A lengthening of the time between Q, the beginning of the ventricles squeezing shut, and T, the repolarization wave, could mean that the electronic signal for the atria to contract comes later than it should. The heart muscle fibers "expect" a conduction wave to pass and when the electrical message is late, other parts of the heart sometimes fire off their own impulses, causing the heart muscle to contract irregularly in what is called an "ectopic beat." Once in a great while, these ectopic beats continue in a disorganized fashion, which is disastrous for the flow of blood through the heart. The heart can sometimes be shocked back into its normal rhythm, if a defibrillator and a trained operator are readily available, which unfortunately is seldom the case. Death occurs if the heart's normal rhythm cannot be reestablished.

Rarely, babies whose deaths were labeled SIDS have actually been murdered. Between 1965 and 1971, in a rural family near Syracuse, five infants died one after another, without obvious cause. A clinical researcher, Dr. Alfred Steinschneider of Upstate Medical Center, published a case-study description of the deaths of these five infants, which he attributed to a familial pattern of SIDS.[36] For years, based on his study, authorities assumed that multiple SIDS deaths occurred in families due to some hereditary condition, an assumption that is now recognized as false. The case was re-opened in 1995. During questioning, the children's mother, Waneta Hoyt, confessed to smothering each of her babies because she could not tolerate their crying.[37]

The American Academy of Pediatrics now estimates that 1 percent to 5 percent of SIDS deaths are actually homicides, which go unrecognized because smothering an infant with soft material does not leave characteristic signs.[38] The recognition that a small number of SIDS deaths are actually homicides is important, but problematic, in that parents whose infants die of SIDS are now subject to scrutiny as possible perpetrators of a crime. A mother whose three-month-old infant died of SIDS on the first day in childcare told me that no one would speak with her when she rushed to the childcare provider's home after hearing of her child's death. She stood alone in the street while the ambulance crew, police, and forensic investigators were busy collecting evidence regarding the death. Some questioned her intently, but none offered sympathy or support. All she knew was that her baby had died at the sitter; she spent several hours frantically trying to find out what had happened, while being mostly stonewalled.

I know the forensic investigators who responded to her child's death and they are humane, caring people. Being among the first responders to a potential crime, however, places them in a nearly impossible situation. Most of the sudden, unexplained infant deaths are the kind of shocking traumas of a parent's worst nightmare. But a very few such parents may have caused the death themselves. The first responders must try to save the baby's life if at all possible and, if not, collect evidence. Many of the forensic and emergency staff subsequently underwent training in better ways to speak with grieving parents. A kinder interrogation, however, may still be quite traumatic for newly bereaved family members. The recognition that a few infant fatalities are homicides and not SIDS means that the first responders still need to question the families to determine what role that may or may not have played in the death.

Notes

1. Gary Cunningham, Kenneth J. Leveno, Steven L. Bloom, and John C. Hauth, *Williams Obstetrics, Twenty-second Edition* (McGraw-Hill Professional, March 31, 2005).

2. V. Frisk, R. Amsel, and H. E. Whyte, "The Importance of Head Growth Patterns in Predicting the Cognitive Abilities and Literacy Skills of Small-for-Gestational-Age Children," *Dev Neuropsychol* 22, no. 3 (2002): 565–93.

3. U. Simeoni and R. Zetterstrom, "Long-Term Circulatory and Renal Consequences of Intrauterine Growth Restriction," *Acta Paediatrica* 94, no. 7 (2005): 819–24.

4. P. D. Gluckman and M. A. Hanson, "Maternal Constraint of Fetal Growth and Its Consequences," *Seminars in Fetal and Neonatal Medicine* 9, no. 5 (2004): 419–25.

5. J. F. Ludvigsson, and J. Ludvigsson, "Milk Consumption during Pregnancy and Infant Birthweight, *Acta Paediatrica* 93, no. 11 (2004): 1474–78; E. A. Mitchell, E. Robinson, P. M. Clark, et al., "Maternal Nutritional Risk Factors for Small for Gestational Age Babies in A Developed Country: A Case-Control Study," *Archives of Disease in Childhood Fetal and Neonatal Edition* 89, no. 5 (2004): F431–35; R. J. Sram, B. Binkova, A. Lnenickova, et al., "The Impact of Plasma Folate Levels of Mothers and Newborns on Intrauterine Growth Retardation and Birth Weight," *Mutation Research* 591, nos. 1–2 (December 11, 2005): 302–10; G. Wu, F. W. Bazer, T. A. Cudd, et al., "Maternal Nutrition and Fetal Development," *Journal of Nutrition* 134, no. 9 (2004): 2169–72.

6. M. F. Schreuder, M. Fodor, J. A. Van Wijk, et al., "Association of Birth Weight with Cardiovascular Parameters in Adult Rats during Baseline and Stressed Conditions," *Pediatric Research* 59, no. 1 (2006): 126–30; J. Lesage, F. Del-Favero, M. Leonhardt, H. Louvart, et al., "Prenatal Stress Induces

Intrauterine Growth Restriction and Programs Glucose Intolerance and Feeding Behavior Disturbances in the Aged Rat," *Journal of Endocrinology* 181, no. 2 (2004): 291–96; P. J. Landrigan, P. J. Lioy, G. Thurston, et al., "Health and Environmental Consequences of The World Trade Center Disaster," *Environmental Health Perspectives* 112, no. 6 (2004): 731–39.

7. S. Oppenheimer and G. Lefevre, *Introduction to Embryonic Development,* Third Edition (Prentice Hall, October 21, 1996).

8. A. J. Wilcox, C. R. Weinberg, J. F. O'Connor, D. D. Baird, J. P. Schlatterer, R. E. Canfield, E. G. Armstrong, and B. C. Nisula, "Incidence of Early Loss of Pregnancy," *New England Journal of Medicine* 319, no. 4 (July 28, 1988): 189–94.

9. Medline Plus, online medical encyclopedia, http://www.nlm.nih.gov/medlineplus/ency/article/002398.htm.

10. The following quote regarding quickening and common law is from the text of *Roe v. Wade,* Section VI, cited from http://www.sacred-texts.com/wmn/rvw/rvw06.htm.
"3. The common law. It is undisputed that at common law, abortion performed before "quickening"—the first recognizable movement of the fetus in utero, appearing usually from the 16th to the 18th week of pregnancy 20—was not an indictable offense. 21 The absence [410 U.S. 113, 133] of a common-law crime for pre-quickening abortion appears to have developed from a confluence of earlier philosophical, theological, and civil and canon law concepts of when life begins. These disciplines variously approached the question in terms of the point at which the embryo or fetus became 'formed' or recognizably human, or in terms of when a 'person' came into being, that is, infused with a 'soul' or 'animated.'"

11. A. Spinillo, B. Gardella, E. Preti, S. Zanchi, M. Stronati, and E. Fazzi, "Rates of Neonatal Death and Cerebral Palsy Associated with Fetal Growth Restriction among Very Low Birthweight Infants: A Temporal Analysis," *American Journal of Obstetric Gynecology* 113, no.7 (July 2006): 775–80. Published online June 2, 2006; See also L. A. Agustines, Y. G. Lin, P. J. Rumney, M. C. Lu, R. Bonebrake, T. Asrat, and M. Nageotte, "Outcomes of Extremely Low-Birth-Weight Infants Between 500 and 750 g.," *American Journal of Obstetric Gynecology* 182, no. 5 (May 2000): 1113–16; G. R. Burgio, A. Paganelli, P. Sampaolo, and P. Gancia, *Ethics in Perinatology* 58, no. 1 (February 2006): 77–89; O. Genzel-Boroviczeny, S. MacWilliams, M. Von Poblotzki, and L. Zoppelli, "Mortality and Major Morbidity in Premature Infants Less Than 31 Weeks Gestational Age in the Decade After Introduction of Surfactant," *Acta Obstetric Gynecology Scandanavia* 85, no. 1 (2006): 68–73; S. Hosono, T. Ohno, H. Kimoto, M. Shimizu, and K. Harada, "Morbidity and Mortality of Infants Born at the Threshold of Viability: Ten Years' Experience in a Single Neonatal Intensive Care Unit, 1991–2000," *Pediatric*

Int. 48, no. 1 (February 2006): 33–39; D. A. Paul, K. H. Leef, R. G. Locke, L. Bartoshesky, J. Walrath, and J. L. Stefano, "Increasing Illness Severity in Very Low Birth Weight Infants Over a 9-Year Period," *BMC Pediatric* 6, no. 6 (February 2006): 2.

12. J. L. Smith, "Foodborne Infections during Pregnancy," *Journal of Food Protection* 62, no. 7 (July 1999): 818–29.; E. Simpson, "Immunology: Why the Baby Isn't Thrown Out...." *Current Biology* 6, no. 1 (January 1996): 43–44.

13. "Malaria in Pregnancy: An Overview," *MJM* 8 (2004): 66–71.

14. "Listeriosis," CDC website, http://www.cdc.gov/ncidod/dbmd/diseaseinfo/listeriosis_g.htm.

15. K. Deb, M. M. Chaturvedi, and Y. K. Jaiswal, "Comprehending the Role of LPS in Gram-Negative Bacterial Vaginosis: Ogling into the Causes of Unfulfilled Child-Wish," *Arch Gynecology Obstetric* 270, no. 3 (November 2004): 133–46. Published online June 18, 2004; M. Wilks, R. Wiggins, A. Whiley, E. Hennessy, S. Warwick, H. Porter, A. Corfield, and M. Millar, "Identification and H(2)O(2) Production of Vaginal Lactobacilli from Pregnant Women at High Risk of Preterm Birth and Relation with Outcome," *Journal of Clinical Microbiology* 42, no. 2 (February 2004): 713–17; R. Romero, J. Espinoza, T. Chaiworapongsa, and K. Kalache, "Infection and Prematurity and the Role of Preventive Strategies," *Seminar on Neonatology* 7, no. 4 (August 2002): 259–74; S. M. Garland, F. Ni Chuileannain, C. Satzke, and R. Robins-Browne, "Mechanisms, Organisms and Markers of Infection in Pregnancy," *Journal of Reproductive Immunology* 57, nos. 1–2 (October-November 2002): 169–83.

16. B. Basso, F. Gimenez, and C. Lopez, "IL-1beta, IL-6 and IL-8 Levels in Gyneco-Obstetric Infections," *Infectious Diseases Obstetric Gynecology* 13, no. 4 (December 2005): 207–11.

17. B. H. Cottrell and M. Shannahan, "Maternal Bacterial Vaginosis and Fetal/Infant Mortality in Eight Florida Counties, 1999 to 2000," *Public Health Nursing* 21, no. 5 (September-October 2004): 395–403; V. A. Rauh, J. F. Culhane, and V. K. Hogan, "Bacterial Vaginosis: A Public Health Problem for Women," *Journal of American Medical Womens Association* 55, no. 4 (Summer 2000): 220–24; K. Fiscella, "Racial Disparities in Preterm Births: The Role of Urogenital Infections," *Public Health Report* 111, no. 2 (March-April 1996): 104–13.

18. S. O. Aral, W. D. Mosher, and W. Cares Jr., "Vaginal Douching among Women of Reproductive Age in the United States: 1988," *American Journal of Public Health* 82 (1992): 210.

19. "Don't Douche," *Mother Jones* (November/December 1992).

20. M. A. Klebanoff, W. W. Andrews, K. F. Yu, R. M. Brotman, T. R. Nansel, J. Zhang, S. P. Cliver, and J. R. Schwebke, "A Pilot Study of Vaginal Flora Changes with Randomization to Cessation of Douching," *Sexually Transmitted*

Diseases 33, no. 10 (October 2006): 610–13; B. H. Cottrell, "Vaginal Douching Practices of Women in Eight Florida Panhandle Counties," *Journal of Obstetric Gynecology Neonatal Nursing* 35, no. 1 (January-February 2006): 24–33; L. Myer, L. Kuhn, Z. A. Stein, T. C. Wright, Jr., and L. Denny, "Intravaginal Practices, Bacterial Vaginosis, and Women's Susceptibility to HIV Infection: Epidemiological Evidence and Biological Mechanisms," *Lancet Infectious Diseases* 5, no. 12 (December 2005): 786–94; A. Karaer, M. Boylu, and A. F. Avsar, "Vaginitis in Turkish Women: Symptoms, Epidemiologic—Microbiologic Association," *European Journal of Obstetric Gynecology and Reproductive Biology* 121, no. 2 (August 1, 2005): 211–15; M. E. Mbizvo, S. E. Musya, B. Stray-Pedersen, Z. Chirenje, and A. Hussain, "Bacterial Vaginosis and Intravaginal Practices: Association with HIV," *Central African Journal of Medicine* 50, nos. 5–6 (May-June 2004): 41–46; W. Watcharotone, K. Sirimai, O. Kiriwat, P. Nukoolkarn, O. Watcharaprapapong, S. Pibulmanee, S. Chandanabodhi, N. A. Leckyim, and G. Chiravacharadej, "Prevalence of Bacterial Vaginosis in Thai Women Attending the Family Planning Clinic, Siriraj Hospital," *Journal of the Medical Association Thailand* 87, no. 12 (December 2004): 1419–24; R. H. Beigi, H. C. Wiesenfeld, S. L. Hillier, T. Straw, and M. A. Krohn, "Factors Associated with Absence of H2O2-Producing Lactobacillus among Women with Bacterial Vaginosis," *Journal of Infectious Diseases* 191, no. 6 (March 15, 2005): 924–29. Published online February 8, 2005. Erratum in: *Journal of Infectious Diseases* 191, no. 10 (May 15, 2005): 1785; R. B. Ness, S. L. Hillier, K. E. Kip, H. E. Richter, D. E. Soper, C. A. Stamm, J. A. McGregor, D. C. Bass, P. Rice, and R. L. Sweet, "Douching, Pelvic Inflammatory Disease, and Incident Gonococcal and Chlamydial Genital Infection in a Cohort of High-Risk Women," *American Journal of Epidemiology* 161, no. 2 (January 15, 2005): 186–95; F. Chiaffarino, F. Parazzini, P. De Besi, and M. Lavezzari, "Risk Factors for Bacterial Vaginosis," *European Journal of Obstetric Gynecology and Reproductive Biology* 117, no. 2 (December 1, 2004): 222–26.

21. S. L. Hillier, "The Vaginal Microbial Ecosystem and Resistance to HIV," *AIDS Res. Human Retroviruses* 14. supp. 1 (1998): S17–21.

22. C. S. Bradshaw, A. N. Morton, J. Hocking, S. M. Garland, M. B. Morris, L. M. Moss, L. B. Horvath, I. Kuzevska, and C. K. Fairley, "High Recurrence Rates of Bacterial Vaginosis over the Course of 12 Months after Oral Metronidazole Therapy and Factors Associated with Recurrence," *Journal of Infectious Diseases* 193, no. 11 (June 1, 2006): 1478–86. Published online April 26, 2006; L. Myer, L. Kuhn, Z. A. Stein, T. C. Wright Jr., and L. Denny, "Intravaginal Practices, Bacterial Vaginosis, and Women's Susceptibility to HIV Infection: Epidemiological Evidence and Biological Mechanisms," *Lancet Infectious Diseases* 5, no. 12 (December 2005): 786–94; J. R. Schwebke amd R. Desmond, "Risk Factors for Bacterial Vaginosis in Women at High Risk for Sexually Transmitted Diseases," *Sexually Transmitted Diseases* 32, no.

11 (November 2005): 654–58; V. M. Pinto, M. V. Tancredi, A. Neto, and C. M. Buchalla, "Sexually Transmitted Disease/HIV Risk Behaviour among Women Who Have Sex with Women," *AIDS* 19, supp. 4 (October 2005): S64–69; C. S. Bradshaw, A. N. Morton, S. M. Garland, M. B. Morris, L. M. Moss, and C. K. Fairley, "Higher-Risk Behavioral Practices Associated with Bacterial Vaginosis Compared with Vaginal Candidiasis," *Obstetric Gynecology* 106, no. 1 (July 2005): 105–14; J. M. Marrazzo, P. Coffey, and M. N. Elliott, "Sexual Practices, Risk Perception and Knowledge of Sexually Transmitted Disease Risk among Lesbian and Bisexual Women," *Perspectives on Sexual & Reproductive Health* 37, no. 1 (March 2005): 6–12.

23. M. A. Klebanoff, S. L. Hillier, R. P. Nugent, C. A. MacPherson, J. C. Hauth, J. C. Carey, M. Harper, R. J. Wapner, W. Trout, A. Moawad, K. J. Leveno, M. Miodovnik, B. M. Sibai, J. P. Vandorsten, M. P. Dombrowski, M. J. O'Sullivan, M. Varner, and O. Langer, National Institute of Child Health and Human Development Maternal-Fetal Medicine Units Network, "Is Bacterial Vaginosis a Stronger Risk Factor for Preterm Birth When It Is Diagnosed Earlier in Gestation?" *American Journal of Obstetric Gynecology* 192, no. 2 (February 2005): 470–77; S. L. Hillier, R. P. Nugent, D. A. Eschenbach, M. A. Krohn, R. S. Gibbs, D. H. Martin, M. F. Cotch, R. Edelman, J. G. Pastorek II, A. V. Rao, et al., The Vaginal Infections and Prematurity Study Group, "Association between Bacterial Vaginosis and Preterm Delivery of a Low-Birth-Weight Infant," *New England Journal of Medicine* 333, no. 26 (December 28, 1995): 1737–42.

24. Dr. Aubry's protocol included screening all pregnant women and treating those with positive or intermediate scores for bacterial vaginosis (on the Nugent gram stain criteria) with metronidizole.

25. New York State Vital Records.

26. Virginia Apgar, "A Proposal for a New Method of Evaluation of the Newborn Infant, New York, N.Y.," *Current Researches in Anesthesia and Analgesia* (July-August 1953): 260.

27. The formula is: (fetal deaths >20 weeks + neonatal deaths)/(fetal deaths >20 weeks + live births)*1000.

28. The data for this analysis is from the study fully described in note 52, p. 28.

29. Sudden Infant Death Syndrome (SIDS), CDC Infant Death Investigation, http://www.cdc.gov/SIDS/index.htm.

30. K. Perrizo and S. Pustilnik, "Association between Sudden Death in Infancy and Co-Sleeping: A Look at Investigative Methods for Galveston County Medical Examiners Office from 1978–2002," *American Journal Forensic Medical Pathology* 27, no. 2 (June 2006): 169–72; R. T. Alexander and D. Radisch, "Sudden Infant Death Syndrome Risk Factors with Regards to

Sleep Position, Sleep Surface, and Co-Sleeping," *Journal of Forensic Science* 50, no. 1 (January 2005): 147–51.

31. On September 29, 1999, the Consumer Product Safety Commission issued a warning against placing babies in adult beds. CPSC, *Mothering* (January-February 2000).

32. J. J. McKenna and T. McDade, "Why Babies Should Never Sleep Alone: A Review of the Co-Sleeping Controversy in Relation to SIDS, Bedsharing and Breast Feeding," *Pediatric Respiratory Review* 6, no. 2 (June 2005): 134–52.

33. http://www.armsreach.com.

34. A Message from James McKenna by Doctor James McKenna, Ph.D., http://www.armsreach.com/article.php?ID=9.

35. H. Wedekind, T. Bajanowski, P. Friederich, G. Breithardt, T. Wulfing, C. Siebrands, B. Engeland, G. Monnig, W. Haverkamp, B. Brinkmann, and E. Schulze-Bahr, "Sudden Infant Death Syndrome and Long QT Syndrome: An Epidemiological and Genetic Study," *International Journal of Legal Medicine* 120, no. 3 (May 2006): 129–37. Published online July 13, 2005.

36. A. Steinschneider, "Prolonged Apnea and the Sudden Infant Death Syndrome: Clinical and Laboratory Observations," *Pediatrics* 50, no. 4 (October 1972): 646–54.

37. John O'Brien, "Mom Who Killed 5 Children Dies in Jail: Waneta Hoyt's Story Was a Landmark SIDS Case Before It Became a Homicide Investigation," *Syracuse Post-Standard*, sec. A., Tuesday Metro Edition, August 11, 1998.

38. American Academy of Pediatrics, Committee on Child Abuse and Neglect, "Distinguishing Sudden Infant Death Syndrome from Child Abuse Fatalities," *Pediatrics* 107, no. 2 (February 2001): 437–41.

Chapter 4

Risk in Social Context

When we started Syracuse Healthy Start (SHS), we developed a risk assessment system that would help public health nurses and other paraprofessional home visiting staff to identify each pregnant woman's specific needs.[1] All pregnant women in Syracuse were eligible for SHS services, so the system was not used to decide who would or would not receive services. It was used instead to tailor interventions or referrals.

In developing the risk assessment system, one of the first questions that we asked ourselves was, "Is race a risk factor?" SHS African American staff members expressed how offended they were by systems that featured race as a risk in and of itself. Using race as a risk factor, moreover, potentially leads to thinking that blames the victim or presents a category of persons as being the problem. Risk factors, we decided at Syracuse Healthy Start, would be limited to those social, behavioral, or environmental phenomena for which a public health intervention can be fashioned. The level of risk may vary among groups, but all groups include individuals with risks. We addressed those social, behavioral, or environmental risks—*and not the person's ancestry.*

Some clinical researchers, looking at low birth weight, for example, continue to speak of "race" as a risk factor, although race as a measurable biological variable has been widely discredited. The human genome project did not find a gene, or genes, that distinguish between the broad categories that we call races. Race, whether being discussed in the most typical way, a division of the world's population into Caucasian, African, and Asian, or in a more elaborate system, does not map onto discrete genetic groups.[2] The designation of racial groups has been based historically on the extent of difference in skin color and hair texture from the European adventurers and colonists who made the distinctions.[3] Racial categories have also been used to justify the social stigmatization of certain groups; both the Irish and Jews were at times labeled as races for this reason.

When I raise the issue of race as a largely social category with students, someone always asks, "What about sickle cell anemia?" Sickle cell anemia happens when an individual receives two sickle cell genes, one from each parent, and afflicts those whose ancestors lived historically in areas endemic for malaria, for example in West Africa. When a person inherits a sickle cell gene from only one parent, he or she is said to have sickle cell "trait," an inherited condition that does not make the carrier sick but provides some protection from malaria.[4] Although most individuals with sickle cell inheritance are of African ancestry, there are parts of Africa without malaria and there are many African descendants from non-malarial geographies who lack the genes for sickle cell anemia.

Cystic fibrosis is inherited in the same manner, but by those of Western European ancestry. Children with cystic fibrosis genes from both parents can be quite sick and die young from lung and intestinal problems, but carriers of the trait—those with a single cystic fibrosis gene—were historically much less likely to die from cholera. In western Europe, where epidemics of cholera in the pre-antibiotic era used to decimate the population, carriers of the cystic fibrosis trait were genetically protected.[5] We would not say, however, that the evidence for Caucasians constituting a race is that some of them have cystic fibrosis. The forebearers of those who inherited the genes for cystic fibrosis came from European cities where poor sanitation led to frequent cholera epidemics. The cystic fibrosis carriers are overwhelmingly of European ancestry, but there are populations of "Caucasians" in which cystic fibrosis is rare. While there are genetic causes to disease, and descendants from a given locality may share increased frequencies of genetic diseases that arose in that locality, the concept of race is too large and too imprecise to be a biologically useful explanation.

Given the controversy about what race means and how it should be interpreted, some scholars advise abandoning race-based analyses and the collection of race in public records altogether.[6] But, as the data presented in this book make clear, there are large differences in health and survival between people of color and their white neighbors. If we forgo collecting data on race and ethnicity we will not be able to measure those differences and may not be able to eliminate the inequality. Despite the evidence that race does not constitute a homogeneous biological category and that the data are fraught with classification errors, these public data sources remain the best measure currently available to examine disparities in health outcomes. Tragically, substantial racial disparities begin in infancy and continue throughout the life span. While the results must be interpreted cautiously, the potential bias in the data should not cause us to abandon the search for effective strategies to eliminate these disparities; to fashion such strategies we need to measure the disparities among racial and ethnic groups.

African and Hispanic immigrants to the United States have fewer low birth weight births than African American and Latin American women who are born in the United States.[7] This foreign-born advantage is strongest among women of African ancestry; in 1998 more than 11 percent of U.S.-born African Americans gave birth to low birth weight babies, compared with less than 8 percent among foreign-born African women who migrated to the United States. This difference is not found among either white or Asian women. The rates of low birth weight among foreign-born white women do not differ from their native-born white counterparts. Foreign-born Asian women have *higher* rates of low birth weight than U.S.-born Asian women. Clearly something in the United States is unhealthy for African American and Hispanic women and their babies, but genetic causes cannot be the main answer since the examples above compare immigrants and native-born individuals from the same groups.

To further complicate matters, African Americans, Latin Americans, and European Americans are not homogeneous groups. In addition to African, Latin American, or European heritage, many United States residents trace ancestors from a variety of the world's regions—northern and southern Europe, central and south

America, Asia, and Native America. A study of race and ethnicity of babies born in central New York found that mothers identifying as "White" represented 143 different ethnic groups and those identifying as "Black" represented 52 different ethnic groups.[8] Even those who do not know about their heterogeneous ancestry still probably have distant progenitors from a variety of areas. According to archeologists, migration and intermarriage have been common throughout human evolution.

An additional layer of confusion emerges from the way that ancestry is tallied in the various public data sources. The United States Census treats race as a self-defined category and allows individuals to choose more than one category, whereas in the Vital Records data race varies from being self-defined to circumstances where a busy clinician fills in the category. Some of the analyses, such as low birth weight, use only the mother's race, because so many of the birth certificates lack paternal data. The infant death certificates, in contrast, indicate the infant's own racial category. These infant death certificates are the basis of the Infant Mortality Rates reported by county and state health departments.

An analysis of Syracuse infant death certificates from 1998 to 2001 indicated that the categorization of deceased biracial children was somewhat capricious. Among African American infant deaths, on average two to three infants per year were classified as "African American," when their mothers identified themselves as "white." A few deceased infants were classified as "white" but their mothers as "Asian." While I was never able to determine precisely how these classifications were made, it seemed from my discussions with hospital personnel that a busy clinician writing up the paperwork after an infant death often filled in the category based on his or her impression of the infant's race or ethnic group. In small cities like Syracuse, moving even a few infant deaths from one racial/ethnic category to another may greatly alter the infant mortality rate of one or another group. From 1998 to 2001 this "misclassification" increased the African American infant mortality by as much as 18 percent when the rate was based upon the baby's racial classification instead of the mother's. Calculations that I made for White and African American infant mortality in two ways—based on the baby's race and the mother's race—are presented in Table 4.1.

Table 4.1 Infant Mortality Rates (IMR), Calculated by the Baby's Race and Mother's Race, Syracuse

	IMR*—African American— calculated by mother's race	IMR*—African American— calculated by baby's race
1998	8.61	12.30
1999	14.82	17.06
2000	8.84	12.11
2001	28.15	31.71

Source data: New York State Vital Records, analysis by the author.
*per 1,000 live births (includes multiples births).

We spend a lot of time thinking about the mother's racial or ethnic heritage and the baby's, but what about the father's background? An analysis of infant death that looks at the race of the baby's father is complicated by the number of births in which the baby's father's information is not listed; these total about 22 percent of white births and 46 percent of African American births. (Chapter 7 goes into greater depth about these "missing fathers" and the impact of their non-involvement on infant survival.) As shown in Table 4.2, among births in which the father's information was listed, those with African American fathers had much higher infant mortality than those in which the father was white, among mothers of both races.

Jail, poverty, and low levels of education shape the lives of numerous African American fathers, many of whom were not adequately fathered themselves. African American males in Syracuse are incarcerated at more than seven times the white rate; they have almost

Table 4.2 Infant Mortality Rate (IMR*) of Infants of White and African American Fathers

	White Mother IMR* (actual number of births)	African American Mother IMR*(actual number of births)
White father	8.45 (n=1657)	0 (n=54)
African American father	16.95 (n=177)	12.85 (n=778)

Source: New York State Vital Records and Perinatal Database, analysis by the author.
* per 1,000 live births (includes multiple births).

twice the rate of non-completion of high school of white males and have more than twice the rate of unemployment of white males. Policymakers sometimes wrongly assume that such fathers lack parental love for their infants, an assumption that I have found to be false. African American fathers in Syracuse whom my colleagues and I have interviewed have expressed enormous love and concern for their children, despite not being able to offer the amount of financial support that they would like to provide. One African American father of four children said,

> Right now I just got a job that is helping me a little bit, I try to be there so they know who I am and respect me when they get older, they can say he didn't live with me but he was around. [Also] ... my little brother helps me, my mom helps me sometimes too because it's her grandchild.

A second African American father of two expressed his frustration with trying to find employment in a situation of few jobs and with a criminal record:

> I'm just in a tunnel of nothing but war right now, it is hard for some people to have jobs [with] old misdemeanors or warrants or felonies, that don't mean nothing. People want to work for their kids and they don't have no money, but they keep pushing us back so we can't get a job. It forces a lot of people that live in the hood to hustle.

A third African American father describes his efforts to stay involved with his son:

> Well my child is currently living with his aunt ... so she has taken over responsibility as mother for my son. She calls me and tells me he needs Pampers, he need new shoes or clothes; that's there without a problem, consistent ... Three or four times a week, I go pick him up at his aunt's house, ride around, take him to the park, or the mall, stuff like that, spend quality time with him, let him know I'm in his life.... I'm his daddy and he knows that.

Despite these fathers' sometimes-extraordinary efforts to nurture their children, the support that they are able to provide to their baby's mothers is limited. An African American man who was incarcerated when his child was born said, "Because I [was] not there for them, it's just not the place to be when you got kids. Especially, like, a Black man like me don't have much to do."

Poverty

One of the most common questions that people ask about racial and ethnic health disparities is whether the unequal health and survival is not simply due to poverty. The Institute of Medicine report *Unequal Treatment* concluded that even with equal education, income, and health insurance people of color receive less adequate health care.[9] Poverty itself, however, often results from institutional racism, including barriers such as inadequate education and discrimination in hiring that face many minorities in the United States. Among families with children under age five, African Americans and Latinos have over twice the poverty of white families in Syracuse. The median family income for white families in Syracuse, at just over $40,000, is $16,000 lower than the median family income for the United States.[10] The African American median family income for Syracuse is only slightly more than half of the white income and the Latino median family income, at $15,899, is less than less than half of the Syracuse white income and less than a third of the median family income for the United States.

Among pregnant women in Syracuse (2000–2001), nearly half were covered by Medicaid insurance for their health care, which is an indirect measure of poverty. Pregnant women in New York State who lack health insurance can receive Medicaid if their family earns less than 200 percent of the federal poverty level. For a family of four in 2005, the federal poverty level was $19,350 or less, so a woman in a four-person family earning up to $38,700 could be covered by Medicaid during pregnancy.[11] Many women who lack health insurance are employed but have jobs that do not provide health benefits. An uninsured twenty-one-year-old African American woman, whom I will call Monique, worked full time at KFC in Syracuse. When I spoke with her early in her pregnancy she said that KFC only provided health insurance to the managerial employees. Later she telephoned me to ask for help because KFC had fired her; she said that as soon as they noticed her growing pregnant belly the manager called her into his office and said that they could not keep her on any longer. Monique provided support for both herself and her baby's father, who told me that he could not find a job.

Figure 4.1 shows the proportion of women age 20 and older who receive Medicaid insurance for their prenatal care and hospital delivery costs. More than two thirds of women of color, compared with less than 40 percent of white women, receive Medicaid. About half of employed women of color who are uninsured by their employers, compared with a quarter of white women, require Medicaid coverage for their prenatal care and delivery. When a woman lacks health insurance prior to pregnancy, she often goes without regular primary care. Women with undiagnosed diabetes or high blood pressure, smokers, or those with other health risks would have much healthier pregnancies if those conditions could be addressed before they got pregnant. But the sad truth is that many low-income women only get good health care when they are pregnant. Obstetricians and midwives thus have to fit into their already time-constrained prenatal appointments essential clinical care that should have been taken care of before the pregnancy began.

Prior to 1996, Medicaid was administered as a fee-for-service insurance program, in which physicians, hospitals, and clinics billed the government for each procedure or visit a patient received.[12] In August 1996, the federal government gave its approval for states to use a managed care model for Medicaid funding. Under Medicaid Managed Care (MMC), the government pays a lump sum per patient per month, an amount that is sometimes called a "capitation fee,"

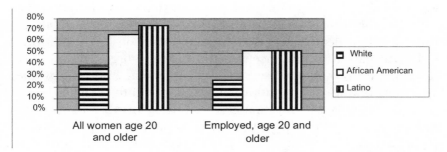

Figure 4.1 Percent of Pregnant Women in Syracuse Uninsured prior to Pregnancy, 1996–2003
Data source: Central New York Regional Perinatal Data System.

indicating that it is based on a per person (literally "head" or "caput"), rather than per procedure, system. Policymakers who voted for MMC hoped that this new billing system would hold down health care costs. According to the Consumers Union, MMC saves taxpayers about 4 percent, compared with Medicaid fee-for-service. MMC also widens the network of doctors and midwives who care for pregnant women, which has both potential benefits and liabilities.[13]

A key benefit in having more providers care for MMC-covered patients is that pregnant women can begin prenatal care earlier, whereas under the old system they often had to wait until they were well along in pregnancy because a paucity of providers took Medicaid-covered patients. Many of the private providers in this expanded network, however, have little experience in caring for impoverished patients, who may be unemployed, need food stamps and WIC, and have poor transportation access, inadequate child care for other children, and low rates of literacy. Few of these providers employ social workers and many lack the resources to help their patients with housing, domestic violence referrals, case management, and the many other social needs that complicate their pregnancies. To help address the multifaceted problems of Medicaid-covered pregnant women and infants, in 1997 the Onondaga County Health Department negotiated agreements with local MMC organizations to fund the county public health nurses to provide public health preventive services to their members. By 1998 about 50 percent of Medicaid-covered pregnant women in Onondaga County were covered by MMC. The implementation of MMC overlapped with the start of Syracuse Healthy Start. From 1997 onward we evaluated the pregnancy outcomes of Medicaid-covered women to assess the impact of the shift to MMC. From 1998 to 2000 the rates of infant death decreased among women on Medicaid, which indirectly gave us confidence that this major re-organization in the funding and provision of services to low income and poor women and their infants did not appear to be harmful to them.

A second major policy change—welfare reform—was much less benign, at least in the beginning of its implementation. Temporary Assistance to Needy Families (TANF), created in 1996 under the Clinton Administration, replaced Aid to Families with Dependent Children (AFDC), which was known as "Welfare."[14] In 1996, as a part of Welfare reform, Onondaga County began the shift from AFDC to

TANF. The goals of TANF are cost savings and, according to the Bush White House, encouraging families to "work toward independence and self-reliance."[15] TANF places a five-year cap on eligibility for support; the first Syracuse-area TANF recipients reached their five-year limit in 2001, but prior to that date tightened regulations resulted in fewer potential clients being approved for support.

Public assistance to pregnant Medicaid-insured recipients in Syracuse fell from about 25 percent in 1996 to 3 percent by 2002. Among African American Medicaid recipients giving birth in Syracuse, the drop in public assistance was steeper, falling from nearly 50 percent in 1996 to about 5 percent in 2003. Even if welfare reform eventually becomes recognized as a successful policy shift—and scholars are still in the midst of such evaluations—its implementation was draconian. A key aspect of welfare reform seeks to help recipients secure employment, as touted on the New York State website: "The JOBSplus! program is designed to provide employment and training opportunities to employable Temporary Assistance (TA) recipients. ... Under JOBS, a TA recipient determined employable is referred to the JOBS Unit. For each employable client, an employability plan is developed which outlines vocational goals and the steps necessary to achieve them."[16]

New York State Law requires pregnant TANF recipients to attend work or actively look for work at least thirty-six hours per week until thirty days before the expected date of her baby's birth.[17] Recipients have three months after the birth per lifetime before they must begin working or searching for work. TANF recipients who used up their lifetime allotment of post-pregnancy leave following the births of previous children must resume looking for work or working six weeks after giving birth.

Employment is not widely available in Syracuse, especially for the half of pregnant TANF recipients over eighteen who have not completed high school. About six months of the year piles of poorly shoveled snow block city sidewalks, making transportation hazardous. Childcare funding depends upon the receipt of public assistance. Since this assistance often stops and starts with the mother's compliance in submitting the numerous required documents, children of public assistance recipients are sometimes moved into and out of crowded child care facilities. Sometimes mothers are forced to leave their children in far-from-optimal care settings to continue to search for work, in order to continue to receive support. When I have spoken about this situation with my students I have asked them to imagine how likely it is that an employer will take a chance on hiring a non–high school graduate in her eighth month of pregnancy.

The humiliation of being rejected for work over and over, combined with the physical stress of waiting in the cold for city buses to attend job interviews, may negatively affect the outcome of pregnancy. Nurse midwife Kathy DeMott brought to my attention the potential risk that the public assistance work requirement placed on the health and survival of the infants of recipients. As she describes below, she tried unsuccessfully to modify this punitive protocol:

> Onondaga County's welfare-to-work program, JOBSplus!, was unrelenting in its requirements for pregnant clients. Women were mandated to participate in the program until their thirty-sixth week of pregnancy and threatened with loss of benefits if they did not comply. Daily I counseled women in my midwifery practice who were trying to cope with the discomforts of advancing pregnancy, overwhelming family responsibilities, and the difficulty of searching for work or getting out to their minimum wage JOBSplus! positions through the hazardous Syracuse winter weather conditions, on foot or by public transportation. Complaints of fatigue, back pain, and preterm contractions were common. The only hope of relief was a medical excuse from a health care provider.
>
> In an attempt to address this situation I, and several community health care workers, arranged a meeting with the director of the JOBSplus! program. We described our concerns for pregnant clients and suggested an alternative program for women more than twenty weeks pregnant. Rather than focusing on active employment, we proposed that women prepare for their impending "job" as new parents. Prenatal and parenting classes could be provided and "work credit" given for attendance. Likewise, credit for keeping prenatal care appointments could be offered. Such a program would benefit mothers and babies and the community at large. And, doctors and midwives would no longer have to negotiate between the needs of their patients and the demands of the welfare system.

Unfortunately, Kathy DeMott's suggestions to modify JOBSplus! for women in late pregnancy failed to be implemented, because the policies are set by the state and cannot be altered by individual counties.

So, how did the JOBSplus! recipients fare in their pregnancies, compared with other pregnant women covered by Medicaid? Among women delivering in the largest birth hospital in Syracuse from January 2000 to March 2002, 15.7 percent of the infants of TANF clients required care in the NICU, compared with 6.5 percent of infants of women covered by Medicaid, who did not receive public assistance. The TANF babies spent a total of 902 days in the NICU; on average TANF babies spent just over 15 days each in the NICU, compared with just over 13 days for all other babies. Since NICU care costs between $1,500 to $3,000 per day per infant, the bill for the TANF babies cost taxpayers between $1,352,655 to $2,705,310.[18] One might characterize the punitive zeal of the JOBSplus! program as penny wise, pound foolish. If Kathy DeMott's suggestion to loosen up on the JOBSplus! requirements for women in late pregnancy had been implemented, it is possible that fewer of their babies would have required expensive NICU care. In 2004, New York State reported a savings of nearly $13 million on public assistance for that year, which includes the TANF program.[19] If the JOBSplus! work requirements for late pregnancy increased the risk of need for neonatal intensive care in some of the babies, however, the program may simply have shifted the cost—in a tragic shell game—from the TANF program to the Medicaid NICU bill. Postneonatal deaths were also 45 percent higher among TANF babies, compared with other Medicaid covered babies in Syracuse during 2000–2001. The TANF mothers might also have benefited from Kathy DeMott's suggested parenting classes in ways that might have reduced their infants' postneonatal deaths.

Substance Abuse

Tobacco

Compared with a national average of 13 percent of pregnant women who smoke, in Syracuse 30 percent of White women, 26 percent of African Americans, and 22 percent of Latinas smoke during pregnancy.[20] Among the youngest Syracuse teen mothers (ages 13 and 14), more than a fifth smoke during the pregnancy, a figure that reaches one third among pregnant teens ages 18 and 19. Of the various substances taken in by pregnant women, tobacco arguably causes the most widespread harm because so many women smoke and smokers light up many times per day. Cigarette smoke constricts the blood vessels that carry oxygen and nutrients to the fetus and remove its waste. Like a plant rooted in rocky soil, deep in the shade, the cigarette-laced fetus cannot grow to its full potential. Various researchers estimate that a full-term baby born to a smoker weighs about 6 oz. less, and one whose mother was exposed to second-hand smoke weighs nearly 3 oz. less, than a baby who was not exposed to tobacco in utero.[21]

My students sometimes wonder why 6 oz. of birth weight is so important, since it seems a rather small amount. But tobacco exposure limits the growth of fetal brain, lungs, and other essential organs. Fried, Watkinson, and Gray demonstrated that prenatal tobacco use impairs a child's lifelong cognitive ability, and the more cigarettes smoked the greater the blunting of the child's ability to reason and learn. Middle school students whose mothers smoked fifteen or more cigarettes per day while pregnant lagged an average of eight IQ points below children whose mothers did not smoke during pregnancy.[22] Those eight points for some children mean the difference between a potential for low average intelligence and more serious cognitive impairment. The same three researchers compared prenatal tobacco to prenatal marijuana; cigarettes stunted fetal brain development more than marijuana.[23]

My colleagues and I assessed the impact of prenatal smoking on the fetal growth of African American and white births among Syracuse residents who gave birth during 2000–2001. We removed from the analysis other biological causes of intrauterine growth restriction (IUGR). The sample contained only full-term births of singletons; births affected by preeclampsia, fertility medications, alcohol, and cocaine were removed. In this group, 28.8 percent of white mothers smoked, compared with 24.2 percent of African American mothers. Not only were white women more likely to smoke during pregnancy, but also white pregnant smokers consumed more total cigarettes than African American pregnant smokers; 53.3 percent of white mothers smoked more than ten cigarettes per day, compared with 34.4 percent of African American mothers. Yet, African American pregnant smokers gave birth to babies who weighed 209.5 grams less than the babies of white smokers, a result that was significant.[24] When we controlled for the number of cigarettes smoked per day, by comparing white and African American pregnant smokers who consumed less than ten cigarettes per day, the African American smokers had nearly 3.5 times the full-term IUGR of white smokers.[25]

Why the racial disparity in birth weight, when we have controlled for other known biological variables, as well as the number of cigarettes consumed per day? A potential explanation for this mystery is the greater use of mentholated cigarettes by people of color, which are much more pathogenic than non-mentholated cigarettes.

> We don't smoke this shit, we just sell it. We reserve that right for the young, the poor, the black, and stupid.
> —R. J. Reynolds Tobacco Company Executive[26]

Beginning in the late 1960s, the tobacco industry sought to fill a market niche by targeting African Americans to consume mentholated cigarettes.[27] Internal records from R.J. Reynolds Tobacco Company, for example, describe strategically produced ads featuring African American models portraying smoking as "hip" and even healthy.[28] The marketing strategy was successful. Nationally, more than 75 percent of African American smokers smoke mentholated cigarettes, with Newport, Kool, and Salem comprising 55 percent of total cigarettes consumed by African Americans. Among African American teenagers, 61.3 percent favor Newport, 10.9 percent Kool, and 9.7 percent Salem cigarettes. Compared with the three quarters of African American smokers who prefer mentholated brands, less than 25 percent of white smokers smoke menthol cigarettes.[29]

Mentholated cigarettes stimulate the lung's cold receptors, which slows respiration and encourages the smoker to hold the smoke in his/her lungs for a longer period of time.[30] The menthol inhibits the metabolism of nicotine, allowing toxins to remain in the smoker's body for a longer period of time,[31] causing mentholated cigarettes to be more addictive[32] and harder to give up than non-mentholated brands.[33] Smoking mentholated cigarettes leads to greater pulmonary complications than non-mentholated cigarettes, in part because they mask symptoms of respiratory distress, thus increasing the risk of lung cancer and other ailments.[34]

Exposure to tobacco smoke after birth continues to wreak havoc with a child's health and survival. Cigarette smoke inflames the breathing passages of young children, triggering asthma, ear infections, bronchitis, and pneumonia. During an asthma study, on which I was a member of the research team, our study nurse collected urine from more than one hundred babies every three months during their first year. We asked our research lab to measure cotinine in the infants' urine, which is a breakdown product of nicotine.[35] Although 54 percent of the mothers smoked, 87 percent of the babies had cotinine in their urine, indicating that many were exposed to secondhand smoke from other members of the household.

Exposure to tobacco, both before and after birth, is a key risk factor for sudden infant death syndrome. Hafstrom and her colleagues, who exposed fetal lambs to nicotine, found that the newborn baby lambs could not take in as much air as those who were not exposed.[36] The prenatal nicotine literally stunted their capacity to breathe. When I tell students about this lamb study, they always grimace in sympathy, while imagining the wooly newborn lambs having been poisoned. I puzzle over the fact that when I tell the students that about one quarter of infants born in Syracuse are similarly exposed, it does not provoke in them the same deep sympathy. Two other studies on this issue are especially striking: the research team of Klonoff-Cohen examined the cases of two hundred white, African American, and Asian infants in Los Angeles who had died of SIDS and two hundred babies whose deaths were due to other causes.[37] They found a dose-response with increasing "numbers of cigarettes, as well as total number of smokers [in the home or doing child care]." Milerad and her colleagues measured nicotine and cotinine levels in the pericardial fluids of twenty-four consecutively autopsied infants who died of SIDS.[38] Of these twenty-four infants, 70 percent had been exposed to nicotine (five moderately, seven markedly and four heavily.) Among the sixteen Syracuse infants who died of SIDS or positional asphyxia from 1998 to 2001, 75 percent had mothers who smoked during pregnancy.

Alcohol, marijuana, and cocaine

Although drinking alcohol remains legal for pregnant women, the harm it can cause to a developing fetus rivals marijuana or cocaine. Home visitors, following the Syracuse Healthy Start protocol, asked women early in pregnancy about their intake of alcohol and illicit drugs. The goal of this early assessment was to target interventions to help the women avoid further substance use. The proportion of African American, Latin American, and European American Syracuse Healthy Start participants who reported drinking alcohol or taking illicit drugs during pregnancy (about 5 percent to 12 percent) was quite similar among the three groups. Among women delivering at the largest birth hospital between January 2000 and March 2002, 4.4 percent had tested positive for a urine drug screen during the pregnancy. When screened for substance use at the time of the birth, more than 5 percent of women reported having used drugs during pregnancy. Roughly equal proportions of African American and white women asked by providers at the time of delivery reported using cocaine and drinking alcohol during pregnancy; about 1.2 percent reported using cocaine and 1.8 percent drinking alcohol. African American women (5.5 percent) were statistically significantly more likely than white women (3.7 percent) to report marijuana use in pregnancy, although the actual difference is not large.[39]

Syracuse Healthy Start provided funds to help three local chemical dependency treatment facilities reach more pregnant women and mothers of infants. With this funding, Syracuse Behavioral Healthcare (SBH) converted two in-patient treatment beds into mother and infant units, so that drug- and alcohol-dependent pregnant women undergoing in-patient treatment can return to treatment with their newborn infants. This facility is linked with a landmark program run by the Onondaga County Probation Department, in which substance-using pregnant women who are arrested may be mandated for drug treatment in lieu of incarceration. In the first year of the program more than thirty-three babies were born drug-free to previously drug-using mothers. Prior to this initiative, the facilities could not care for mothers with newborn infants. Once the babies were born the mothers were faced with a no-win choice: they were obliged to either leave in-patient treatment or be separated from their babies. With Healthy Start funding, newly delivered mothers have been able to remain in drug treatment while bonding with their infants and establishing a nurturing tie that may strengthen their recovery. Public health nurses and other home visiting staff also visit the mother in the treatment facility, to assess her ability to care for her infant and to help develop her parenting skills.

Pregnant Inmates

In the Onondaga County jail, a pregnant woman bled to death from a ruptured ectopic pregnancy in 1996.[40] The inmate, who did not realize she was pregnant, complained of extreme cramps for several hours. According to news reports, a nurse practitioner forced the inmate to climb down a flight of stairs to be examined and, when the woman stopped breathing, the physician merely watched on the television monitor, rather than performing CPR.[41] A state inquiry into the death found that a physician, nurse practitioner, and three nurses were negligent. Upon reading the state report, County Legislator Sid Oglesby said, "Her death certificate should not read that she bled to death. Based on this report, it should say she died from incompetence and indifference." The inmate was African American, the Jail Health staff were white.[42]

In response to this tragedy, and in part funded by Syracuse Healthy Start, the Onondaga County Health Department overhauled the care of pregnant inmates. There are three correctional facilities in Onondaga County. In addition to the county jail, a state correctional facility, and a juvenile detention center, all house women of reproductive age. During 2000, 136 pregnant women passed through these facilities. As the director of Syracuse Healthy Start at that time, I was occasionally very involved with helping individual women get the care they needed as they passed into and out of correctional facilities, chemical dependency treatment facilities, and back to the street. The women nearly universally were drug users, often of crack and other substances. They were such heavy smokers that their teeth and fingers were stained yellow. Some were infected with HIV; many were homeless and had long psychiatric histories with borderline personality disorder, depression, and other diagnoses. They often supported themselves by selling sex, usually oral sex, to men in cars. One day I was searching for a Healthy Start client who had stopped going to prenatal care. I was told that she took her lunch daily at St. Francis of Assumption, where the nuns provide free food to the homeless and destitute. The nuns said that she ate the lunch outside in fair weather, across the street on the steps of a boarded-up, but once majestic, church. As I waited on the corner, where this homeless, pregnant, drug-using woman typically hung out, I noticed that cars with single male drivers swerved close to the sidewalk where I stood. I had, without realizing it, staked out a corner where sex workers ply their trade. As the first several men drove by, they looked expectantly at me and I looked back a bit sternly, but puzzled. I think that they must have taken me for a female police officer, because they drove quickly away after our mutual looks of inquiry. Finally, the woman passed by and I was able to encourage her to return to prenatal care and to enter drug treatment.

Because most pregnant inmates in these facilities have problems with chemical dependency, SHS coordinates with local chemical dependency treatment agencies, the probation department, obstetrical providers, correctional health, and, at times, the Syracuse Community Policing program. When a pregnant woman is arrested, staff from each of these agencies interacts to help her get the clinical care and social support needed for her to have a healthy baby. Usually the pregnant women are arrested for prostitution; about 150 women are arrested for prostitution each year in the City of Syracuse, but since some women may have been arrested more than once this may not be an unduplicated number. The chemical dependency agencies try immediately to open up treatment slots. Correctional health ensures that the women see an obstetrician, according to the following protocol: Pregnant women in jail for at least 7 days receive (1) an initial prenatal history, (2) a physical exam, and (3) an obstetric ultrasound. All pregnant women in jail receive regular prenatal visits from an obstetric physician on a schedule recommended by the American College of Obstetrics and Gynecologists. Public health nurses also begin "home visiting" the client while she is incarcerated, to provide support, education, and coordination of services.

SHS and Correctional Health staff evaluated this protocol from October 1, 2001 through September 30, 2002.[43] During that year, a total of 103 pregnant inmates were incarcerated in the local correctional facilities. The average number of days per inmate was 12.3, but some inmates stayed for lengthy periods. The majority of inmates were in and out of the facility within two days. The speed with which the women come and go makes it very difficult to provide services to them, especially any services—such as tuberculosis testing—that require at least two days to assess. Often the women give false addresses upon release, which makes it difficult or impossible to provide ongoing services. Nevertheless, more than 80 percent of women incarcerated for two weeks or more received adequate prenatal care in the jail. The evaluation tracked the birth outcomes of sixty of the infants of these inmates, most of whom had been released from the incarceration facility prior to their baby's birth; the remaining inmates, whose births were not assessed, may have given birth outside of Syracuse. Two of the infants died, but the birth weights and gestational ages of the other infants were similar to babies of non-incarcerated Syracuse mothers. Of course, we wished that all of the infants had survived, but given how difficult it was to provide care to women who were in and out of jail, often homeless, drug using, and surviving on sex work, we were pleased that the large majority of infants appeared to have been born healthy.[44]

Unintended Pregnancy

In graduate school in the 1980s, I recall discussing the issue of pregnancy planning with one of my fellow doctoral students, a young woman from Egypt. She at first did not understand what I meant by "planned pregnancy," upon which I explained that the couple has sexual relations with the intention of conceiving. "Ya Haram, Ya Sandy!" (Oh sin, Sandy!), she exclaimed. The hubris of planning an event that she believed to be an act of God seemed to her to be utterly presumptuous. She helped me to see that the Western concept of planning, in fact, our entire approach to engineering biological processes in the world and in our bodies, is not traditionally shared by much of the world. Yet, when women are ready for pregnancy, and when they want to be pregnant, their rates of low birth weight are lower and fewer of their babies die.[45] It is true that women who are not at all happy to find themselves pregnant often adjust and look forward to their baby's birth. But, women with unintended pregnancies frequently lack the resources—health insurance, a reliable partner, even a washer/dryer in the home—that would help them to take better care of themselves during pregnancy and better care of the baby after the birth.

As a part of the documentation of their birth data in the Perinatal Data System, women who deliver infants in Central New York are asked the following question, "Thinking back to when you first became pregnant, did you want to be pregnant (1) then, (2) sooner, (3) later, (4) not at all, or (5) were you unsure of how you felt?" Among mothers delivering infants in Syracuse during 2000–2001, about half wanted to be pregnant at that time or sooner. One third of all new mothers would have preferred to give birth at a later time, and nearly one fifth did not want the pregnancy at all or were unsure of how they felt about being pregnant.

Perinatal Depression and Domestic Violence

Pregnant women suffer a staggering burden of mental and emotional illness, but too often their distress goes unrecognized. Among women who delivered at the largest Syracuse birth hospital (between January 2000 to March 2002), 3.8 percent had received some type of psychiatric diagnosis during their pregnancies, including depression (2.6 percent), bipolar disorder (0.6 percent), and schizophrenia (0.4 percent). Some had previously attempted suicide, had current suicidal thoughts, or had an unspecified history of psychiatric hospitalization. Among Syracuse women whose babies died (1999–2001), 11 percent had been diagnosed with depression during pregnancy, and others had schizophrenia or had unsuccessfully attempted suicide.

New fathers also respond to the emotional roller coaster of pregnancy and birth. Among a group of fathers and mothers that my colleagues and I interviewed just after their babies' births, we administered the Edinburgh Depression questions. This list of ten questions about mood, crying, laughter, and thoughts of harming oneself are most commonly used to screen new mothers for postpartum depression.[46] To my knowledge, we were the first researchers to use the Edinburgh questions with new fathers, 40 percent of whom had higher scores for emotional distress than their baby's mothers.

This stress on the baby's fathers may help to explain why domestic violence occurs so frequently during pregnancy.[47] Among pregnant SHS participants (1998 to 2002), 10 percent of white women, 7 percent of African American women, and 8 percent of Latinas reported being hit, punched, or otherwise physically hurt by their partners in the previous year. Women who reported being hurt by their partners in the previous year were more than 2.5 times as likely to be admitted to the hospital during their pregnancies to treat traumatic injuries, compared with women who did not report histories of abuse.[48] We do not know, from the available information, how many of these traumatic injuries were directly caused by partner violence, in large part because women often hide the cause of their injuries from healthcare providers. In some cases abuse clearly caused the injury: for example, women who were stabbed or shot in the abdomen while pregnant, pregnancy resulting from rape, and/or physical assault to the abdomen precipitating premature delivery. Among women delivering in Syracuse's largest birth hospital between January 1, 2000, and March 31, 2002, 4 percent reported partner abuse during their pregnancies; the rates of domestic violence during pregnancy among white (3.5 percent) and African American women (3.9 percent) were nearly identical, whereas Latinas reported more abuse (6.3 percent). Many of the women reporting domestic violence during their pregnancies also have substantial substance use, as well as depression and other mental illnesses.

Unfortunately, social workers, who could provide much of the counseling for parents with depression, domestic violence, or other psychosocial problems have been cut from local health care facilities because of inadequate funds. In Syracuse-area prenatal and pediatric clinics, the few remaining social workers often struggle heroically to patch together sufficient services to meet the enormous needs of some three hundred patients or more each per year. The patients helped by these overburdened social workers often live with multiple and complex problems. One pregnant woman, for example, abused cocaine, had been in a drug rehabilitation facility, had been exposed to tuberculosis, was sexually abused as a child, entered prenatal care very late, and was diagnosed with depression. Another woman with prenatal depression had lost previous children to the foster care system because of her drug use. A third, with a history of preterm labor and paranoid schizophrenia, was a poly-substance abuser, had asthma and depression, and had begun prenatal care quite late. Although these women's troubles seem extreme, they are not uncommon.

The image many folks have of a teaching hospital obstetrical service is one where skilled staff members care for life-threatening clinical conditions. University-based obstetricians at our birth hospitals daily deliver care to women whose pregnancies are complicated by such life-threatening clinical conditions as advanced diabetes; twins, triplets and quadruplets; severe heart disease; alarmingly elevated blood pressure; and many other medical risks. Obstetricians know how to resolve clinical risks and they are very good at doing so. I watched a maternal-fetal specialist obstetrician, for example, perform a cesarean section in the space of minutes to rescue a baby who would otherwise have perished; it was nearly 5:00 a.m., he had been up all night, and while he operated he calmly taught the obstetrical resident who was assisting him. The non-clinical risks that at least partially arise from hopelessness and harmful environments—drug abuse, smoking, homelessness, and domestic violence—are much harder for these overburdened providers to resolve.

Inadequate Medical Translation

A newly arrived immigrant in late pregnancy was examined at a Syracuse area prenatal clinic. The obstetrician could not hear a fetal heartbeat, so a sonogram was performed. The baby was dead. The physician and clinic staff became alarmed and tried to explain to the mother what had happened. I do not know precisely what words the staff used, but I imagine they included "fetal death" and "absent heartbeat" and "no signs of life." The mother could converse a bit in English, which led the staff to believe that she understood them. She understood simple questions, such as "what is your name?" and "how are you?" She nodded to the providers, as they nodded when speaking with her. In her culture such non-verbal responses are a sign of respect and physicians are held in high regard. The mother left the clinic thinking all was well with her baby. Within a few days she felt the unmistakable signs of labor and went to the hospital. When she gave birth to a dead, macerated baby her shock and panic were extreme. Her provider, both troubled and puzzled by her response, had not realized the profound barrier to communication posed by her limited English.[49]

In 2004, I translated during the labor and delivery for a refugee who escaped from Sudan, where the Sudanese government's treatment of her people can be described as genocide. I was visiting the woman with two medical students as a part of a course that I was teaching. When the labor and delivery nurses wanted to explain in detail to the woman that her physician planned to induce her labor they called a commercial language line and asked for a translator fluent in the woman's tribal language. The language line employee had never heard of the women's language. Fortunately, the woman understood Egyptian dialect Arabic, having fled to Cairo from Sudan; she had lived in Cairo for some time before being accepted for asylum in the United States and had taught herself Arabic by watching television.

During the next fourteen hours I, and an obstetrical resident who was a native speaker of Arabic, translated for the woman, who gave birth to a healthy baby. However good the outcome, the situation was far from ideal. The woman had grown up in a traditional village and had never attended school. Explaining about the various high-tech pieces of equipment and techniques in a modern hospital delivery took all of the creative use of Arabic vocabulary that my brain could muster. Arabic was the second language for both the patient and me. It was the first language of the obstetrical resident, but since the resident's home country was not Egypt, and dialects of Arabic differ considerably by region, her spoken Arabic proved somewhat difficult for the refugee patient to understand. Despite my atrocious grammar, the woman understood my Arabic dialect somewhat better.

All of us need health information in a format that is respectful, clear, and comprehensible. Healthcare providers are extremely limited in the amount of time that they can spend with each patient. Explaining complex procedures to pregnant women, such as home blood glucose monitoring, for example, takes time and patience. Even native English speakers often leave the provider's office with prescriptions for drugs or tests that they do not fully understand. In Syracuse, 13.2 percent of the population speaks a language other than English at home; the majority of them speak Spanish. Many of those individuals require the assistance of translators in the medical setting. We also have newly arrived refugees from ever-increasing geographies where civil conflict forces people to flee. The provision of adequate translation services in healthcare settings is often limited to a telephone translator via a commercial translation service, who cannot see the patient or physician to directly translate the physician's jargon-laden medical language. Some local clinics, emergency rooms, and other facilities require patients to come in with their own interpreter. Often, the interpreter is a young child in the family who is more proficient in English than the parent, but obviously not sufficiently proficient to do medical interpretation. To partially make up for this serious deficit in spoken communication, medical providers give their patients written material to take home, which they hope will explain to the patient how to follow the home-based care procedures. These written materials are usually in English; even for those whose first language is English the materials are often at too high a reading level. When the materials are translated into Spanish, for example, the reading level is also often too advanced. Many Latinos in Syracuse are less than fully literate in either Spanish or English, so materials that are simply translated into fluent Spanish are also likely to fail at helping them to care for their critically important medical needs.

The Cross Cultural Health Care Program categorizes medical translation into seven levels of service[50]: (1) *No interpreter*; (2) *Chance interpreters*, such as a friend, family member, or staff member who speaks the needed language but is not specifically designated or trained to be a medical interpreter; (3) *Bilingual support staff*, who may be hired for their language skills to assist patients, but who lack full understanding of the clinical aspects of what they are translating; (4) *Professional on-site interpreters* with appropriate training, who are expensive for the institution, but are in many cases one of the better options; (5) *Telephonic interpretation,* which can provide a larger number of languages, but is expensive and lacks the nonverbal cues in face-to-face communication; (6) *Remote interpreting,* which has trained interpreters hired by the health care facility and two headsets, one each for the provider and patient; and (7) *Bilingual providers,* which is wonderful when the provider speaks the needed language, but given the continual influx of refugees with uncommon native languages, cannot serve all patients who require translation.

In 2000, in response to situations like those described above, the federal Office of Minority Health published the National Standard for Culturally and Linguistically Appropriate Healthcare (CLAS), which states,

> Standard 6. Health care organizations must assure the competence of language assistance provided to limited English proficient patients/ consumers by interpreters and bilingual staff. Family and friends should not be used to provide interpretation services (except on request by the patient/consumer).[51]

To assure compliance with this standard, in 2000 the Office for Civil Rights published a guidance memorandum, detailing how, under Title VI legislation, all health care facilities that take federal dollars must offer Limited English Proficient (LEP) services.[52]

Since 2005, several Syracuse area health care, community based, and educational organizations have sent bilingual staff to the Cross Cultural Health Care Program to become Certified Medical Interpreters, and other agencies have offered such training locally. In 2005, the New York Immigration Coalition requested New York State to take action against four big city hospitals that did not provide translation for emergency patients. In response to this civil rights complaint, the New York State Health Department issued regulations mandating translation services that must be available to those with limited English proficiency. Dr. Antonia Novello, New York State's then-commissioner of health, explained, "The new regulation requires hospitals statewide to avoid the use of family members, as well as individuals under sixteen years of age, as interpreters, except in extremely unusual situations. This will help ensure the quality of interpreter services and protect a patient's right to confidentiality."[53]

Adequate medical translation and interpretation is a partial success story. We now have the regulations in place, considerable political will, and an emerging cohort of trained medical interpreters. In two or three years we can evaluate this new initiative to see how well it is working.

Notes

1. T. Dye, S. D. Lane, and L. F. Novick, "A Population-Based, Race-Independent Public Health Assessment for Identifying Pregnant Women in Need of Healthy Start Services" (Centers for Disease Control and Prevention, November 30, 1998). Syracuse Healthy Start Risk Assessment System: We assessed relative risk, population attributable risk, sensitivity, and specificity for five variables: (1) mothers' age less than twenty-one years, (2) education less than high school completion, (3) Medicaid enrollee, (4) smoker, and/or (5) unintended or mistimed pregnancy. The risk system identifies a woman as being at risk if she has one or more of these risk factors. The model does not include inadequate prenatal care, because all pregnant participants receive a prenatal care appointment and are followed up to ensure that they receive ongoing prenatal care. The risk associated with Medicaid enrollment involves potential difficulties with access to care. The five risk factors each have greater than or equal to 10 percent population attributable risk (PAR percent) for low birth weight or infant death. Clinical risks that may be grave for an individual woman (i.e., placenta previa or abruptio, gestational diabetes, hypertensive disorder of pregnancy) occur sufficiently rarely that they represent much less than 10 percent PAR. The five risk factors in the model are widespread; together they accounted for 75 percent of the City of Syracuse population of women giving birth during 1996–7. A stepwise model examined the contribution to a cumulative PAR with the addition of

each variable for two outcomes: (1) low birth weight and (2) infant death. The cumulative PAR for the model was 48.4 percent for low birth weight and 61 percent for infant death. Our assessment indicates that this system identified 409 out of 470 women with low birth weight infants and 47 out of 52 mothers whose infants died had at least one of the five risk factors cited above. To make sure that bias is not introduced in not using race as a risk factor, we assessed the same five variables in the risk assessment model with and without the inclusion of race. These two models differed only slightly. The largest difference we found was with infant mortality as an outcome, in which case the difference in sensitivity with and without African American race in the model was 3.8 percent (the sensitivity was 90.4 percent without African American race and increased to 94.2 percent with African American race).

2. D. M. Charmaine, Royal Dunston, and M. Georgia, "Changing the Paradigm from 'Race' to Human Genome Variation," *Nature Genetics* 36 (2004): S5–7. Online publication: ; | doi:10.1038/ng1454.

3. American Anthropological Association Statement on "Race" (May 17, 1998).

4. R. C. Williams, "The Mind of Primitive Anthropologists: Hemoglobin and HLA, Patterns of Molecular Evolution," *Human Biology* 75, no. 4 (August 2003): 577–84; J. R. Aluoch, "Higher Resistance to Plasmodium Falciparum Infection in Patients with Homozygous Sickle Cell Disease in Western Kenya," *Tropical Medicine & International Health* 2, no. 6 (June 1997): 568–71.

5. M. Dean, M. Carrington, and S. J. O'Brien, "Balanced Polymorphism Selected by Genetic Versus Infectious Human Disease," *Annual Review Genomics Human Genetics* 3 (2002): 263–92; B. A. Kotsias, "The Advantage of Heterozygotes," *Medicina* 64, no. 1 (B. Aires, 2004): 79–83; S. M. Kavic, E. J. Frehm, and A. S. Segal, "Case Studies in Cholera: Lessons in Medical History and Science," *Yale Journal of Biological Medicine* 72, no. 6 (November-December 1999): 393–408; J. Bertranpetit and F. Calafell, "Genetic and Geographical Variability in Cystic Fibrosis: Evolutionary Considerations," *Ciba Foundation Symposium* 197 (1996): 97–114.

6. Audrey Smedley and Brian D. Smedley, "Race as Biology Is Fiction, Racism as a Social Problem Is Real," *Anthropological and Historical Perspectives on the Social Construction of Race, American Psychologist* (January 2005).

7. D. Acevedo-Garcia, M. J. Soobader, and L. F. Berkman, "The Differential Effect of Foreign-Born Status on Low Birth Weight by Race/Ethnicity and Education," *Pediatrics* 115, no. 1 (January 2005): e20–30.

8. This unpublished study was conducted by Tim Dye and is cited in: S. D. Lane, D. Cibula, L. P. Milano, M. Shaw, B. Bourgeois, F. Schweitzer, C. Steiner, K. Dygert, K. Demott, K. Wilson, R. Gregg, N. Webster, D. Milton, R. Aubry, and L. F. Novick, "Racial and Ethnic Disparities in Infant

Mortality: Risk in Social Context," *Journal of Public Health Management and Practice* 7 no. 3 (2001): 30–46.

9. Brian D. Smedley, Adrienne Y. Stith, and Alan R. Nelson, "Unequal Treatment: Confronting Racial and Ethnic Disparities in Health Care," *Eds. Institute of Medicine* (2003).

10. Data are from the U.S. Census 2000. Analysis by the author.

11. *Annual Update of the HHS Poverty Guidelines, Federal Register* 70, no. 33 (February 18, 2005): 8373–8375.

12. Managed Care, New York State Department of Health, http://www. health.state.ny.us/health_care/managed_care/index.htm; Medicaid Managed Care, "Overview of Medicaid Managed Care Provisions in the Balanced Budget Act of 1997," Kaiser Family Foundation.

13. "The Promises of Medicaid Managed Care, Consumer's Union," www. consumersunion.org/health/txmedicaid/txmed-5.htm.

14. U.S. Department of Health and Human Services, Administration of Children and Families, Office of Public Affairs, "Welfare Reform: Interim Final Regulations Fact Sheet," Washington, D.C., http://www.acf.hhs.gov/programs/ofa/regfact.htm.

15. "Welfare Reform," http://www.whitehouse.gov/infocus/welfarereform/.

16. "Welfare-To-Work Policy and Program Framework," Welfare-To-Work Division, NYS Department of Labor, March 2000.

17. "State Plan, Outline of the General Provisions of Its Temporary Assistance for Needy Families (TANF) Program," http://www.otda.state. ny.us/tanf/09_06/TANF0609Plan.

18. Kalchbrenner, "Clinical Review of Home Uterine Activity Monitoring," *JAOA* 101, no. 2, supplement (February 2001): 18–24.

19. "State Success Stories and Examples of Savings Using PARIS," U.S. Department of Health and Human Services, http://www.acf.hhs.gov/nhsitrc/paris/succ_par.html.

20. The proportions of white and African American groups do not include Latinas, whose rate is reported separately.

21. H. K. Hegaard, H. Kjaergaard, L. F. Moller, H. Wachmann, and B. Ottesen, "The Effect of Environmental Tobacco Smoke during Pregnancy on Birth Weight," *Acta Obstetricia et Gynecologica Scandinavica* 85, no. 6 (2006): 675–81; R. Adamek, E. Florek, W. Piekoszewski, A. Anholcer, and E. Kaczmarek, "Effect of Exposure to Tobacco Smoke and Selected Socioeconomic Factors in Occurrence of Low Birth Weight," *Przegl Lek* 62, no. 10 (2005): 965–9; K. Steyn, T. de Wet, Y. Saloojee, H. Nel, and D. Yach, "The Influence of Maternal Cigarette Smoking, Snuff Use and Passive Smoking on Pregnancy Outcomes: The Birth to Ten Study," *Pediatric Perinatal Epidemiology* 20, no. 2 (March 2006): 90–9.

22. P. A. Fried, B. Watkinson, and R. Gray, "Neurocognitive Consequences of Cigarette Smoking in Young Adults—A Comparison with Pre-Drug Performance," *Neurotoxicological Teratology* 28, no. 4 (July-August 2006): 517–25. Published online June 29, 2006.

23. P. A. Fried, B. Watkinson, and R. Gray, "Neurocognitive Consequences of Marijuana—A Comparison with Pre-Drug Performance," *Neurotoxicological Teratology* 27, no. 2 (March-April 2005): 231–9. Published online December 9, 2004.

24. Mean birth weights of white and African American smokers were significantly different. Student's t-test, p=0.014.

25. Odds ratio=3.48, 95 percent CI 1.19-10.22, p=0.008.

26. D. B. Goerlitz, "Steven R. Arch, et al. vs. the American Tobacco Company, et al. Videotape Deposition of David B. Goerlitz. Exhibits 1–17" (August 6, 1997). Bates: 517706191-517706708. http://tobaccodocuments. org/rjr/517706191-6708.html.

27. I am grateful to my student, Jessica Brill, whose term paper titled "Structural Violence and Tobacco" provided the background to this section.

28. E. D. Balbach, R. J. Gasior, and E. M. Barbeau, "R.J. Reynolds' Targeting of African Americans: 1988–2000," *American Journal of Public Health* 93, no 5. (2003): 822–27.

29. E. T. Moolchan, "Adolescent Menthol Smokers: Will They Be a Harder Target for Cessation?" *Nicotine and Tobacco Research* 6, supp. 1 (2004): S93–95.

30. S. Garten and R. V. Falkner, "Role of Mentholated Cigarettes in Increased Nicotine Dependence and Greater Risk of Tobacco-Attributable Disease," *Preventative Medicine* 38, no. 6 (June 2004): 793–8.

31. N. L. Benowitz, B. Herrera, and P. Jacob, "Mentholated Cigarette Smoking Inhibits Nicotine Metabolism," *Journal of Pharmacology and Experimental Therapeutics* 310, no. 3 (2004): 1208–15.

32. K. S. Okuyemi, M. Ebersol-Robinson, N. Nazir, et al., "African-American Menthol and Nonmenthol Smokers: Differences in Smoking and Cessation Experiences," *Journal of the National Medical Association* 96, no. 9 (2004): 1208–11.

33. G. A. Giovino, S. Sidney, J. C. Gfroerer, et al., "Epidemiology of Menthol Cigarette Use," *Nicotine Tobacco Research* 7, supp. 1 (2004): S67–81.

34. M. K. Formica, J. R. Palmer, L. Rosenberg, et al., "Smoking, Alcohol Consumption, and Risk of Systemic Lupus Erythematosus in the Black Women's Health Study," *The Journal of Rheumatology* 30, no. 6 (2003): 1222–26; K. S. Okuyemi, J. S. Ahluwalia, M. Ebersole-Robinson, et al., "Does Menthol Attenuate the Effect of Bupropion among African American Smokers?" *Addiction* 98, no. 10 (2003): 1387–93.

35. Judith, A. Crawford, Teresa M. Hargrave, Andrew Hunt, Chien-Chih Liu, Ran D. Anbar, Geralyn E. Hall, Deepa Naishadham, Maria H. Czerwinski, Noah Webster, Sandra D. Lane, and Jerrold L. Abraham, "Issues in Design and Implementation of an Urban Birth Cohort Study: The Syracuse AUDIT Project," *The Journal of Urban Health* (2006); P. F. Rosenbaum, T. Hargrave, J. L. Abraham, J. A. Crawford, C. Liu, S. D. Lane, D. Naishadham, G. Hall, R. Anbar, and A. Hunt, "Risk Factors for Wheeze in the First Year of Life in Inner-City Infants at Risk for Asthma," *Proceedings of the American Thoracic Society* 2 (2005): A694. Presented at the American Thoracic Society Meeting, May 2005. Published online by the American Thoracic Society, "ATS Abstracts2 View." (http://www.abstracts2view.com/atsall/).

36. O. Hafstrom, J. Milerad, and H. W. Sundell, "Prenatal Nicotine Exposure Blunts the Cardiorespiratory Response to Hypoxia in Lambs," *American Journal of Respiratory Critical Care Medicine* 166, no. 12, pt. 1 (December 15, 2002): 1544–9; O. Hafstrom, J. Milerad, K. L. Sandberg, and H. W. Sundell, "Cardiorespiratory Effects of Nicotine Exposure during Development," *Respiratory Physiology Neurobiology* 149, nos. 1–3 (November 15, 2005): 325–41. Published online June 20, 2005.

37. H. S. Klonoff-Cohen, S. L. Edelstein, E. S. Lefkowitz, I. P. Srinivasan, D. Kaegi, J. C. Chang, and K. J. Wiley, "The Effect of Passive Smoking and Tobacco Exposure through Breast Milk on Sudden Infant Death Syndrome," *Journal of the American Medical Association* 273, no. 10 (March 8, 1995): 795–8.

38. J. Milerad, A. Vege, S. H. Opdal, and T. O. Rognum, "Objective Measurements of Nicotine Exposure in Victims of Sudden Infant Death Syndrome and in Other Unexpected Child Deaths," *Journal of Pediatrics* 133, no. 2 (August 1998): 232–6. Comment in: *Journal of Pediatrics* 135, no. 1 (July 1999): 132–3.

39. Relative risk=1.49 (95 percent CI 1.12 —1.99).

40. John O'Brien, Jacqueline Arnold, and Maureen Sieh, "Inmate Described Bleeding in Note as Part of Their Review of Lucinda Batts' Death: County Officials Are Looking at What Happened to Her Note to a Nurse," *Syracuse Post-Standard,* sec. A, March 20, 1996.

41. Jacqueline Arnold, "Inmate in Coma After She Collapses. Justice Center Officials Say the Inmate Had Been Checked on Regularly After She Complained of Pain," *Syracuse Post-Standard,* sec. C, March 14, 1996.

42. John O'Brien, "State Faults Care of Inmate: A Report Cites a Doctor and Three Nurses at The Justice Center Jail for Ignoring Signs That Lucinda Batts Was Seriously Ill Before She Collapsed and Died," *Syracuse Post-Standard,* sec. A, November 2, 1996.

43. B. Levandowski, S. Teran, F. Schweitzer, D. Buchanan, B. Paul, and S. D. Lane, "Obstetrical Care Coordination for Incarcerated Women,"

(National Centers of Excellence in Women's Health: Second National Forum, "Understanding Health Differences and Disparities in Women: Closing the Gap," Virginia, May 13–14, 2003.)

44. See also J. A. Stein, M. C. Lu, and L. Gelberg, "Severity of Homelessness and Adverse Birth Outcomes," *Health Psychology* 19, no. 6 (November 2000): 524–34.

45. S. D. Lane, S. Teran, C. Morrow, and L. F. Novick, "Racial and Ethnic Disparity in Low Birth Weight in Syracuse, New York," *American Journal of Preventive Medicine* 24, supp. 4 (May 2003): 128–32, http://www.curriculum.som.vcu.edu/popmed/.

46. B. Hanna, H. Jarman, and S. Savage, "The Clinical Application of Three Screening Tools for Recognizing Post-Partum Depression," *International Journal of Nurse Practitioners* 10, no. 2 (April 2004): 72–79.

47. J. G. Silverman, M. R. Decker, E. Reed, and A. Raj, "Intimate Partner Violence Victimization Prior to and during Pregnancy among Women Residing in 26 U.S. States: Associations with Maternal and Neonatal Health," *American Journal of Obstetric Gynecology* 195, no. 1 (July 2006): 140–8.

48. Relative risk = 2.52 (95 percent CI, 1.09–5.83, p<0.042).

49. I am grateful to my colleague Llamara Padro Milano for this case description.

50. http://www.xculture.org/interpreter/overview/models.html.

51. "National Standards for Culturally and Linguistically Appropriate Services in Health Care," U.S. Department of Health and Human Services, Office of Minority Health, March 2001, prepared by IQ Solutions, Inc., 38.

52. "Guidance to Federal Financial Assistance Recipients Regarding Title VI Prohibition against National Origin Discrimination Affecting Limited English Proficient Persons," Health and Human Services Agency, 2000, http://www.hhs.gov/ocr/lep/revisedlep.html.

53. "A Matter of Life and Death: State Creates Patient Protections to Overcome Hospital Communication Barriers: Civil Rights Complaints Bring About Reforms," New York Immigrant Coalition Press Release, September 13, 2006.

Chapter 5

Babies Having Babies

"The issue is, you just got babies having babies."
—*African American man, Syracuse, 2006.*

We evolved as a species with teen pregnancy. Before the modern era, without antibiotics and vaccinations to prevent lingering illnesses and attendant delayed growth, and without packaged, frozen foods to stave off periodic starvation, girls often began menstruating at about age fifteen or even later.[1] As a girl's body packed on the pubertal pounds, which gradually arranged themselves into the pleasing curves of breasts and buttocks, family elders would make plans for her marriage. In most traditional societies—both hunter-gatherer and subsistence agriculturalists—a girl married soon after her first menses. Fecundity, the regular ovulation of viable eggs, generally begins about a year or longer after the first bleeding, resulting in the traditional pattern of the first birth within two years of the marriage. Families, who well realized the vulnerability of infants born to inexperienced young women, carefully tended the pregnancies of those traditional teen mothers.

Now at the turn of the twenty-first century, menstruation begins on average at twelve, an age that dropped throughout the twentieth century, paradoxically, as the average age of marriage increased.[2] My grandmother, for example, born in Glasgow, Scotland, in 1901, began menstruating at age sixteen; my mother, born in 1929 in Glasgow and raised in the United States during the depression, was fourteen. Born in 1951, the beneficiary of polio vaccines, penicillin, and plentiful food, I began bleeding at eleven.

Whether we are socially conservative and want teens to abstain from all sex until marriage, or socially liberal and want teens to avoid unwanted pregnancy and disease, we are up against the most powerful human drive. In our postmodern era, Madison Avenue manipulates this biological imperative. As the mother of a now-fifteen-year-old girl, with whom I do battle on shopping expeditions for her clothes, I am appalled at how the purveyors of teen fashions exploit this preternatural puberty by promoting hooker clothes to middle-schoolers. I am surely not the only parent to puzzle at the bitter irony of endless televised dramas of real or fictional missing girls, snatched from their parents' false security, in the midst of massive advertisements luring girls to dress as pedophilic bait.

Beginning in the late 1990s, and increasing under the George W. Bush administration, federal and state governments began funding abstinence-only, or abstinence-until-marriage, education in lieu of programs that comprehensively teach teens about sexuality, including birth control and the avoidance of both sexually transmitted diseases and sexual violence.[3] Federal guidelines released in 2006 further seek to meddle with adult unmarried sexuality, pushing the target age for premarital sex prevention to twenty-nine years old.[4] In 2005, new federal guidelines for overseas AIDS funding required that two-thirds of the money be spent on "abstinence-until-marriage" programs teaching "faithfulness."[5] As a mother of a teen I can sympathize with the desire for youth to delay sexual involvement, although having served on our county's Child Fatality Review Team for seven years I am much more frightened of teens in cars together than teens in bed together. But whether one is old-fashioned or permissive about teen sexuality, we all care about how our taxes are spent. Representative Henry Waxman and several other members of Congress asked the federal General Accounting Office (GAO) to evaluate the HIV/AIDS abstinence funding.[6] The GAO concluded that such programs divert funding from essential prevention programs, such as mother-to-child transmission of the virus during pregnancy and birth.

In Syracuse since mid-2000, well over three-quarters of a million dollars in federal and state grants have funded abstinence-only programs designed to get teens to "just say no." Prior to this single-minded abstinence funding, a variety of programs received support that encouraged abstinence while also helping sexually active teens to delay childbearing and avoid infection. As with the overseas HIV/AIDS abstinence-until-marriage funds, the abstinence-only funding in New York State diverted funds from comprehensive adolescent risk reduction. These abstinence-only pregnancy-prevention programs, with their virginity pledges, have been evaluated by teams of researchers who found the programs to be largely a waste of tax dollars.[7] Virginity pledges did not delay sexual experience, but teens who publicly pledged to maintain their chastity were less likely than other teens to use condoms when they did succumb. So, how did we fare in Syracuse with our abstinence-only funding? As Table 5.1 indicates, from 1997 to 2001 the actual number of teen pregnancies and the overall rate dropped each year. Beginning in 2002, however, the rate began to climb, just as the abstinence-only programs reached full swing. On average about 38 percent of teen pregnancies are terminated, a proportion that had also dropped by the years 1999–2000 and rose again beginning in 2001. I cannot say, with certainty, that this climb in Syracuse teen pregnancies resulted from the diversion of essential funds to help teens avoid pregnancy. But, it does not look like abstinence-only funding has been a roaring success.

African American women become mothers at an earlier age than their white counterparts and finish with childbearing sooner as well. Twice as many African American babies (12 percent) as white

Table 5.1　Syracuse Teen Births and Fertility Rates, 1997–2003

Year	Actual number of teenage pregnancies, maternal age 15–19 years, Syracuse	Fertility rate 15–19 years, Syracuse
1997	719	101.8
1998	689	97.6
1999	648	91.8
2000	635	89.9
2001	583	82.6
2002	623	88.2
2003	641	90.8

Data source: New York State Department of Health, analysis by author.

babies (6 percent) in Syracuse are born to teens under age eighteen. The peak age for giving birth among African American Syracuse residents is 24.7 years and the range is 12.5 to 42.5 years, compared with the white peak age of 27.2 years and the range of 12.5 to 47.5 years. African Americans not only become parents earlier, they die sooner than their white neighbors, two factors that I believe are probably related. Figure 5.1, which presents data from Onondaga County, illustrates that in the year 2000 more than half of African American males who died were younger than sixty-five, compared with 23.9 percent of white males; 38.8 percent of African American females died before sixty-five, compared with 14.2 percent of white females. Overall, 17 percent of the white population is age sixty-five or older, compared with just 6 percent of the African American population in Syracuse. I can only speculate, but it seems to me that the earlier deaths may indirectly lead to earlier births. I have asked African American colleagues why they timed their births during their twenties, whereas I gave birth to my daughter at the relatively geriatric maternal age of forty. My African American colleagues said that they were afraid of becoming too old. Many had already suffered the loss of their parents and had seen neighbors and friends die tragically early. Their sense of urgency to become parents before it was too late was completely foreign to me, as a relatively privileged white baby boomer.

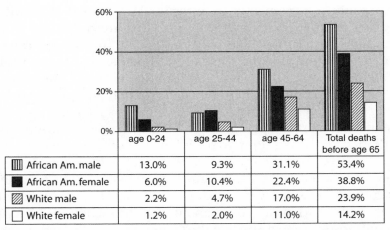

	age 0-24	age 25-44	age 45-64	Total deaths before age 65
African Am. male	13.0%	9.3%	31.1%	53.4%
African Am. female	6.0%	10.4%	22.4%	38.8%
White male	2.2%	4.7%	17.0%	23.9%
White female	1.2%	2.0%	11.0%	14.2%

Figure 5.1 Age at Death by Race and Gender, Onondaga County, 2000

Syracuse Healthy Start and Teen Birth Outcomes

One of the key areas in which Syracuse Healthy Start appears to have considerable success is with the babies of teen mothers. The babies born to teens in Syracuse have *lower* rates of death than babies born to adult women, whereas across the United States the infants born to adolescents have higher infant mortality than those of older mothers.[8]

The network of partner agencies working together with Syracuse Healthy Start provides comprehensive services to pregnant and parenting teens, including coordinated case management, outreach, and prenatal programs. While SHS seeks to reach pregnant women of all ages, teen parents often receive more attention than adult parents. Case managers assisted teens with scheduling their prenatal and pediatric care, made sure that they attended their appointments, coordinated these preventive and clinical services with school health personnel to help the teens stay in school, provided transportation, and gave many other types of assistance. By 2000, some 90 percent of pregnant teens were reached by at least some SHS services; of these, 79 percent received comprehensive care. In contrast, only 29 percent of women age twenty and older received comprehensive care.

We focused a lot on making the services "teen friendly." For example, one of the prenatal clinics serving low income women grouped the teen appointments on Thursday afternoons, when a nurse practitioner and physician who were particularly skilled at caring for pregnant teens were on duty. Sister Ida Gregoire, a Roman Catholic nun who is both a nurse and social worker, sat in a waiting room allocated specifically for the teens each Thursday afternoon, feeding the young clients granola bars and listening to them. Everyone who knows Sister Ida smiles when they speak of her. So tiny that she was often dwarfed by her teen patients, she exudes such compassion and acceptance that they opened up with their life stories, brought their friends to the waiting room to meet her, and often came to the waiting room on Thursdays even when they did not have appointments. Sister Ida resisted well-meaning attempts to have her teach the teens in structured sessions, which I think would have turned them off. I once asked her what she talked about with the teens and she replied that she mostly listened and that the teens themselves raised the issues with which they were struggling. I cannot quantify in an evaluation the magnitude of Sister Ida's contribution to the good outcomes of her teen patients, but my hunch is that it was considerable. Additional teen services include school-based early identification of pregnancy, risk assessment and referral, as well as case management and public health home visiting. The school-based program not only sought to promote the health of both mother and child, but also to encourage and support the academic progress of pregnant teens and new teen parents.

A number of authors have speculated as to whether the frequent finding of poorer pregnancy outcomes experienced by teen mothers are attributable to biological factors associated with their young age, or to a combination of teen life patterns and poverty.[9] In Syracuse during 2000–2001, as illustrated in Figure 5.2, the youngest teens had higher rates of low birth weight and premature birth, which adds weight to the argument that younger teens may be physically less able to carry a baby to term or to nourish the fetus in ways that promote adequate growth.

Yet, Syracuse infants born to teen mothers have the lowest infant mortality, as shown in Figure 5.3. Nationally in 1998, teen mothers had higher infant mortality than mothers of all other ages; national infant mortality rates by mothers' age follow a U-shaped curve that is highest among the teens, dips down to about a third of the teen rate

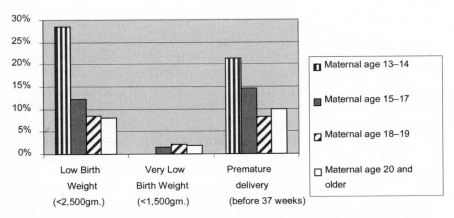

Figure 5.2 Pregnancy Outcomes, Singleton Births, by Maternal Age, Syracuse 2000–2001

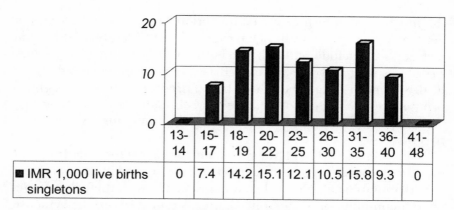

	13-14	15-17	18-19	20-22	23-25	26-30	31-35	36-40	41-48
■ IMR 1,000 live births singletons	0	7.4	14.2	15.1	12.1	10.5	15.8	9.3	0

Figure 5.3 Infant Mortality Rate by Mother's Age, Singleton Births, Syracuse, 2000–2001

among mothers age twenty-five to thirty, then goes up slightly among mothers age thirty-five and older. In Syracuse, in contrast, the curve is *reversed,* in that teens less than age fifteen had no infant deaths during 2000–2001 and infant mortality peaked among mothers in their mid-twenties and their late thirties.

A second encouraging finding is that the racial gap in low birth weight, premature births, and infant death was *eliminated* among teens ages thirteen to seventeen years, whereas among adult mothers (age twenty and older) the racial disparity persists. African American babies born to adult mothers have higher low birth weight, preterm delivery, and infant mortality than babies born to adult white mothers. The racial gap in low birth weight begins in the late teen years and the gap in preterm births and infant deaths begins at age twenty.

Did the comprehensive case management, outreach, and teen-friendly prenatal services lead to lower infant mortality among teen mothers and the elimination of the racial gap in pregnancy outcomes? It seems quite likely that they did, but since SHS is not an experiment with a control group, I can only speculate that the case management and teen friendly services were what worked. The projects' success in reaching so many teens in the city of Syracuse with the various clinical, case management, and home visiting services means that there is no comparison group of pregnant teens within the city who were not served. In truth I would much rather reach the vast majority of teens with needed services than have a comparison group who lacked services.

Other Teen Risks Remain Alarming

Although my colleagues and I were quite pleased about the good results of the teen births, we were well aware that a number of problems
persist among pregnant teens, particularly with regard to drugs and
other risk factors. Smoking, drinking, marijuana, and other drug use
begin very early for some teens. Table 5.2 presents the proportion of
substance use, STDs, and other risk factors among pregnant women
by the age of the mother.

Teens report getting high from an alarming number of substances.
Young adults in Syracuse have told our research team that ecstasy,
heroin, methamphetamines, and various designer drugs named after
luxury cars—Lexus and Mercedes—are commonly available. One of
the newer trends involves soaking a cigarette or marijuana joint in
embalming fluid and smoking it. Many teens also were diagnosed with
an STD during pregnancy, most notably in the youngest cohort.

While unintended pregnancy is a recognized risk factor, I was struck
by our finding that approximately a quarter of teens *wanted* to become
pregnant. These social risk factors, including intentional pregnancy

Table 5.2 Risk Factors among Pregnant Women, Syracuse 2000–2001

Maternal Age	13–14 years	15–17 years	18–19 years	20 years and older
Intended Pregnancy (wanted to be pregnant then or sooner)	21.4%	25.1%	32.9%	58.5%
Unintended Pregnancy (wanted to be pregnant later, not at all, or was unsure)	78.6%	72.8%	65.7%	39.1%
Medicaid Insurance	71.4%	53.4%	66.2%	39.0%
Late Entry to Prenatal Care (after first trimester)	78.6%	55.2%	47.2%	33.3%
Tobacco Use	21.4%	26.5%	33.9%	26.8%
Alcohol Use	0.0%	1.8%	1.6%	1.9%
Marijuana Use	7.1%	9.0%	8.9%	3.3%
Cocaine Use	0.0%	0.4%	0.5%	1.4%
STD Diagnosed during Pregnancy	42.9%	16.9%	19.2%	13.3%

among those as young as thirteen years, need further exploration. Teen mothers in Syracuse face considerably higher proportions of social risk factors, compared with adults, as presented in Table 5.2. Younger mothers were more likely to be covered by Medicaid insurance, indicating fewer economic resources. More than three quarters of very young teens (13–14) and more than half of those 15–17 years entered prenatal care late—after their first trimester of pregnancy—compared with one third of adults.

The youngest teens have only slightly lower levels of tobacco use in pregnancy (21.4 percent), and teens aged eighteen to nineteen years had the highest amount of smoking (33.9 percent). All groups reported relatively low rates of alcohol ingestion during pregnancy (less than 2 percent), but the proportion of mothers who reported drinking was nearly identical from age fifteen though adulthood, indicating that young teens are at risk for alcohol abuse despite it being illegal for them to consume. Cocaine abuse was low, with adults reporting the highest use at 1.4 percent. Marijuana, in contrast, was highest among the teens, with 7.1 percent of those ages thirteen to fourteen years reporting marijuana use during their pregnancies. Exposure to sexually transmitted infections during pregnancy was much higher in younger mothers, with more than 40 percent of the youngest teens affected.

Unequal Partners

Adult males father about half of the births in the United States to mothers younger than fifteen years old.[10] Among adolescent births in Syracuse during 2000–2001, 45 percent of births to teens ages thirteen to sixteen years list no father on the birth certificate, 32 percent of the fathers are between fifteen to eighteen years old, and among 23 percent of the births the baby's father is age nineteen or older. In one case, an over-forty-year-old male impregnated an under-fifteen-year-old. I became quite concerned about the problem of older males preying on teenage or pre-teenage girls when I was speaking with a group of twelve-year-old African American girls at a local community center. I had set up a meeting between the girls at the center and two female medical students, because I thought that having the young girls interact with the medical students informally might help the girls to envision advanced education for themselves. I brought pizza and soft drinks and during the wide-ranging discussions the African American pre-teens began to tell us about how they are followed by older men, mostly white men, in cars as they walk home from school. I asked if there were any girls who got into the cars, and if so, what happened to them. The girls affirmed that they knew that a couple of their classmates entered the vehicles of older males, who took them to the mall for treats in exchange for sexual favors. After this conversation, I reported the issue to the police and spoke about it widely with community groups.

My colleagues in a local HIV prevention program serving people of color included the issue of older males and younger females in a focus group of African American women (ages fourteen to twenty-one) because it is a potential risk factor for HIV transmission. The focus group facilitator asked, "What is the situation with older males and younger females in the Syracuse community?" The young women answered:

> Person #1: "[Young] women like it this way [older men] because males buy them drugs and stuff."

> Person #2: "Many of the men are married and still refuse to use condoms."

> Person #3: "Women want an older guy because they think they are going to be taken care of."

My colleagues and I asked a similar question in several focus groups of adult African American and Latino Syracuse residents, who responded:

> Person #1: "The younger girls now are more developed ... and they catch older guys' eyes ... and that's just what it is."

> Person #2: "It's strong in our community [the African American community] because a lot of younger sisters seek what they call "sugar daddies" or whatever for money, for rides, for getting high, or whatever."

> Person #3: You know, a lot of them young girls' mama's kick them to the curb. They're gonna find somebody who's gonna take care of them.

That's all right, most of the time they end up with an older person and most girls [who] end up with an older person are well taken care of. They eat, everything is taken care of."

Nearly all focus group members and other community members condemn sexual relations between older males and young teen females. However, in one of our focus groups, an older male appeared to speak from direct experience as the older partner in such a relationship:

The younger ladies are impressionable. You give them a little trinket here or jewelry there, some sneakers and some nice jeans and stuff, labels—Jean Paul, you know things like that, Gucci bag, Louis Vuitton—and you got it, you got it. It's a shame that you got to trade, you make a bargain with the devil. You gonna get me something and it's not for free—everything has a price.

From our ethnographic analysis, briefly outlined above, it is clear that although most adult community members strongly disapprove of these pairings, some older white males and males of color prey on very young teens. We still know relatively little about these relationships, some of which are consensual, some coercive, and some probably incestuous. But even those relationships that the young woman claims to have entered voluntarily have an inevitable age-related power difference.

The Onondaga County District Attorney's office has led in the development of a model program to prosecute perpetrators of statutory rape, defined as cases involving any type of sexual contact between an adult male and a female age sixteen or younger.[11] At the request of state-level health policy planners, my colleagues and I spoke with local reproductive health providers to understand their perspective on the problem of older sexual partners of young teens. Health care and social service providers are mandated by law to report child abuse. Although the providers we interviewed were unclear about which type of adult/teen sexual partnerships fell into the reportable category, New York State Law designates vaginal, oral, or anal sex with a teen fewer than seventeen years old by a person age twenty-one or older to be a class E felony.[12] Every provider with whom we spoke was deeply concerned, but most described this as a "no-win" situation. If teen patients believe that their older partners will be reported, the health care providers say, the teens will be much less likely to come for care. The providers, steeped in patient confidentiality, believe that reporting on their teen patients' adult partners will breach any trust between themselves and their young patients. The teens may then go without necessary STD treatment, birth control, and prenatal care. Some of the providers have, in response, adopted an unwritten "don't ask, don't tell" policy. This situation remains unresolved. Law enforcement personnel view this as a crime to be prosecuted; the providers remain torn between not wanting to drive their teen female patients away and concerns that they may be putting their licenses at risk if they don't report.

Teens who give birth are much less likely to go as far in school as those who delay motherhood. But, what comes first? Are failing students more drawn into sexual relationships, or less able to negotiate contraception, than academically achieving students? Or, perhaps morning sickness, childbirth, and the demands of colicky infants leave little time for study? The answer to this question is both: academically troubled teens disproportionately become mothers and motherhood is not conducive to high school completion even among bright adolescents. I looked at the highest school grade completed among teen mothers (ages thirteen through nineteen) in Syracuse. One quarter of teen mothers at the time of their first birth were already more than one full academic year behind their expected grade level. By their second or higher birth, half of the teen mothers lagged more than a year behind their expected grade.

Developmental Delay and Teen Pregnancy

Cognitively challenged individuals can be effective parents with enough supportive services. When teen females are developmentally delayed, however, even their ability to consent to sexual relations and to envision the possibility of parenthood resulting from such intimacy may be limited. SHS staff provided services to about twenty developmentally delayed pregnant adolescent students in Syracuse each year during 1999–2000, many of whom, I suspect, became pregnant in abusive, coercive relationships. In a national female sample of 6,283, studied as a part of the National Longitudinal Survey of Youth, women with lower scores on the Armed Services Vocational Aptitude Battery (a test of arithmetic reasoning, math knowledge, word knowledge, and paragraph comprehension) were significantly more likely to have become mothers prior to age twenty, regardless of racial or ethnic background.[13] A nested case-control comparison within this sample demonstrated that women with low cognitive ability had nearly three times the odds of a second birth in their teen years than those with higher cognitive ability.

Environmental Injustice: Lead Poisoning, Teen Pregnancy, and Tobacco

My colleagues and I found childhood lead poisoning in Syracuse to be significantly associated with subsequent repeat teen pregnancy and cigarette smoking. Lead entering the bodies of babies and toddlers affects their developing brains in ways that continue to influence their behavior years later. Lead poisoning thus becomes a cumulative environmental injustice. Children's greatest exposure to lead comes from old paint in dilapidated buildings, especially around windowsills and doorframes, which yield powdery paint dust and chips each time they are opened.[14] To a lesser, but still important extent, lead is found in soil surrounding houses whose exteriors have peeling lead paint. Finally, lead-tainted water from corroded lead solder in old copper pipes potentially contributes a modest amount to children's exposure to lead. The level of blood lead considered harmful has decreased over time, as research identified health consequences at increasingly lower levels. Before 1970, a blood lead level of 60 mcg/dl was considered dangerous, by 1985 the level for concern had dropped to 25 mcg/dl, and in 1991 it was changed to 10 mcg/dl. A longitudinal study of 172 children followed from the ages of six months to five years found that IQ, measured on the Stanford-Binet Intelligence Scale, fell by 7.4 points as blood lead rose from 1 mcg/dl to 10 mcg/dl.[15] Currie estimates that lead poisoning and other health disparities account for up to a quarter of the racial gap in school readiness.[16]

Lead's neurotoxicity is not simply a blunt instrument damaging cognitive capacity, but it diminishes the ability to plan, learn from prior experience, and control impulsive behavior, impairments that are collectively termed deficits in "executive function." Observational studies with exposed children have found associations between lead exposure and what has been variously termed impulsive behavior, delinquency, and aggressive/anti-social behavior.[17] Adults occupationally exposed to lead also exhibit neurobehavioral deficits, including diminished cognitive ability and executive function.[18]

Experimental animal studies have demonstrated early lead exposure to be a risk for impulse control, failure to delay gratification,
and increased sensitivity to drug-seeking behavior.[19] A possible
biological pathway for lead's promotion of maladaptive behavior
has been identified in experimental trials in which lead-dosed rat
pups developed disruptions in their neurochemistry (dopamine,
norepinephrine, serotonin, and monoamine oxidase).[20] According
to Bellinger, the neurotoxic effects of lead on children's development appear to be irreversible.[21]

Our analysis on lead, repeat pregnancy, and tobacco used data
from 1998 to the first quarter of 2002, which was compiled to monitor the receipt of preventive care of pregnant Syracuse Healthy Start
participants. As a part of routine screening, the SHS staff looked
up the pregnant participants' childhood lead levels in archived
paper files in the OCHD. If the participant's childhood lead level
is elevated, SHS staff reports this finding to the woman's obstetrician. SHS staff also completes a risk-screening questionnaire with
participants, which asks about tobacco use, in order to make a
plan for intervention. This analysis includes only those aged fifteen
to nineteen years, who were born after the phase-out of leaded
gasoline and after the ban on lead-based residential paint. During
the time period covered in this analysis, SHS enrolled more than
three quarters of all mothers less than age twenty in Syracuse. The
variables that are part of this analysis are:

- Childhood lead level of currently pregnant teens: The pregnant teens in this sample were between ages zero to twenty-four
  months during the years 1981 to 1989, at which time a blood
  lead level of below 25 mcg/dl was considered "acceptable" by the
  Centers for Disease Control and Prevention. In the lead records
  on file in the Onondaga County Health Department during
  this era, if a child's lead level was less than 20 mcg/dl the staff
  wrote, "OK," rather than the exact number. If the child's blood
  lead level was 20 mcg/dl or greater, the staff recorded the exact
  number. In cases where participants had more than one childhood lead level on file, we used the highest lead level recorded.
  Childhood blood lead level was coded as a dichotomous variable
  (<20 mcg/dl, 20 mcg/dl, or greater).
- Tobacco use: SHS participants were asked about tobacco use
  early in the pregnancy as a part of routine screening and were

offered assistance with reducing or quitting smoking. Tobacco use was coded as a dichotomous variable (any, none).

- Repeat pregnancy: Participants were asked about their previous pregnancies. If a participant has had a previous pregnancy, then the current pregnancy is called a "repeat teen pregnancy." Repeat pregnancy was coded as a dichotomous variable (first pregnancy, second, or higher pregnancy).
- Maternal age: Maternal age was calculated by subtracting the maternal date of birth from the expected date of her baby's birth (EDC, or expected date of confinement). The analyses, below, use maternal age as a dichotomous variable (fifteen through seventeen years, eighteen through nineteen years).

Of the 1,111 pregnant teens served by the Syracuse Healthy Start program, we found documentation of the highest childhood lead level for 719 (65 percent) pregnant teens, of whom 26.7 percent were white, 48.4 percent African American, 5.7 percent Latina, 1.2 percent Native American, 0.8 percent Asian, and 16.7 percent unknown/other. Among these pregnant teens 73 percent had childhood lead levels less than 20 mcg/dl, 14 percent between 20–29 mcg/dl, 9 percent between 30–39 mcg/dl, and 5 percent between 40–99 mcg/dl.

Repeat pregnancy was significantly associated with elevated childhood lead and mother's age (older teens were more likely to have a repeat birth), findings that were each statistically significant. Tobacco use was also significantly associated with maternal race (white teens smoked more than African American teens). We performed two separate logistic regression analyses with childhood lead level as the exposure, or risk factor. In the first analysis repeat birth was the outcome variable and in the second tobacco use was the outcome variable. In each logistic regression, we controlled for maternal race, mother's age, and Medicaid insurance as a proxy for poverty. These logistic regressions found childhood lead poisoning to be a risk factor for repeat birth, with the lead-exposed group of teens having a 59 percent increased risk of repeat pregnancies. The risk of smoking in those exposed to lead was significantly increased only in those not receiving Medicaid, or higher income, teens.[22]

Next we examined the ecological association of lead poisoning and teen birth in the five high-lead zip codes in Onandaga County exclusive of the five zip codes. A caveat is that ecological analysis cannot tell us about individuals, but can only provide insight into the aggregate levels of each factor in the geographical area. Nevertheless, this ecological analysis echoes the link between lead poisoning and repeat teen pregnancy, found in the individual-level analysis described above. As shown in Table 5.3, the teen birth rate (maternal age 15 to 19 years) and the percent of repeat births to teens increase in proportion to the percent of elevated blood lead in children in that zip code. The chi-square for trend among these strata is statistically significant, with the odds ratio of each stratum increasing in proportion to the increased lead poisoning. Of course, the elevated lead blood lead occurs in contemporary infants and toddlers, whereas the pregnancies occur in teens, who would have been tested for lead 13 or more years

Table 5.3 Zip Code–Level Association of Lead Poisoning and Teen Birth (2000–2001)

Zip codes	% of children tested (age 0–24 months) with elevated blood lead (2000–2001)[v]	Population of females (15–19 years)[ii]	# of Births to teens (15–19 years) 2000–2001[i]	Birth rate (15–19 years) per year, per 1,000 births[iv]	% of all births (to mothers age 15–19) that are repeat births	Chi square for linear trend of lead and pregnancy rate (26.170 p<0.00001)
13203	6.7 %	444	45	50.7	14%	1.00[vi]
13208	8.05%	683	111	81.3	14%	1.72
13207	9.25%	544	89	81.8	12%	1.73
13205	10.6 %	775	129	83.2	16%	1.77
13204	11.2 %	746	175	117.3	22%	2.72
Onondaga County excluding the above Zip codes	1.3 %	16,863	627	18.6	n/a	

Sources:
i New York State Vital Records
ii 2000 Census
iii Calculations by author
iv Electronic birth certificate data, Syracuse births 2000–2001, calculations by authors.
v Data from New York State DOH, calculations by authors
vi Referent stratum

previously. Therefore, we do not know for certain if the pregnant teens currently residing in the zip code lived there as young children.

Lead and Executive Function

Most of the studies cited earlier linking prior lead exposure to deficits in executive functioning have been conducted with adolescent and adult males. Among lead-poisoned adolescent males, according to these studies, poorer planning ability, the reduced capacity to learn from prior behavior or to delay gratification lead to higher rates of socially deviant, and sometimes law-breaking, behavior. But, teenage girls are much less likely to be arrested or labeled "delinquent." A key area in which executive function influences the lives of teenage females is choices about their intimate partners, including when and with whom to express their sexuality and the effective use of both contraception and protection from sexually transmitted infections. An important caveat in applying the concept of executive function to teen sexuality is that many births to younger teens are the result of coercive sex. As mentioned earlier, nationally, adult males father about half of the births to mothers less than fifteen years old[23]; thus, even in relationships that are not overtly coercive there may be an age-related power differential. Since lead poisoning potentially impacts both cognitive ability and executive functioning, these two factors may operate synergistically in reducing the teen's ability to avoid pregnancy. Teen women with less strong cognitive or judgment capacity—secondary to lead poisoning—may be less able to perceive whether potential partners sincerely care about their welfare or are manipulating them. Reduced cognitive competence, and being less able to plan ahead or be mindful of consequences, may also impede the effective and consistent use of birth control.

Lead and Propensity to Addiction

As described in Chapter 8, many small corner stores in inner-city Syracuse neighborhoods sell loose cigarettes—"loosies"—to minors, thus facilitating their potential addiction to tobacco. The 1999 Youth Risk Behavior Survey, conducted with all tenth grade students in Syracuse, revealed that 97.5 percent had tried cigarette smoking at least once; 24 percent had smoked within the past thirty days; and 9 percent reported smoking more than two cigarettes per day within the past thirty days.[24] These data demonstrate that an alarming proportion of Syracuse youth risk lifetime tobacco addiction. Even in an environment in which nearly all youth have tried tobacco, however, only about a quarter continue to smoke. The higher-income teens with childhood lead exposure, in our analysis, were significantly more likely to use tobacco. To date only two articles have linked lead exposure to addiction, both of which focus on cocaine. The first posits lead poisoning in childhood as a theoretical risk factor for subsequent cocaine addiction.[25] The second, an experimental study in which rats were exposed to lead in utero and before weaning, found that the perinatally-lead-exposed rats exhibited "increase[d] sensitivity to cocaine later in the life cycle."[26] The lead-dosed rats, which went on to self-administer low doses of cocaine at higher rates than the lead-free rats, no longer had traces of lead in their blood or body tissues. The rats' perinatal lead poisoning caused irreversible developmental changes that left them at greater risk for later addiction. An editorial in *Environmental Health Perspectives* commented that the results in the rat study, described above, may come from lead's disruptive effect—demonstrated in other animal research—on the dopamine reward center in the developing brain.[27] Our study is the first that we are aware of to find an association between elevated childhood lead and cigarette smoking in teen years. Two potentially-related findings in lead exposure/behavioral studies appear to be pertinent in evaluating the potential for early lead exposure to increase sensitivity to tobacco addiction: (1) the association of early lead exposure with a decreased ability to delay gratification—found in both observational human and experimental animal studies and (2) the aforementioned alterations in the dopamine system and other mood-regulating neurochemicals, found in the experimental rat studies. These two factors suggest biological plausibility that early lead exposure could increase sensitivity to tobacco addiction.

Lead and School Readiness

Chapter 6 on education inequality and infant death presents the shocking rates of school failure among children in Syracuse. While there are many reasons why schoolchildren fail, surely lead poisoning accounts for a portion of this tragedy. Consider that the five "high lead" zip codes in

Syracuse account for 7.7 percent of the total incidence of elevated lead in children in *all of New York State*. Children in those zip codes arrived at school much less cognitively ready to learn. In Syracuse during the years 2000–2003, as presented earlier, 10.8 percent of white children and 22.7 percent of African American children had lead levels of 10 mcg/dl or greater. The potential IQ deficit associated with blood lead of 10 mcg/dl is 7.4 points. One in ten white children and nearly one quarter of African American children in Syracuse suffer this lifetime neurotoxic insult; the population-level loss of human potential is staggering.[28]

Notes

1. Hardy, Sarah, *Mother Nature: A History of Mothers, Infants, and Natural Selection* (Pantheon, September 21, 1999).

2. B. Towne, S. A. Czerwinski, E. W. Demerath, J. Blangero, A. F. Roche, and R. M. Siervogel, "Heritability of Age at Menarche in Girls from the Fels Longitudinal Study," *American Journal of Physical Anthropology* 128, no. 1 (September 2005): 210–19.

3. F. E. Mebane, E. A. Yam, and B. K. Rimer, "Sex Education and the News: Lessons from How Journalists Framed Virginity Pledges," *Journal of Health Communications* 11, no. 6 (September 2006): 583–606; H. Klaus, "Abstinence and Abstinence-Only Education," *Journal of Adolescent Health* 39, no. 2 (August 2006): 151, discussion 152, author reply 152–4; A. L. Golden, "Abstinence and Abstinence-Only Education," *Journal of Adolescent Health* 39, no. 2 (August 2006): 151–2, discussion 152, author reply 152–4; A. Elster and M. Fleming, "Abstinence and Abstinence-Only Education," *Journal of Adolescent Health* 39, no. 2 (August 2006): 150, discussion 152; D. Kittredge, "Abstinence and Abstinence-Only Education," *Journal of Adolescent Health* 39, no. 2 (August 2006): 150–1, discussion 152, author reply 152–4.

4. "Section 510 Abstinence Education Program (CFDA #93.235)," U.S. Department of Health and Human Services, Administration for Children and Families, Administration on Children, Youth and Families, Family and Youth Services Bureau, August 2006, http://www.acf.hhs.gov/grants/open/HHS-2007-ACF-ACYF-AEGP-0143.html#_Toc142296169.

5. "Revamped Federal Abstinence-Only-Until-Marriage Programs Go Extreme," http://www.siecus.org/media/press/press0124.html.

6. The content of federally funded abstinence-only education programs, prepared for Rep. Henry A. Waxman, United States House of Representatives, Committee on Government Reform–Minority Staff, Special Investigations Division, December 2004, http://www.democrats.reform.house.gov/Documents/20041201102153-50247.pdf.

7. "United States Ignorance Only: HIV/AIDS, Human Rights and Federally Funded Abstinence-Only Programs in the United States, Texas: A Case Study," Human Rights Watch report, http://hrw.org/reports/2002/usa0902/; J. Santelli, M. A. Ott, M. Lyon, J. Rogers, and D. Summers, "Abstinence-Only Education Policies and Programs: A Position Paper of the Society for Adolescent Medicine," *Journal of Adolescent Health* 38, no. 1 (January 2006): 83–7; J. Santelli, M. A. Ott, M. Lyon, J. Rogers, D. Summers, and R. Schleifer, "Abstinence and Abstinence-Only Education: A Review of U.S. Policies and Programs," *Journal of Adolescent Health* 38, no. 1 (January 2006): 72–81; "Abstinence-Only Programs Challenged," *AIDS Patient Care STDS* 19, no. 11 (November 2005): 783–4; E. A. Borawski, E. S. Trapl, L. D. Lovegreen, N. Colabianchi, and T. Block, "Effectiveness of Abstinence-Only Intervention in Middle School Teens," *American Journal of Health Behavior* 29, no. 5 (September-October 2005): 423–34; J. H. Tanne, "Abstinence Only Programs Do Not Change Sexual Behaviour, Texas Study Shows," *BMJ* 330, no. 7487 (February 12, 2005): 326; S. E. Bennett and N. P. Assefi, "School-Based Teenage Pregnancy Prevention Programs: A Systematic Review of Randomized Controlled Trials," *Journal of Adolescent Health* 36, no. 1 (January 2005): 72–81.

8. "Healthy People 2010," http://wonder.cdc.gov/.

9. A. A. da Silva, V. M. Simoes, M. A. Barbieri, H. Bettiol, F. Lamy-Filho, L. C. Coimbra, and M. T. Alves, "Young Maternal Age and Preterm Birth," *Pediatric Perinatal Epidemiology* 17, no. 4 (October 2003): 332–9; B. Zuckerman, J. J. Alpert, E. Dooling, R. Hingson, H. Kayne, S. Morelock, and E. Oppenheimer, "Neonatal Outcome: Is Adolescent Pregnancy a Risk Factor?" *Pediatrics* 71, no. 4 (April 1983): 489–93.

10. P. Donovan, "Can Statutory Rape Laws Be Effective in Preventing Adolescent Pregnancy?" *Family Planning Perspectives* 29, no. 1 (January/February 1997): 30–34, 40.

11. P. Donovan, "Can Statutory Rape Laws Be Effective in Preventing Adolescent Pregnancy?" *Family Planning Perspectives*, special report 29, no. 1 (January/February 1996), http://www.guttmacher.org/pubs/journals/2903097.html.

12. http://public.leginfo.state.ny.us/menugetf.cgi. The exact wording of the relevant passages of two laws is cited below:

Penal Law § 130.25, Rape in the third degree: A person is guilty of rape in the third degree when: ... 2. Being twenty-one years old or more, he or she engages in sexual intercourse with another person less than seventeen years old ... Rape in the third degree is a class E felony. Penal Law § 130.40, Criminal sexual act in the third degree: A person is guilty of criminal sexual act in the third degree when: ... 2. Being twenty-one years old or more, he or she engages in oral sexual conduct or anal sexual conduct with a person less than seventeen years old … Criminal sexual act in the third degree is a class E felony.

13. D. L. Shearer, B. A. Mulvilhill, L. V. Klerman, et al., "Association of Early Childbearing and Low Cognitive Ability," *Perspectives on Sexual and Reproductive Health* 34, no. 5 (2002): 236–43.

14. New York State Department of Health, "Eliminating Childhood Lead Poisoning in New York State by 2010," (Albany: New York State Department of Health, 2004.)

15. R. L. Canfield, C. R. Henderson, D. A. Cory-Slechta, et al., "Intellectual Impairment in Children with Blood Lead Concentrations below 10 mcg per Deciliter," *New England Journal of Medicine* 348, no. 15 (2003): 1517–26.

16. J. M. Currie, "Health Disparities and Gaps in School Readiness," *The Future of Children* 15, no. 1 (2005): 117–38.

17. A. K. Leung, W. L. Robson, J. E. Fagan, et al., "Attention Deficit Hyperactivity Disorder: Getting Control of Impulsive Behavior," *Journal of Postgraduate Medicine* 95, no. 2 (1994): 153–60; H. L. Needleman, C. McFarland, R. B. Ness, et al., "Bone Lead Levels in Adjudicated Delinquents: A Case Control Study," *Neurotoxicology and Teratology* 24, no. 6 (2002): 711–17; R. L. Canfield, M. H. Gendle, and D. A. Cory-Slechta, "Impaired Neuropsychological Functioning in Lead-Exposed Children," *Developmental Neuropsychology* 26, no. 1 (2004): 513–40; K. A. Espy, "Using Developmental, Cognitive, and Neuroscience Approaches to Understand Executive Control in Young Children," *Developmental Neuropsychology* 26, no. 1 (2004): 379–84; L. M. Chiodo, S. W. Jacobson, and J. L. Jacobson, "Neurodevelopmental Effects of Postnatal Lead Exposure at Very Low Levels,"*Neurotoxicology and Teratology* 26, no. 3 (2004): 359–71; R. L. Canfield, D. A. Kreher, C. Cornwell, et al., "Low-Level Lead Exposure, Executive Functioning, and Learning in Early Childhood," *Neuropsychology, Development, and Cognition* 9, no. 1, Section C, Child Neuropsychology (2003): 35–53.

18. B. S. Schwartz, B. K. Lee, K. Bandeen-Roche, et al., "Occupational Lead Exposure and Longitudinal Decline in Neurobehavioral Test Scores," *Epidemiology* 16, no. 1 (2005): 106–113; M. G. Weisskopf, H. Hu, R. V. Mulkern, et al., "Cognitive Deficits and Magnetic Resonance Spectroscopy in Adult Monozygotic Twins with Lead Poisoning," *Environmental Health Perspectives* 112, no. 5 (2004): 620–25; A. Barth, A. W. Schaffer, W. Osterode, et al., "Reduced Cognitive Abilities in Lead-Exposed Men," *International Archives of Occupational and Environmental Health* 75, no. 6 (2002): 394–98; B. S. Schwartz, W. F. Stewart, K. L. Bolla, et al., "Past Adult Lead Exposure Is Associated with Longitudinal Decline in Cognitive Function," *Neurology* 55, no. 8 (2000): 1144–50. Erratum in *Neurology* 56, no. 2 (2001): 283.

19. D. A. Cory-Slechta, "Lead-Induced Impairments in Complex Cognitive Function: Offerings from Experimental Studies," *Neuropsychology,*

Development, and Cognition 9, no. 1, Section C, Child Neuropsychology (2003): 54–75; J. F. Nation, A. L. Cardon, H. M. Heard, et al., "Perinatal Lead Exposure and Relapse to Drug-Seeking Behavior in the Rat: A Cocaine Reinstatement Study," *Psychopharmacology* 168, nos. 1–2 (2003): 163–74.

20. C. B. Devi, G. H. Reddy, R. P. Prasanthi, et al., "Developmental Lead Exposure Alters Mitochondrial Monoamine Oxidase and Synaptosomal Catecholamine Levels in Rat Brain," *International Journal of Developmental Neuroscience* 23, no. 4 (2005): 375–81; Y. Xu, G. Li, C. Han, et al., "Protective Effects of Hippophae Rhamnoides L. Juice on Lead-Induced Neurotoxicity in Mice," *Biological & Pharmaceutical Bulletin* 28, no. 3 (2005): 490–94; S. Fazli-Tabaei, M. Fahim, and M. R. Zarrindast, "Effect of Acute and Chronic Lead Exposure on Apomorpine-Induced Sniffing in Rats," *Pharmacology & Toxicology* 92, no. 2 (2003): 88–93.

21. D. C. Bellinger, "Lead," *Pediatrics* 113, supp. 4 (2004): 1016–22.

22. Among teens not covered by Medicaid, the odds of having an elevated childhood lead level among smokers was 4.25 (95 percent CI 1.89, 9.57) times the odds of having an elevated childhood blood lead among non-smokers, controlling for maternal race and age. Among those receiving Medicaid, the odds of elevated childhood lead level among smokers was 1.26 (95 percent CI 0.79, 2.03) times the odds of elevated childhood blood lead among non-smokers, controlling for maternal race and age. Controlling for maternal age, maternal race, and Medicaid use, the odds of elevated childhood lead level among those women having their second pregnancy was 1.59 (95 percent CI 1.04, 2.43) times the odds of elevated childhood blood lead among those having their first child.

23. P. Donovan, "Can Statutory Rape Laws Be Effective?"

24. Onondaga County Health Department, "Youth Risk Behavior Survey," 1999. (The YRBH is conducted in collaboration with the Centers for Disease Control and Prevention.)

25. M. D. Majewska, "Cocaine Addiction as a Neurological Disorder: Implications for Treatment," *NIDA Research Monograph* 163 (1996): 1–26.

26. J. R. Nation, K. R. Smith, and G. R. Bratton, "Early Developmental Lead Exposure Increases Sensitivity to Cocaine in a Self-Administration Paradigm," *Pharmacology Biochemistry and Behavior* 77, no. 1 (2004): 127–35.

27. J. Wakefield, "Leading to Drug Abuse," *Environmental Health Perspectives* 109, no. 2 (2001): A68.

28. Data are from the Onondaga County Health Department, analysis by the author. Presented by the author at an Onondaga County and New York State Lead Program meeting, "Racial and Ethnic Disparity in Lead Exposure," September 2003.

Chapter 6

Health Literacy

People with more education live longer and mothers with more education have fewer infant deaths.[1] Just completing high school confers greater longevity; compared with high school graduates, the lives of those who dropped out before getting a diploma are almost two and one half times more likely to end before age sixty-five.[2] Nationally, in 2002, among mothers of all racial and ethnic groups, those who left high school between the ninth and eleventh grades had the highest rates of infant death, followed by those who finished twelve years of education.[3] Mothers with at least some post-secondary education had the lowest infant mortality.

Educational inequality is a cornerstone of many disparities in pregnancy and infant health in Syracuse. The Syracuse City School District, for example, was one of five school districts statewide in a 1998 class-action lawsuit that were characterized by the American Civil Liberties Union as failing to deliver on the constitutional promise of a sound education.[4] A New York State appellate court, ruling on the matter, initially concluded that the state's constitution only guarantees education to a literacy level of the eighth or ninth grade. Fortunately, this decision was overturned on appeal in 2003.[5]

A nationwide analysis of high school graduation rates for the class of 2001, conducted by The Urban Institute, demonstrated that only 68 percent of students who started ninth grade received a high school diploma on time in June.[6] This is not the eventual proportion of students who obtain high school graduation certificates; some students graduate at a later date, after making up failed or missed classes; some repeat a grade in high school and graduate the following year; and some finish with a GED. While it is important to help as many students as possible to graduate from high school, The Urban Institute's measure of the proportion of the original ninth-grade cohort earning diplomas *on time* in June illuminates large disparities between wealthy and impoverished school districts.

In The Urban Institute's report, the City of Syracuse School District had the lowest graduation rate in New York State (of the seven large city school districts in the analysis), with only 26.2 percent of its 2001 cohort receiving a diploma *of any type* on time. These alarmingly low rates of on-time receipt of a high school diploma differ greatly from the published rates put out by the Syracuse City School District (SCSD). I double checked The Urban Institute's findings, because they were so different from the SCSD's own published graduation rates. Using data from the Syracuse City School District's Web site, covering the period from 1998 to 2002, I calculated the proportion of the original ninth-grade cohort who graduated at the completion of twelfth grade in 2002. As shown in Table 6.1, only 28.4 percent of the original ninth-grade cohort graduated in 2002 with a diploma of any type.

For the academic year 2001–2002, the Syracuse City School District reported a dropout rate for general education students of 3.6 percent. When I was in the midst of reading through the SCSD's reports, I frequently became confused when the numbers just did not add up. From Table 6.1 it is clear that from ninth grade to twelfth grade there are between 15 percent to 30 percent fewer students each year, when compared with the count of students in the previous year. How can a cohort, I wondered, lose a fifth or more of its membership from one year to the next and have a dropout rate that is less than 5 percent? Two investigative journalists, Paul Riede and Maureen Nolan, answered my question. I quote from their report in the Syracuse *Post-Standard* below:

> Syracuse tells the state each year that its districtwide dropout rate is less than 6 percent. Last year it reported a rate of 5.3 percent—just above the state's standard of 5 percent. But students in any city high school can tell you there's more to it than that. In any given year, city ninth-graders can look around them and be assured that by the time they finish their senior year, more than half their classmates will be

Table 6.1 School Enrollment by Grade, Syracuse City School District, Class of 2002

	Month and Year	Actual Number and/or Percentage
9th grade cohort— reported by the SCSD	September 1998	1,848 students
10th grade cohort— reported by the SCSD	September 1999	1,250 students
11th grade cohort— reported by the SCSD	September 2000	1,059 students
12th grade cohort— reported by the SCSD	September 2001	828 students entered 12th grade in September 2001
		805 students were in the "graduation rate cohort" reported by the SCSD that academic year
# and % receiving a diploma of any type— reported by the SCSD	June 2002	524 students SCSD Reported graduation rate 65%
% of original 9th grade cohort receiving a diploma of any type	June 2002	28.4%

Data source: Syracuse City School District, analysis by author.

gone. Not all will have dropped out—some will have transferred to other schools or to GED programs; others will spend an extra year in school to try to graduate. But even if all those transfers and held-back students succeed, more than 40 percent of the original ninth-graders will fail to earn a high school diploma. It isn't only a Syracuse problem. Dropout rates have been obscured for years in local schools because the state reporting system minimizes the numbers and school districts often fail to follow up on students who leave. Yet those rates are published in widely distributed state report cards each year to help parents and taxpayers evaluate their schools. Schools are under growing pressure to count dropouts better. State audits have criticized districts for faulty numbers. Starting next fall, state officials plan to make their boldest move to get the job done right: They'll add up the numbers themselves.[7]

New York State high school graduates have historically received either a *local* or a *Regents diploma.* Under the old system, local diploma graduates were considered sufficiently educated for non-professional jobs, whereas Regents diploma holders were college-bound. Local diploma graduates formerly demonstrated their English language proficiency with a passing grade on the RCT exam, set at about the eighth-grade literacy level.[8] However, a switch from a two-tiered diploma to the Regents-for-all is being "phased in" over the course of several years.[9] All students now take Regents exams in a series of subjects. The graduating cohort of 2002 was the last to have the local diploma option. For the class of 2002, a score of fifty-five to sixty-four on the Regents exams was accepted to receive a local diploma and a score of sixty-five or higher became required for a Regents Diploma.[10] A score of eighty-five or better on a Regents exam is considered "mastery" of the subject. To get a sense of what these scores mean, consider that the City University of New York requires entering freshman to achieve a Regents Exam English score of seventy-five to meet their "basic skills" requirements.[11] In the Syracuse City School District graduating class of 2002, 262 students earned Regents diplomas.[12] These Regents graduates represent less than 14 percent of their original ninth-grade cohort.

Educational inequality affects health indirectly because less education translates to lower income and more job instability, which too often mean that a person cannot afford health insurance. It is also a key area of racial and ethnic disparity. Among new mothers in Syracuse, African Americans and Latinas fare worse educationally than other racial/ethnic groups, with white mothers having the highest rates of post–high school education, as shown in Figure 6.1.

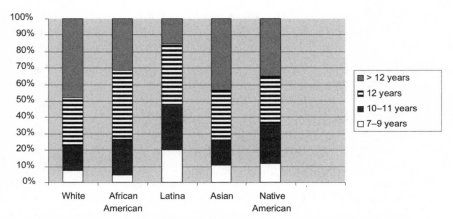

Figure 6.1 Highest Grade Attained by New Mothers Age 19 and Older, Syracuse, 2000–2001

Health Literacy[13]

According to the Literacy Coalition of Onondaga County, more than half of the adults in the City of Syracuse read at or below the eighth grade reading level and one quarter read at or below the fifth grade level. A growing number of studies on low literacy and health have led to the recognition that information distributed by health care providers must be easy-to-read, of a literacy level that is comprehensible to the majority of consumers, and culturally appropriate to the priority population. Nearly half of all Americans have difficulties in comprehending written health information in a manner that may seriously impact their health. On average, reading comprehension is about four years below a person's highest grade completed. Even those who graduate from high school may have low literacy; among adults who have graduated from high school about 15 percent read at or below a sixth-grade level.[14] To illustrate this point, a study of the functional health literacy of patients in two public hospitals found that 15 percent could not read a prescription bottle with enough accuracy to correctly identify the dosage as one pill four times a day.[15] Research has also documented low literacy as associated with self-perception of poor health by patients and as a barrier to care.[16] Health literacy encompasses the following aspects:

I. *The ability to learn and read health information.* Patients ashamed of their low literacy often rely on cues such as oral instructions, demonstrations, or the aid of a literate friend or family member. However, once they leave the physician's office, they are left with a brochure to answer questions concerning dosage or procedures. Health literacy in this regard encompasses instrumental literacy—using print to solve problems—such as determining how much medicine to give to a sick baby. For example, acetaminophen overdose in babies and children has recently been recognized as an important avoidable cause of liver failure. According to a researcher familiar with the problem, the package label instructions "may exceed the reading comprehension of as many as 50 percent of parents."[17] An analysis performed by our research team found that directions (on the side of the can) for preparing the powdered infant formula Enfamil are written at the seventh-grade level.

II. *Preparation of written health education for patients.* Informed consent documents, discharge papers, and health education brochures are often written by public health professionals without regard to the literacy levels of patients. Emergency department discharge instructions used in three rural hospitals are written at a ninth-grade reading level.[18] Similarly, the standard Southwestern Oncology Group consent form and other medical consent forms fall into college-grade reading levels.[19] Information about correct usage of contraceptives was found to be above the average reading level of contraceptive users, leading to a documented relationship between unplanned pregnancy and lower literacy.[20] Due to the discrepancy between the reading level of pamphlets and consequent poor comprehension by the general population, in 1993 the Joint Commission on Accreditation of Health Organizations mandated that "patient instructions must be provided in ways the patient can understand."[21]

III. *Strengthening the link between comprehension and behavior change.* Even when health promotional literature is prepared at the appropriate reading level, it may not positively influence health behavior. A study of the efficacy of patient literature on smoking cessation found that pregnant women with higher literacy levels were more cognizant of the harmful effects of smoking on their fetus. However, this knowledge did not result in comparable levels of smoking cessation.[22]

Evidence-Based Health Literacy Interventions

My colleagues and I in Syracuse Healthy Start developed an evidence-based model for our interventions, directed toward parents with low literacy. The steps in our model (Figure 6.2) involve (1) analyzing local data, (2) reviewing published studies, (3) assessing available materials, (4) initiating programmatic interventions, and (5) evaluating the outcomes. Our review of the scientific literature on health literacy was described in the last section. The remainder of this chapter describes the SHS planning, programs, and outcomes to address health literacy. In this work we were guided by Paulo Freire's call, in *Pedagogy of the Oppressed,* to empower the disadvantaged to positively impact

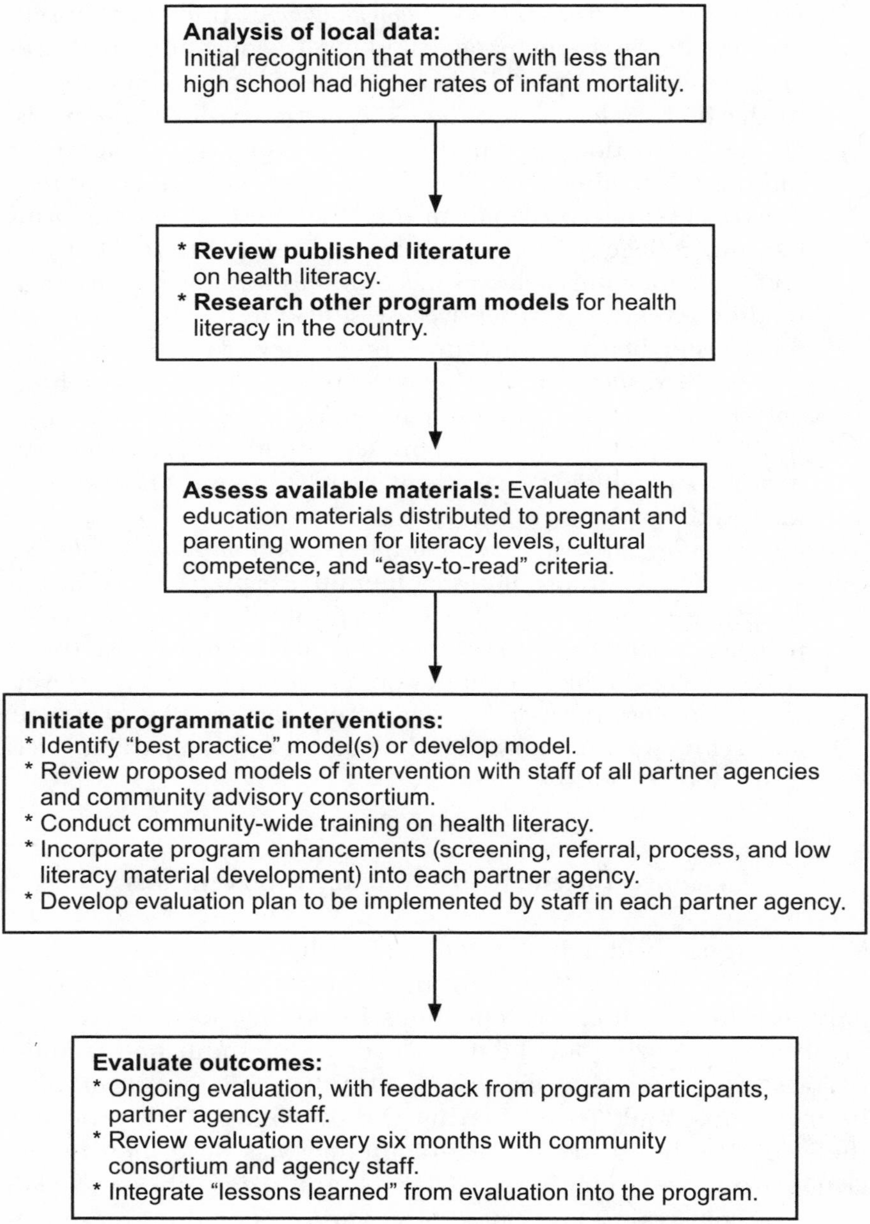

Analysis of local data:
Initial recognition that mothers with less than high school had higher rates of infant mortality.

↓

* **Review published literature** on health literacy.
* **Research other program models** for health literacy in the country.

↓

Assess available materials: Evaluate health education materials distributed to pregnant and parenting women for literacy levels, cultural competence, and "easy-to-read" criteria.

↓

Initiate programmatic interventions:
* Identify "best practice" model(s) or develop model.
* Review proposed models of intervention with staff of all partner agencies and community advisory consortium.
* Conduct community-wide training on health literacy.
* Incorporate program enhancements (screening, referral, process, and low literacy material development) into each partner agency.
* Develop evaluation plan to be implemented by staff in each partner agency.

↓

Evaluate outcomes:
* Ongoing evaluation, with feedback from program participants, partner agency staff.
* Review evaluation every six months with community consortium and agency staff.
* Integrate "lessons learned" from evaluation into the program.

Figure 6.2 Evidence-Based Health Literacy Model

their health and the health of their infants, toward the reduction of infant mortality.[23]

Analyzing local data

We reviewed local epidemiological data on maternal education and infant mortality from the New York State Vital Records. Among all births in Syracuse during 1996–1997, having only a high school education or less was the leading population attributable risk factor, meaning that this risk factor accounted for 25 percent of the infant deaths among mothers age twenty and older. An analysis of Onondaga County matched birth and death cohorts from 1992–1994 found an infant mortality rate of 11.3 per one thousand live births for mothers without a high school education, compared with 7.4 per one thousand for those with high school or more education, a difference that was significant.[24] Sudden Infant Death Syndrome (SIDS) was the single cause of infant death significantly associated with the mother's non–high school graduation in an analysis of 205 infant consecutive deaths in Onondaga County between 1993 and 1996. During this period there were a total of fourteen SIDS deaths, thirteen of which were to infants whose mothers had not completed high school. Within these 205 infant deaths, we compared SIDS with non-SIDS causes of death, and non-high school graduation as a risk factor. The odds of a non-high school graduate adult mother having a baby die of SIDS were nearly nine times that of a high school graduate.[25]

Assessing available materials

Our research team conducted an analysis of twenty-eight health education materials given to pregnant women and families by local providers and by national agencies. We wanted to make sure that the printed health advice for pregnant women was written at a level that they could actually read. The analysis is based on materials provided to pregnant women by local prenatal care providers, consumer-education brochures sent to Syracuse Healthy Start from local and national agencies, and an Internet search of the Web sites of organizations disseminating health information focused on prenatal and postpartum care. The organizations producing these documents included the Centers for Disease Control and Prevention, the American Academy of Pediatrics, the American College of Obstetrics and Gynecology, the March of Dimes, and the National Institute of Child Health and Human Development.

These documents were evaluated according to three criteria: (1) The Fry Readability Index, which is a standardized method of determining reading level.[26] (2) The "easy-to-read" criteria developed by Stableford,[27] which assesses inclusion of white space, inclusion of culturally appropriate pictures, the type of material, and length of material. "White space" refers to short statements surrounded by ample space. (3) Cultural competence: Since it is difficult to analyze materials directed to a general audience in terms of cultural competence, we focused on the addition of graphics that represented a diverse audience.[28] A three-person panel of graduate students in medicine, public health, and medical sociology reviewed each of the documents. The panel reviewers had attended health literacy training where the Fry Readability index and other measures used in this analysis were fully covered. The reviewers jointly discussed the document analysis to arrive at consensus.

The documents ranged in type from one-page tear sheets and pamphlets, a book, Web site booklets, and other Web site formats. About half (57 percent) of the materials were equal to five pages or less. Of the documents reviewed, 78.5 percent were above seventh-grade reading level; 100 percent were above the sixth-grade reading level. Only 53.6 percent of the documents included enough white space. Of the 25 percent of the materials that included pictures, almost all had culturally appropriate and inclusive graphics. However, three quarters of the materials did not contain pictures. More than three quarters of the printed health education materials for pregnant women and parents were above the reading ability of nearly half of the parents in Syracuse. When I discuss this point with students, I ask the class how many can easily read their VCR instruction manuals. Usually, only one or two students raise a hand. The printed materials, often produced at considerable expense, are as useless as VCR instruction manuals for the disadvantaged half of the population.

Initiating Programmatic Interventions

Based on the findings reviewed above, we revised our interventions so that we could better help mothers with low educational attainment to have healthy babies. This section presents five levels of intervention for low educational attainment and infant health undertaken by Syracuse Healthy Start.

1. *Written Health Materials:* First, we initiated a multi-agency approach to changing how written health materials were prepared and what types of materials were purchased to use. To do this, we provided training the staff of local health care, public health, human service, outreach, case management, and community-based agencies in how to write materials that are "easy-to-read." Following Freire's admonition to ensure that theory once learned was translated into action we conducted a follow-up assessment of whether the trained staff used these principles in their work. Of the approximately twenty-one agencies or programs whose staff attended one or more of the training sessions, fifteen agencies/programs subsequently used the approach to prepare or purchase materials. In more than three-quarters of these agencies or programs, the staff reported that their approach to preparation or selection of health materials had been fundamentally revised.

2. *Health Education:* Second, we put ads on television, trained hairstylists to impart our health messages, and increased the number of outreach staff who engaged community members in face-to-face communication.

3. *Ensuring That Adolescents Complete Their Schooling:* Third, we provided funding to fourteen peer leadership/education programs to help adolescents complete their education. This network of after school, summer, and school-based programs went beyond simply imparting information to the teens or monitoring their healthcare. The staff shared our vision of helping adolescents to imagine a productive future for themselves, which includes completing their education.

4. *Appropriate Screening and Referral of Parents to Adult Literacy Programs:* Fourth, we referred parents with low literacy to adult education programs. Parents who read to their children are

more likely to raise children who are competent readers and, in turn, increase their own literacy.[29] Syracuse has a local literacy coalition and two nonprofit agencies devoted to increasing adult literacy, which helped to increase the reading ability of some of the parents in our project. Too few adults with low reading ability, however, took advantage of the free tutoring. Parents who were already overwhelmed with work, childcare, and daily life, combined with the shame of admitting to their low literacy, were reluctant to participate in adult literacy education.

5. *Paternal Involvement:* Fifth, we added a fatherhood component to the SHS program that included a paternal case manager to work with the fathers of the babies of adolescent mothers. The fathers were encouraged to read to their babies during two half-hour periods per week and were given culturally appropriate children's books such as *Guess How Much I Love You, Good Morning Baby,* and *Good Night Baby.* To help us inspire fathers to read to their children, our local baseball team, the Syracuse SkyChiefs, held a father's reading event at one of their games.

Outcome Evaluation

So, how did these low literacy interventions work? We evaluated these efforts by looking at the pregnancy outcomes of adult women in Syracuse who did not graduate from high school. Among these births, we compared women who were or were not Healthy Start participants. Just as in our earlier analysis, SIDS and other causes of infant deaths that occurred after the babies reached one month of age—postneonatal deaths— were higher among mothers who had not graduated from high school. This evaluation has some limitations. First, because "social promotion" used to be common, a high school diploma does not guarantee adequate literacy. But, since we were not able to test the literacy level of each pregnant participant, education was the best measure that we had. Second, since SHS involves a multifaceted set of interventions, we cannot in this analysis tease apart which specific intervention made the greatest difference.

We conducted this evaluation on all singleton births in the City of Syracuse for the years 2000–2001. Among these births, we compared non-high school graduate mothers who were or were not Healthy Start participants. Our analysis was conducted on mothers aged nineteen and older, to include only mothers who were old enough to complete high school. High school dropout was not statistically associated with low birth weight, very low birth weight, neonatal mortality, or infant death. Postneonatal infant mortality, however, was increased among mothers who had not graduated from high school, a finding that was consistent with our analyses prior to beginning SHS.[30]

We were very pleased to find that Healthy Start participants were 75 percent less likely to have an infant die in the postneonatal period than non-participants, a result that was statistically significant.[31] The finding that SHS participation was associated with lower postneonatal death for mothers with less than twelve years of education suggests that our overall interventions are effective in reducing infant mortality in this group. The health literacy interventions are a large part of the overall interventions.

The evidence-based steps that we followed—analyzing local data, reviewing published studies, assessing available materials, initiating programmatic interventions, and evaluating the outcomes—are applicable to a wide variety of community-based programs. This method can potentially enhance the development of health promotion activities, by fitting the interventions to the needs of the population as well as by learning about the successes and failures of other similar initiatives.

A potential limitation is that in order to reserve project funds for direct service, we preferred to use available data for formative analysis and evaluation rather than spend money on additional data collection. Publicly collected epidemiological data, such as the vital records data that we used in this evaluation, can be enormously helpful in program planning, development, and assessment. Since the data are not collected specifically for program purposes, however, it may not precisely fit as a measure of individual program interventions. This was an issue with the analysis of the SHS interventions. We were only able to measure maternal years of education completed, whereas the optimal measurement would have been maternal literacy level. Similarly, in the program evaluation, we were not able to separate the overall program inputs from those specifically targeting health literacy.

Notes

1. M. Murphy, M. Bobak, A. Nicholson, R. Rose, and M. Marmot, "The Widening Gap in Mortality by Educational Level in the Russian Federation, 1980–2001," *American Journal of Public Health* 96, no. 7 (July 2006): 1293–9. Published online May 30, 2006; D. H. Jaffe, Z. Eisenbach, Y. D. Neumark, and O. Manor, "Effects of Husbands' and Wives' Education on Each Other's Mortality," *Social Science Medicine* 62, no. 8 (April 2006): 2014–23; W. J. Nusselder, C. W. Looman, J. P. Mackenbach, M. Huisman, H. van Oyen, P. Deboosere, S. Gadeyne, and A. E. Kunst, "The Contribution of Specific Diseases to Educational Disparities in Disability-Free Life Expectancy," *American Journal of Public Health* 95, no. 11 (November 2005): 2035–41; J. Fawcett, T. Blakely, and A. Kunst, "Are Mortality Differences and Trends by Education Any Better or Worse in New Zealand? A Comparison Study with Norway, Denmark and Finland, 1980–1990s," *European Journal of Epidemiology* 20, no. 8 (2005): 683–91.

2. M. Arialdi, M. P. H. Miniño, Elizabeth Arias, Kenneth D. Kochanek, Sherry L. Murphy, and Betty L. Smith, "Deaths: Final Data for 2000," *National Vital Statistics Reports* 50, no. 15 (September 16, 2002).

3. T. J. Mathews, Fay Menacker, and Marian F. MacDorman, "Infant Mortality Statistics from the 2002 Period Linked Birth/Infant Death Data Set," *Division of Vital Statistics National Vital Statistics Reports* 53, no. 10 (November 24, 2004).

4. Merri Rosenberg, "Suit Filed to Challenge Disparities in Schools," *New York Times,* January 17, 1999.

5. Greg Winter, "New York Schools Ruling: Overview, State Underfinancing Damages City Schools, New York Court Finds," *New York Times,* June 27, 2003.

6. Christopher B. Swanson, "Who Graduates? Who Doesn't? A Statistical Portrait of Public High School Graduation, Class of 2001," Education Policy Center, The Urban Institute. Published online February 25, 2004.

7. Paul Riede and Maureen Nolan, "Schools Undercount Dropouts. Central New York High Schools Fail to Graduate About 7,000 Students," *Syracuse Post-Standard,* sec. A, July 3, 2002.

8. These pieces originally appeared as a weekly column entitled "Lessons" in the *New York Times* between 1999 and 2003. This article first appeared in the *New York Times* on January 11, 2001: "The Challenge: The Unforeseen Costs of Raising Academic Standards," by Richard Rothstein.

9. "Regents Keep Local Diploma Option (10/13/03), 55 Remains Passing Grade on Key Regents Exams," New York State School Boards Association, http://www.nyssba.org/.

10. Overview of district performance in English language arts, mathematics, and science and analysis of student subgroup performance for Syracuse City School District, March 2003.

11. "How Can Students Meet City University's Basic Skills Requirements?" http://rwc.hunter.cuny.edu/cuny-act/overview.html.

12. The number 262 comes from the Syracuse City School District, New York State District Report Card Comprehensive Information Report, April 9, 2003.

13. The remainder of this chapter is adapted from B. Levandowski, P. Sharma, S. D. Lane, N. Webster, A. Nestor, D. Cibula, and S. Huntington, "Parental Literacy and Infant Health: An Evidence-Based Healthy Start Intervention," *Health Promotion Practice* 7, no. 1 (2006): 95–102. Used with permission.

14. National Work Group on Literacy and Health, "Communicating with Patients Who Have Limited Literacy Skills," *Journal of Family Practice* 46 (1998): 168–76.

15. R. M. Parker, D. W. Baker, M. V. Williams, and J. R. Nurss, "The Test of Functional Health Literacy in Adults: A New Instrument for Measuring Patients' Literacy Skills," *Journal of General Internal Medicine* 10 (1995): 537–41.

16. D. W. Baker, R. M. Parker, M. V. Williams, W. S. Clark, and J. Nurss, "The Relationship of Patient Reading Ability to Self-Reported Health and Use of Health Services," *American Journal of Public Health* 87 (1997): 1027–30; M. V. Williams, "Recognizing and Overcoming Inadequate Health Literacy, a Barrier to Care," *Cleveland Clinic Journal of Medicine* 69 (2002): 415–8.

17. Heubi cited J. E. Brody, "With Tylenol and Children, Overdosing Is Perilously Easy," *New York Times,* January 25, 2000.

18. K. S. Hayes, "Literacy for Health Information of Adult Patients and Caregivers in a Rural Emergency Department," *Clinical Excellence for Nurse Practitioners* 4 no. 1 (2000): 35–40.

19. T. C. Davis, R. F. Holcombe, H. J. Berkel, S. Pramanik, and S. G. Divers, "Informed Consent for Clinical Trials: A Comparative Study of Standard versus Simplified Forms," *Journal of the National Cancer Institute* 90 (1998): 668–74.

20. R. M. Parker, M. V. Williams, D. W. Baker, and J. R. Nurss, "Literacy and Contraception: Exploring the Link," *Obstetrics and Gynecology* 88 (1996): 72S–77S.

21. A. Riffenburgh, "Joint Commission of Accreditation of Healthcare Organizations (JCAHO)." *Health Literacy Toolbox* (2000). Retrieved July 30, 2002, from http://www.prenataled.com/healthlit/hlt2k/script/ht2_a_7.asp.

22. C. L. Arnold, T. C. Davis, H. J. Berkel, R. H. Jackson, I. Nandy, and S. London, "Smoking Status, Reading Level, and Knowledge of Tobacco Effects among Low-Income Pregnant Women," *Preventive Medicine* 32 (2001): 313–20.

23. Paulo Freire, *Pedagogy of the Oppressed* (New York: Continuum, 1970).

24. Odds ratio=1.5; 95 percent Confidence Interval: 1.1–2.2; n=20,968.

25. Odds ratio=8.59, 95 percent Confidence Interval: 1.10–67.04.

26. Centers for Disease Control and Prevention, "The Fry Readability Scale," (March 14, 2001). Retrieved January 25, 2001, from http://www.cdc.gov/od/ads/fry.htm.

27. This analysis is based on the format developed by Sue Stableford of the Maine AHEC Health Literacy Center, who was a consultant for Syracuse Healthy Start. It is summarized in her training module, "Write It Easy-To-Read, Level 2: A Training Manual" (n.d.).

28. I. S. Kickbusch, "Health Literacy: Addressing the Health and Education Divide," *Health Promotion International* 16 (2001): 289–97.

29. Department of Education and Department of Health and Human Services, "A Call to Commitment: Father's Involvement in Children's Learning," (March 14, 2001). Retrieved July 22, 2002, from http://www.ed.gov/pubs/parents/calltocommit/chap1.html.

30. Relative risk 2.70 (95 percent CI 1.05–6.98), Chi Square/Fisher's Exact p value: 0.037.

31. To assess the impact of SHS participation on postneonatal death among mothers with lower education, we conducted a two-stratum analysis for relative risk and Chi Square/Fisher's Exact (to account for the cell values of less than five). The sample was divided by mother's education, with SHS participation as the exposure variable and postneonatal death as the outcome. SHS was significantly protective. (Relative risk=0.25 (95 percent CI 0.07–0.93), Chi-square/Fisher's Exact p-value: 0.04.

Chapter 7

Missing Fathers[1]

> It's hard because men have it easy. They have two to three women per man, so it's very easy for him to not stay committed. A woman like me is looking for commitment and will try almost anything just to keep that commitment going ... I'm gonna accept this BS he's giving me because ... without him ... it's gonna be hard for me to find someone else to [be with] ... seeing it as, "If I let him go, this [other] woman's gonna have him ... I don't want to be alone."
> —*African American woman, Syracuse, New York, 2003*

African American women face a classic double bind, as described by Gregory Bateson and his colleagues.[2] Faced with an increasing proportion of single African American mothers, social policy discourse has grown more strident in trying to create incentives that will lead these women to wed, as if their single status were a personal preference that could be changed by social policy bringing forth the right combination of carrots and sticks. Yet, the mathematical fact is that there are fewer African American men than African American women. Two factors account for the dearth of men of color: incarceration and death. By assuming single motherhood to be an idiosyncratic behavioral pattern, and ignoring the disproportionate premature death and incarceration, contemporary marriage promotion policies obscure the pattern of racism constraining African American women's reproductive choices.

Epidemiological data in this chapter tally the skewed sex ratios among African American adults in Syracuse, resulting in large part from the overwhelming inequality in arrest and imprisonment of males of color, which is the context in which women must piece together reproductive and family goals. These "missing men" are often fathers whose infants have a much greater risk of dying in their first year of life. In neighborhoods where fathers are missing, single motherhood, grandparents caring for their grandchildren, and criminal arrests are widespread. These family-level and neighborhood-level factors do not occur in isolation from one another, but are interrelated outcomes of structural violence. To put a human face on these statistical inequalities, my colleagues and I compiled women's narratives that describe the experience of birth when the baby's father is incarcerated and the struggle to make relationships work when there are too few men.

African American Family Formation

During the first half of the twentieth century, female-headed households were in the minority among African American families; a large majority of African American households were composed of two parents and their children. Gutman reported that in 1905 and 1925 only 15 percent and 17 percent, respectively, of African American families in Manhattan were headed by the mother.[3] By 1950, according to Hacker, the nationwide proportion of African American female-headship was 17.2 percent.[4] In his infamous 1965 study, *The Negro Family: The Case for National Action,* Moynihan documented 25 percent of African American households as female headed.[5] Table 7.1 compares the rates of female household headship for African American and white families for the United States, New York State, and Onondaga County in 1990 and 2000.

Clearly, African American families have changed dramatically during the twentieth century. The majority began the century as two-parent units. Single motherhood began to rise in the second half of the century—reaching one-quarter of African American families by 1965. The biggest jump was between 1965 and 1990, when the proportion of female-headed families doubled.

Table 7.1 Percent of Female-Headed Households with Children

	1990 African American	2000 African American	1990 White	2000 White
United States	50%	47%	15.8%	16.8%
New York	52.7%	53.8%	16.4%	16.1%
Onondaga County	61.8%	64.4%	17.5%	20.1%

Source: U.S. Census data, 2000, calculations by the author.

Missing African American Men

> I feel that we don't have enough males around here ... there [are] not too many boys around here because [they're] locking everyone up.
>
> —*African American woman, 2004*

So, how many men are missing? To answer that question, I calculated the sex ratios of the white and African American populations in Syracuse (presented in Figure 7.1), which illustrates the number of women per man enumerated in the 2000 census for each group from birth to eighty-five years and over.

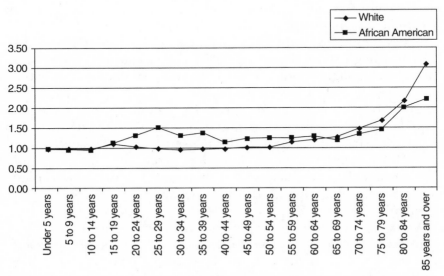

Figure 7.1 Sex Ratio (Women per Men) by Race, Syracuse, 2000 Census

Between the ages of twenty and fifty-nine, for every five African American women there are four African American men, whereas the proportion of white females and males in that age range is nearly equal. This finding has important implications for the promotion of marriage. Generally women choose partners from members of their own group. In Syracuse in 2000, among the births in which the father was named, 93 percent of the fathers of babies born to African American women were themselves African American. Correspondingly, 87 percent of the fathers of babies born to white women were themselves white. As illustrated in Figure 7.1, the male/female sex ratio disparity is highest between the ages of twenty-five to twenty-nine, when for every two African American men there are nearly three African American women. Heterosexual, monogamous marriage is thus an arithmetical impossibility for one-third of African American women in this age group, if they want marital partners near their age and of their race. If the African American group had the same female-to-male sex ratio as their white counterparts, there would be approximately 2,250 more African American men in Syracuse from the ages of twenty through fifty-nine. (This estimate is based on the Syracuse African American male population, enumerated by the 2000 census for the ages twenty through fifty-nine.) The "missing men," who would otherwise be present if the African American population had the same sex ratio as the white population, would represent an additional 22 percent of the total male population in these prime adult years.

What happened to these missing men? Population changes take place through three pathways: birth, death, and migration. In all populations, slightly more male babies are born than female babies, but males generally have higher death rates than females at each age, with the result that male life expectancy is about seven years shorter than female life expectancy in most populations.[6] As the figure makes clear, the African American and white sex ratios in Syracuse do not differ greatly until age twenty, so we can discount an unusual sex ratio at birth as a cause. The second potential pathway—disproportionate and prematurely early male death—does appear to contribute to the gender imbalance.

Vital statistics records for Onondaga County show that African American males and females die earlier than their white counterparts, but the disparity in survival affects African American males most profoundly. As described in the introductory chapter and Chapter

3, more than half of African American men who died during 2000 were younger than age sixty-five, compared with less than a quarter of white men. Migration is the third potential pathway leading to disproportionately fewer men, but we could find no evidence that African American males leave Syracuse more than African American females for work, school, or to reside in other localities, nor during 2000–2001 was there disproportionate male out-migration for military service. The most frequent type of non-voluntary migration, disproportionately affecting African American males, is incarceration.

> [My baby's father] went to jail for about a year, when he came home he was out for a few months and then he went back for seven to eight months, and then he got out and did a month and a half. So since I've known him [he's been incarcerated for] about two years."
>
> —*African American woman, 2004*

Disproportionate Incarceration

Nationally, African Americans make up almost 13 percent of the population, yet they represent 30 percent of the people arrested and 49 percent of the people in prison.[7] In 1995, one in three African American men between the ages of twenty and twenty-nine was either in jail or prison, on parole, or on probation.[8] Nationwide, African American men are incarcerated 9.6 times more than are white men. In New York, African Americans make up 16 percent of the population, but constitute 43 percent of the arrests and 51 percent of the incarcerations.[9]

Due in large part to the War on Drugs and lengthier mandatory sentences, the national incarceration rates have tripled during the past two decades.[10] The Rockefeller Drug Laws, enacted in New York in 1973, were ratcheted up in 1988, when in response to the social harm caused by crack cocaine the state legislature mandated lengthy sentences for the possession or sale of small amounts of the drug.[11] According to Human Rights Watch, "Sentences for drug offenders in New York State are among the most punitive in the country" and people of color make up the largest proportion of this expanded prison population.[12]

Analysis of a three-year period (1997–1999) of data from the Onondaga County Department of Corrections showed that although African Americans make up only 9.4 percent of the population in Onondaga County, they make up 52 percent of the inmates incarcerated in the local correctional facility and 61 percent of the inmates incarcerated in the state prison.[13] Among those individuals arrested, African American residents were nearly four times more likely to be sentenced to jail or prison than white residents, who were more likely to receive probation or a fine.[14] During 2000, 655 white (0.2 percent of the white population) and 980 African American (2.3 percent of the African American population) Onondaga County residents were sentenced to jail or prison.[15] If African Americans were sentenced on the same per capita basis as white Onondaga County residents, only 73 African Americans would have been sentenced that year, instead of 980. Correcting for the fact that about 94 percent of prisoners are male and 87 percent of African Americans live in Syracuse, we estimate that the disproportion in African American men from Syracuse being sentenced in 2000 to jail or prison totaled about 740 men, many of whom were sentenced for a period of greater than one year. This calculation provides indirect evidence that most of the unbalanced sex ratio in Syracuse is due to disproportionate incarceration. Furthermore, the deficit of African American males in the sex ratio occurs not because the men are permanently removed from the Syracuse population, but rather, because the men cycle through correctional facilities, for a period on average of two to three years before release. Recidivism rates (the return to jail or prison) draw more than one-half of the men back to incarceration at some time.

Disproportionate arrest and incarceration affects adolescent males as early as age sixteen. A local social worker with whom I spoke recalled working in the Onondaga County Jail, officially called the Justice Center, one evening in 1999. A total of twenty-one newly arrested males were brought into the facility, of whom nineteen were African American and eighteen were between sixteen and nineteen years old. Among the African American youth arrestees, a large majority were charged with violation-level offences, such as being out doors without identification ("loitering"), playing loud music, having open containers of alcoholic beverages, and being in a park after sunset. These youth spent the night in jail, not having been allowed to make a telephone call until many hours had passed after their arrival at the facility. On three other occasions the social worker saw sixteen-year-old African American males arrested for similar violations on their sixteenth birthdays, as if the arresting officers knew that on that very day the youth became subject to the adult criminal justice system. In one of these cases, the youth reported to the social worker that during the previous week the police officer had asked the youth the date of his birthday. The social worker, who worked in the jail for about one year, reported that she never saw white youth arrested for similar violations.

During 2002, according to a *Post-Standard* report on police records, 93.6 percent of all individuals arrested for loitering were African American.[16] The shocking disparity in these arrests leads many to accuse the police of racial profiling. Former Police Chief Dennis Du-Val parried the criticism by pointing out that the police respond to community requests to control crime. Much of the gun violence and drug dealing in the past few years in Syracuse occurs in and around corner stores, as described in Chapter 8. Chief DuVal, the first African American chief of police in Syracuse, claimed, "To know there's an issue and not do anything about it is more racist, and that's not how I police. Just to ignore it is more of a concern to us here in the community. Senior citizens are afraid to use the stores in their neighborhoods and can't go to other stores because of transportation issues. Our job is not to make the law; it's to enforce it."[17] The community expects the police to "clean up the neighborhoods," a call that sounds chillingly like ethnic cleansing. Examples like the sixteen-year-old African American male whose birthday gift was an arrest indicate that racial profiling may in fact occur. But, the police did not cause the poverty, unemployment, and high rates of high school dropout that leave young males with little else to do but to hang out on street corners. Nevertheless, a loitering arrest initiates a young man into the criminal justice system. On his next arrest, he has a "prior" offence, so his bail will be set higher; because of the previous arrest, instead of probation or a fine he may do time.

Men make up 94 percent of prisoners in both New York and the United States. About two-thirds of these men are fathers, the majority of whom have children under the age of eighteen.[18] A total of 1.5 million children nationwide, and 7 percent of all African American children, have one of their parents in correctional facilities.[19] We do not know, for Onondaga County, how many incarcerated men or women are parents. We have an indirect estimate of the proportion of children fathered by incarcerated men, from the Onondaga County Title X-funded Family Planning Program, which assists women with positive pregnancy tests to apply for Medicaid. The Family Planning Program staff estimate that in about 15 percent of new pregnancies in which the woman's financial resources are sufficiently limited to qualify her for Medicaid, the baby's father is incarcerated. My colleagues and I have also interviewed one hundred women receiving care at the University Hospital prenatal clinic, first during their pregnancies and again just after their births. Among these women, 17 percent of their baby's fathers were incarcerated; 11 percent of the baby's fathers were incarcerated prior to the birth and 6 percent entered correctional facilities around the time of their infant's birth. Two thirds of the inmate fathers were men of color.

The Princeton University Fragile Families Study found that, in contrast to non-incarcerated men, formerly incarcerated men are less likely to reside with the mother of their children or to be employed; their female partners report that they are less likely to compromise in decision making, express affection, or speak encouragingly, and are more likely to criticize, be violent, or abuse substances.[20] Of course, these cross-sectional correlation results do not indicate whether the period of incarceration contributed to the men's behavior or if the behavior pre-dated the incarceration.

HIV in Correctional Facilities

Seroprevalence rates vary among correctional systems, but nationwide estimates indicate that the inmate population is at least five times more likely to be infected with HIV than the general population.[21] AIDS is now the second leading cause of death in U.S. prisons; 20 percent to 26 percent of all people living with HIV in 1997 spent time as inmates that year.[22] Inmates in the New York State system have the highest rate of HIV among inmates nationwide, with more than 10 percent of the male and 20 percent of the female inmates infected.

Substantial evidence suggests that many inmates risk becoming infected while incarcerated, because the risk factors for sexual and blood-born infections occur frequently in correctional facilities. An estimated 7 percent to 12 percent of the inmates across several studies report being raped while incarcerated; inmates who had been raped reported that it occurred an average of nine times during their incarceration.[23] Moreover, prisoners have been found to trade sex for drugs or other items, or to engage in consensual/companionship sexual behavior, which is more often than not unprotected. The Federal Bureau of Prisons provides a conservative estimate of 30 percent of federal inmates engaging in male-with-male sexuality while incarcerated. A case-control study of formerly incarcerated males reported that 23 percent of the males with HIV, and 9 percent of the males without HIV, claimed to have had anal sex while incarcerated.[24]

An estimated 90 percent of the sex in correctional facilities occurs without the use of condoms. In fact, less than 1 percent of all jails and prisons in the U.S. allow inmates access to condoms.[25] Most prison authorities appear to agree with the Pennsylvania Department of Corrections secretary, who claimed, "Sexual activity in prison is against the rules and regulations of the Pennsylvania Department of Corrections for a number of penological reasons. Providing condoms to inmates while they are incarcerated both condones and encourages this behavior. We don't plan to begin providing condoms to inmates while they are incarcerated."[26] A former Onondaga County inmate interviewed by our research team said, "Because you are not supposed to have sex anywhere, condoms are unavailable and it makes sex a high-risk activity. Somebody may get a rubber glove to use, but still, the rules are you should not be having sex. My experience with it was the majority were having sex with other inmates in there."

Injecting drugs and tattooing are also potential routes of HIV transmission among inmates. With respect to intravenous drug use, the Office of National Drug Control Policy concludes that roughly 25 percent of all inmates entering U.S. prisons have injected drugs, which puts them at risk for HIV as well as hepatitis B and C.[27] Some of these inmates continue to inject drugs while in prison, sharing syringes and drugs purchased on the underground prison market. Tattooing, which a former Onondaga County inmate reported being accomplished with metal guitar strings, was reported by 48 percent of inmates in a CDC study.[28]

Only a few studies, however, have assessed the actual incidence of HIV seroconversion occurring in correctional facilities. A 1990 CDC study in the Illinois state correctional system found a rate of three HIV seroconversions per one thousand person years, which was ten times greater than the Illinois non-inmate rate during that time period.[29] Another CDC study of HIV transmission, this time in a Georgia state prison, identified inmates' risk behaviors for HIV infection to be male sex and tattooing. Researchers found the highest infection rates among men who were more slightly built, more than twenty-six years of age, African American, and who had served five or more years in prison.[30]

We conducted two focus groups, led by two African American colleagues, with African American and Latino males to ask about this issue of heightened HIV risk in correctional facilities. Several of the men had been inmates and were quite frank about the HIV risks:

Person #1: "But what's scary is that because of lack of female contact, the men are doing things to each other in there and God only knows—because the judicial system or the way the jails work—they don't care about your health. You're there for a reason we not going to coddle you. So when they go in there and do what they do, and when they come out—they left that behind because that was a need that I had to relieve myself. Then when I get out there I'm gonna get me a good woman. What man is gonna admit, Latino, Black, yellow, orange or green is gonna admit that he was with a dude in jail. He'll come out there and never admit it and he'll bring something to the first girl he gets out there and she has no [idea]."

Person #2: "I've been incarcerated quite a bit myself and I think it's a large contribution towards HIV and STDs disease, because a lot of things going on in the penitentiary a lot of brothers hate to admit or even face or deal with, you know ... some guys that just fall into it and it's just, ain't no thing, and they come right out here and stick with it and they got their wives they're dealing with and other men on the streets."

Person #3: "As far as the impact on HIV and AIDS, sure, it has a lot of impact because you send those individuals upstate, those weak ones, and they fall victim to a lot of things. I've seen guys come up there and never spent a day in prison and get physically abused, you know, gang banged, get raped in the showers, jumped on in the cells and stuff by individuals who are either infected or even they were infected."

Person #4: "When they get your kid [i.e., when they arrest your son] they gonna beat and do whatever they want to your kid. There is nothing you can say or do about it once he get in the system. Up there [in prison] some people are never coming home and they're gonna do that thing and then you got some juveniles that come in there and it's just fresh meat. You get busted inside the head, get raped, and some of them just give it up. There's a whole lot of that."

Person #5: "I would say the same thing, he touched it on the head. Peoples up there, you know, you're coming back home, you're not telling peoples what happened to you or something like that, and you're messing with your female and passing it on and you don't ever know if the female's messing with the next person and on and on and on and that's how I think that it, all this, mostly gets started. It goes from one person to the next by them not telling what happened, you know, to keep that secret within themselves but the secret is not really kept because it's coming out in other ways, you know, that's what I say with that."

Person #6: "I think a lot of brothers go to prison with HIV, through their drug use, their reckless sexual behavior and they go up and a lot of brothers don't get checked, a lot of brothers don't get checked when they up there because it's not mandatory, not obligatory that you get checked when you come through the system. They check you, I guess, for, what's that, DNA now for certain crimes. They got eighty-six crimes that they check you for DNA for. From possession of drugs in the first, to the possession of drugs in the second, to a DWI, to whatever—they take your DNA but it's not mandatory for a confidentiality law for them to take HIV or that it's mandatory for them to take it. So I think a lot of brothers go up there with it [HIV], knowingly and unknowingly and return on the street with ... I know a couple of brothers that done died in prison from HIV, being positive for HIV. But I know a lot of brothers done come home with it. But it's a lot of juveniles, though. You know you got juveniles going up there and have nothing [no HIV infection] and they get up there, they take their manhood and don't say nothing and them ones up there with twenty-five years, fifty years, ain't never coming home and they end up checking one of the young ones and that's why a lot of, majority, like in my community around here I can walk outside and two hours tops I can pick out at least twenty-five people that [as] young boys went upstate [and] got their manhood taken. I ain't saying they got HIV, but you know."

In recognition of the problem of prison rape, in July 2003, the Prison Rape Elimination Act of 2003 was passed unanimously by both the

House of Representatives and the Senate. On September 4, 2003, President Bush signed the bill into law.

In a subsequent focus group with women of color the interviewer asked, "Do you think incarceration contributes to the increase in HIV/AIDS in these communities?" Women tended to doubt the risk of HIV seroconversion among inmates. As it was described by one woman, "I would think not because, I mean, incarceration means, they're in jail at the time. How is that putting them—the increase in HIV—unless they bringing from jail to the streets ... They real restricted in jail [with regard to risk behavior]." In many conversations, women of color in Syracuse have expressed the belief that men are not at risk for HIV in jail or prison and that when they are released they come home "clean." They assume that because the correctional facilities segregate males and females, the men lack sexual partners. Sadly, that is not the case. The HIV seroprevalence of inmates potentially affects the larger communities to which the inmates return once they are released from prison. In research among HIV-infected African American women living in the South, who had fewer than ten lifetime sexual partners and could identify no high-risk behavior, one-quarter reported that one of their last three sexual partners had been incarcerated for more than twenty-four hours. Similarly, a CDC study among African American women in North Carolina found male partner incarceration to be a statistically significant risk factor for a woman being HIV positive.[31]

Missing Fathers and Infant Mortality

> I got to take care of my baby [by myself]. I brought her into the world so she basically depends on me to take care of her until she gets older and be able to do for herself.
> —*African American woman, 2004*

In order to assess the impact of father involvement or non-involvement on pregnancy outcome and infant survival, we used an indirect measure of father involvement, which is whether the father's name and demographic information is entered on the birth certificate at the time of the birth or within forty-eight hours thereafter. The protocol for entering the father's name on the birth certificate is as follows: For births in which the mother is married, her husband's name is automatically entered on the birth certificate, unless either parent objects. If the mother is unmarried, the father must sign a Declaration of Paternity. This document is given to the mother by a Vital Records staff member on the morning following her delivery and left at her bedside during her hospitalization, which in Syracuse averages about two days following the birth. The father's information, along with numerous other details of the pregnancy and birth, are entered into the Electronic Birth Certificate database and the Perinatal Data System database by hospital staff upon the mother's discharge. Whether the fathers' information—date of birth, age, race/ethnicity—are recorded in or missing from these databases gives some indirect evidence of his involvement with his child and his child's mother at the time of the birth. The father may sign the Declaration of Paternity at a later date, but if he signs it after the mother's discharge from the hospital following childbirth his information would not be recorded in these databases.

Our research team asked focus group participants and the family case study respondents the reasons that a father may not be listed on the birth certificate. Their responses included: (1) The mother may have separated from the father and not want him involved. (2) The father sometimes requests that the mother not list him if she is receiving public assistance, because he may not be able to afford the mandated child support payments, especially if he already has other children. (3) The father of the baby of a teen mother may not want to be listed if he is much older, because he may fear being charged with sexual assault. (4) The father may be incarcerated, or otherwise not able to be present to enter his name on the birth certificate.

Despite the imprecision inherent in the multiple reasons that fathers may not be listed on the birth certificate, the reasons cited above indirectly imply a reduction in the amount of paternal financial and social support available to the woman and her baby at the time of the birth. The advantage of using the father's name on the birth certificate, despite its limitations, is that it is a population-based measure of paternal involvement.

The analyses in Table 7.2 compare the demographic factors, risk factors, birth weight, and infant mortality in which the father is listed, or is not listed, on the birth certificate. As Table 7.2 illustrates, among the births in which the father is not listed on the birth certificate the mother is much less likely to have completed high school, more likely to receive public assistance, more likely to abuse substances including tobacco, and to have increased infant mortality. In this analysis we separated neonatal mortality (death in the first twenty-eight days of life) from postneonatal mortality (death after twenty-eight days and before the first birthday), because they have generally different causes. As described more fully in chapter 3, neonatal death more frequently involves complications following premature delivery and severe congenital anomalies; postneonatal mortality is more commonly associated with Sudden Infant Death Syndrome, suffocation on unsafe bedding, and various types of infectious diseases.

Because the father not being listed on the birth certificate is associated with or potentially influenced by African American ancestry, teen birth, Medicaid, and receipt of public assistance, we conducted logistic regression analyses which controlled for these variables. We conducted separate logistic regression analyses with low birth weight, neonatal death, and postneonatal death as the outcome variables,

Table 7.2 Percent of Risk and Outcome Variables in Two Groups, Compared with Father on Birth Certificate, all Syracuse Births 2000–2001

	Father on birth certificate	No father on birth certificate
Total births of singletons (n=4,343)	69.6%	30.4%
African American (n=1,512)	54.0%	46.0%
White (n=2,358)	78.0%	22.0%
1st trimester entry into prenatal care (n=2,783)	70.8%	48.6%
Less than 12 years education, age 20+ (n=906)	18.9%	41.3%
Medicaid (n=1,872)	51.0%	65.0%
Public assistance (n=438)	6.6%	18.0%
Alcohol (n=81)	1.0%	3.9%
Cocaine (n=54)	0.5%	3.0%
Marijuana (n=186)	2.6%	8.2%
Tobacco (n=1,204)	22.6%	39.5%
STD diagnosis during pregnancy (n=623)	13.0%	17.8%
Maternal age less than 20 (n=706)	51.0%	49.0%
Low birth weight (<2,500 gm) (n=367)	7.7%	10.1%
Very low birth weight (<1,500 gm) (n=82)	1.6%	2.7%
Neonatal death (n=33)	0.6%	1.1%
Post neonatal death (n=21)	0.3%	1.0%
Infant death (n=54)	0.9%	2.0%

with the presence or absence of the fathers' information as the risk factor or exposure variable. Postneonatal mortality was the *only* birth outcome significantly associated with the absence of the father's information.[32] Babies whose fathers' information was lacking from the birth certificate were nearly *four times* as likely to die a postneonatal death, compared with babies whose fathers were listed. Many of the risk factors for postneonatal death have a common thread involving inadequate parental care and attention. The statistically significant link between father absence from the birth certificate and postneonatal death may thus indirectly result from a reduction of paternal support.

As mentioned above, the father is not listed on the birth certificate more than twice as often among births to African American mothers compared with white mothers in our sample. When we added the presence or absence of fathers' information to the formula, the postneonatal death racial disparity was no longer statistically significant, meaning that something about the father's information being absent "explained" the unequal postneonatal death between African American and white babies. I was very excited about these findings because it could give us something to work on to reduce the preventable deaths of these babies. I also wanted to be able to say how much of the postneonatal death was associated with father non-involvement, so I did what epidemiologists call a Population Attributable Risk (PAR) assessment. PARs rely on a very long and cumbersome equation, but make good common sense because they tell us how much of a bad outcome could be prevented if we could eliminate the risk factor. I first calculated the singleton postneonatal mortality rate for African American infants (6.4 deaths per one thousand live births) and white infants (3.7 deaths per one thousand births). Then I calculated the proportion of each of these rates that was associated with the father not being listed on the birth certificate and *subtracted* that from the rate for each group. What I had left was the postneonatal mortality rate for each group, if the risk of father non-involvement was removed. Admittedly, this is a theoretical analysis—I wish it were that easy to actually remove such troublesome risk factors. The singleton postneonatal death rates for each group, minus the proportion associated with father absence, is 2.5 per one thousand live births for white and 2.7 for African American infants, or nearly equal.

The Neighborhood Context

Well, basically I would say the neighborhood I live in is nothing but drugs, guns, violence, or whatever and it affects me because I can't really do nothing ... but now I have a baby and things getting harder, there's a lot of trouble out here ... My grandmother brought me up but my grandmother couldn't bring me up the way my mother would bring me up. I never had no real confident parenting so I can give it my son.

—African American woman, 2004

It just basically a community where I don't want to raise my child because it's the ghetto. And when I say the ghetto, I say people living hard, during hard times, and you got to worry about your baby when they outside.

—African American woman, 2004.

My colleagues and I also conducted an environmental analysis, using data compiled as rates at the level of the census tract, for the fifty-seven Syracuse census tracts. Of course, aggregate data for neighborhoods can only illustrate the context in which residents live; it does not provide information about individual lives in that neighborhood. This analysis used the following variables as rates at the level of the census tract: births lacking the father's name on the birth certificate in 2000–2001; families in which children under eighteen were primarily cared for by two parents, single mothers, single fathers, or grandparents caring for their own grandchildren; and arrests (assault, drugs, homicide, rape, arson, burglary, robbery, and prostitution) provided by the Syracuse Police Department for the years 2000–2001.

Figure 7.2 divides Syracuse census tracts into two groups, those in which less than 30 percent of the birth certificates lacked fathers' information and those in which 30 percent or more of the birth certificates lacked fathers' information. Within each of these two groups the figure shows who takes the primary responsibility for children under age eighteen, whether it was both parents, single mothers, single fathers, or grandparents. In the census tracts with the higher proportion of fathers listed on the birth certificates, well over half of the families have two parents; two-parent families are almost double single-mother families and less than 5 percent of children are cared

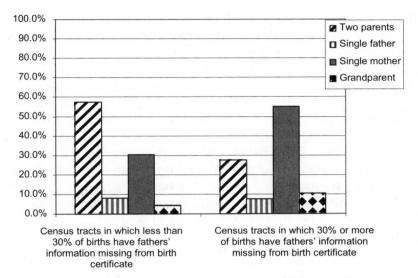

Figure 7.2 Census Tract Analysis: Who Cares for Children <18 Years?

for primarily by grandparents. In the census tracts with the higher numbers of fathers not listed on the birth certificate, in contrast, single mothers outnumber two-parent families by nearly two to one, and grandparent primary caretakers are more than doubled. This group of census tracts with the higher proportion of fathers missing from the birth certificates also had nearly six times the per capita rate of criminal arrests. It is our contention that these findings are not isolated, unrelated phenomena. Female-headed families and grandparents caring for their grandchildren are likely the same families that began with fathers who were less involved at the time of the children's birth. The data suggest, moreover, that arrest and incarceration comprise daily realities for many of the families in those census tracts.

Women's Voices

To get a better idea of the perspectives of women in the affected communities we conducted interviews with three groups of women about the issues of missing men and male incarceration: (1) one hundred women who had just given birth, (2) in-depth interviews with parents of young children who lived in the Syracuse census tracts with the highest rates of health risks, and (3) front-line staff members who provided services to impoverished women and children.

Among the group of one hundred new mothers who had received prenatal care at a university-based clinic, 19 percent were married to their baby's father. Among 16 percent of the births the baby's father was intermittently or inconsistently involved, and among 6 percent the father was not involved at all. More than 40 percent of the babies' fathers were unemployed, and 17 percent were incarcerated either during the pregnancy or just after the birth. Two themes expressed by these women are the male's involvement with other women and keeping in touch with men in correctional facilities:

Person #1: "He comes around sometimes for visits, sometimes emotionally [he is] there. He has a 'girlfriend.' I am not his girlfriend, I am just pregnant by him."

Person #2: "He has problems staying home and helping out. He stays out with other women and doesn't come home for weeks."

Person #3: "He calls me [collect from jail] every day and wants to know how we are doing."

Person #4: "He's been in jail since I found out I was pregnant. But he writes letters and asks questions [about how we are doing]. We also have a seven-year-old and he was never a constant part of his life."

Person #5: "He is incarcerated at this time, but calls [collect] every day for emotional support and I visit him every week."

Person #6: "He calls [collect] from prison to see how the baby and I are doing."

In four of the ten families who lived in the high health risk census tracts and participated in in-depth interviews, the baby's father had been incarcerated during the pregnancy or birth, or the mother specifically mentioned incarceration as a factor influencing relationships; in three of these families the father did not sign the birth certificate. The unpredictability, and fear, of having their baby's father taken away is haunting in these narratives:

Person #1: "My baby's father went to jail when I was pregnant. I told him I was pregnant when I was two or three weeks, then two months after that he went to jail, over something, basically trespassing, hanging out on a corner. He was in there for almost two months, and it had me stressing because I thought he was going to have to do time, and then I was thinking my baby wasn't going to have no father and I'd have to do everything on my own."

Person #2: "My baby's father left me when I was four and a half months pregnant, for two or three other girls that he got another baby on the way [with] ... and it's just, it's hard out here because all the boys [are] in jail. [There is] always violence between females ... over girls messing with somebody else's boyfriend ... All the males I grew up with are incarcerated now. So now, there is really nobody. I feel that it is wrong that everybody is in jail because there is no one out here, there is no money out here, nobody left."

Person #3: "I met him [when] I was still in high school. He had been in jail like maybe once before when we just started dating. ... He had just went to jail [and] I found out I was pregnant maybe two weeks into him being in jail, and then I went through the whole pregnancy by myself and he just wasn't there to sign the birth certificate."

The "missing men" issue struck a chord with many of the front-line staff focus group participants. Rather than being solely a problem that their clients faced, the participants responded to this question in personal terms. Nearly all of the women were mothers, but not one of them expressed a preference for single motherhood. Like the women interviewed for the family case studies, the importance of having a strong relationship with a man, and the difficulty of doing so, were among the topics on which the focus group participants expressed their most passionate opinions. An important point made by both the family case study and focus group participants is that the difficulty in establishing and maintaining relationships influences women to put up with more negative male behavior than they would accept if the sex ratio were different, as exemplified by the following narrative: "So many women are fighting over men for stability ... who wants to be a woman going into old age alone? Who wants to be alone for the rest of their life? Either you have a man or you are alone."

Several women explained how in some cases motherhood might be a strategy to solidify a shaky relationship:

Person #1: "That's where it comes in ... trying to tie a man down. Because that's the man you want, so you start having kids by this man."

Person #2: "[Women think that] if they are pregnant they will ... keep the man."

Person #3: "[If] I have a baby by this person, this person's never going away from my life. He's always going to have to deal with me and that's that."

Person #4: "Some of these young girls go and get themselves pregnant because they think that man will stay with them. They're scared to death that they'll end up like their mother and have no man in their life."

In some cases, the skewed sex ratio results in two women being concurrently pregnant by the same man. Two focus group members spoke about this issue:

Person #1: "You see one man in a house with a woman and a baby ... I go to another house [as a home visitor] and I see that same man in the other woman's house with another baby and you know that man doesn't even blink an eye, and I knew he remembered me from the other day coming to that other house."

Person #2: "Two women were pregnant by the same man and each wanted to give birth first, so that she could name her baby after that man."

In contrast to the family case study respondents, the focus group participants did not specifically comment on disproportionate incarceration as a cause of the skewed sex ratio. When the issue was brought up in one focus group by the facilitator, the women agreed that it made sense, but said that they had not previously thought about the connection.

Structural Violence and Racism in Social Policies

Social policy creates categories through which public goods are distributed. People who do not conform to these categories are considered deviant, abnormal, or stigmatized. Arturo Escobar, drawing on Michel Foucault's analysis of the role of hegemonic discourse defining "normal" and "deviant," described a similar situation in the context of international development, namely, "Development proceeded by creating 'abnormalities,' ... which it would later treat and reform."[33] Marriage-promoting policies construct the monogamous, male-female marriage as the "normal" family, and attempt to advance marriage by stigmatizing women who are deviant in relation to this category. Yet, a demographic double bind is created by draconian drug laws that decrease the potential for marriage by removing eligible men from the community.

A low male-to-female sex ratio has been found to be associated with the presence of concurrent partnerships, in which a male has an intimate relationship with more than one female at the same time. Anthropologists have long observed that a low male sex ratio was associated with polygyny and demographers have found it to be associated with female-headed households.[34] Laumann, in a study of relationship patterns in different neighborhoods in Chicago, found that the ratio of fewer males than females among African Americans was associated with males maintaining sexual partnerships with two or more females simultaneously.[35] A woman who is in a partnership in which her male partner has another female partner is not always aware of the situation and, if aware, is unlikely to approve. A low male-to-female sex ratio robs women of their bargaining power in relationships; as men become scarcer, each relationship becomes harder to secure. Consequently, a woman in such an environment may accept conditions she would not agree to if her bargaining power were greater. Adimora and her colleagues found that among more than 10,000 women nationally, 21 percent of African Americans, 11 percent of whites, 8 percent of Hispanics, and 6 percent of Asian American and Pacific Islanders were in partnerships in which one of the partners was concurrently in another partnership with someone else.[36]

Guttentag and Secord argue that sex ratios with an abundance of women and a paucity of men influence women to have a subjective sense of powerlessness and feel personally devalued by society.[37] The authors label this form of powerlessness a limitation of "dyadic power." Guttentag and Secord, as well as Wilson,[38] provide evidence to show that sex ratios with too few men increase female-headed families markedly and decrease the proportion of women with committed male partners throughout their childbearing years. As a result, men have the opportunities to move successively from woman to woman or to maintain multiple relationships with different women. In turn, some women might double their efforts to attract or keep a man by making sacrifices and going out of their way to please their male partner.

The partners of incarcerated individuals also pay the government for the privilege of receiving their collect calls. In the opening chapter I told the story of Mae, a single mother whose child's father remains incarcerated. Many of the other women whose narratives are presented in this chapter similarly accept regular collect telephone calls from their incarcerated partners. Mae pays about $200 in monthly telephone bills for the collect calls made by her child's father. In much of her working life Mae's income has rarely topped $20,000, so the price for keeping her child's father involved comes to 12 percent of her pre-tax income. A Syracuse *Post-Standard* exposé revealed that Onondaga County government gets a kickback of 45 percent on all collect phone calls made from the jail, according to Onondaga Chief Custody Deputy Anthony Callisto.[39] So, Mae is being taxed by the government because her baby's father is an inmate and because she wants to keep him involved with her child. It would not be overstating this situation to call it collective punishment, making the intimate partners and family members pay for the transgressions of their loved ones, a type of penalty that is contravened by the Geneva Convention.[40]

When I discussed the issue of the health impacts of disproportionate incarceration with a wide number of physicians and public health officials in Onondaga County, I found that not one of the health professionals was previously aware of the issue. Although the rates of incarceration, HIV, and premature death are staggeringly unequal between white and African American residents, many community members viewed them as individual tragedies and public policymakers failed to consider them as relevant to the analysis of poverty, single motherhood, or infant death.

As the policy analysis and the epidemiological, environmental, and ethnographic data presented in this chapter make clear, there is a disconnect between the policymakers' assumptions and the structural violence that forms the context in which women of color live and make decisions about marriage, intimate partnerships, and reproduction. The marriage-promotion policies being advocated by the federal government ignore the unbalanced African American sex ratio and assume that the dramatic rise in African American single motherhood is a capricious choice.

Female-headed families were the minority among African American families in the first half of the twentieth century, yet between 1965 and 1990 they doubled. This doubling is temporally associated with enacting the legislation directed toward the War on Drugs, which resulted in a tripling of the African American prison population. Most of the missing men in the African American population in Syracuse are incarcerated. The "missing men" are thus not permanently removed but rather are cycled for multiple-year periods through correctional facilities. This cycling further impacts families, in that formerly incarcerated men have greater difficulty in establishing secure relationships, maintaining employment, and behaving in ways that nurture intimate relationships. Arguably, the brutality of incarceration itself may be at least in part responsible for the men's less nurturing and less stable behavior.

In Syracuse, the disproportionate African American male incarceration begins at age sixteen, which indicates that it is a likely risk factor for subsequent low educational attainment and future unemployment. Moreover, once arrested, African Americans are nearly four times more likely to be sentenced to jail or prison, whereas their white counterparts receive probation or fines. Disproportionate incarceration may be a key factor in the rising HIV infections among women of color and may be an indirect factor in the white/African American infant mortality gap.

In contrast to the policymakers' assumptions that single motherhood is an individual preference, the African American women with whom my colleagues and I spoke expressed the hope that they could establish stable, nurturing intimate relationships. They indicate that the dearth of African American men has led them and other women to accept male behavior that they otherwise would not accept if they had other options. According to these women, this struggle to maintain relationships appears to have led some women to adopt a strategy of having a baby to "tie" the man, resulting in single motherhood when the strategy failed. Perhaps most stigmatizing and demoralizing for the women is that in some cases an individual man fathers babies with two women concurrently, without the women's knowledge. Clearly, a low male sex ratio robs women of their "bargaining power" in relationships. As men become scarcer, each relationship becomes much harder to achieve. In her effort to hold onto the relationship a woman may accept conditions to which she would not agree if her range of potential partners were wider.

Marriage promotion policies do not take account of these painful realities. The policymakers assume that by educating the poor about how to succeed in the marital relationship, they will coax reluctant African American brides and grooms down the aisle. They further assume that encouraging heterosexual matrimony will solve the problems of poverty and social disruption in communities of color. In Syracuse, as the sex ratio data make clear, for all adult African Americans to marry an opposite sex individual of their racial background, the government would have to legalize polygyny. As one focus group participant put it, there are simply "not enough African American men to go around."

Notes

1. This chapter is adapted from Sandra D. Lane, Robert A. Rubinstein, Robert Keefe, Michael Freedman, Brooke Levandowski, Don Cibula, and Maria Czerwinski, "Marriage Promotion and Missing Men: African American Women in a Demographic Double Bind," *Medical Anthropology Quarterly* 18, no. 4 (December 2004): 405–28. Used with permission.

2. Gregory Bateson, et al., "Toward a Theory of Schizophrenia," *Behavioral Science* 1 (1956): 251–64.

3. Herbert Gutman, *The Black Family in Slavery and Freedom, 1750-1925* (New York: Vintage Books, 1976).

4. Andrew Hacker, *Two Nations: Black and White, Separate, Hostile, Unequal* (New York: Scribners, 1992).

5. Daniel Patrick Moynihan, *The Negro Family: The Case for National Action* (Washington, DC: Office of Policy Planning and Research, U.S. Department of Labor, 1965).

6. S. D. Lane and D. Cibula, "Gender and Health," in *Handbook of Social Studies in Health and Medicine,* eds. S. Scrimshaw and G. Albrecht (SAGE Publications, London, 2000).

7. Jamie Fellner, *Cruel and Usual: Disproportionate Sentences for New York Drug Offenders* (New York: Human Rights Watch, 1997); Jamie Fellner,

Punishment and Prejudice: Racial Disparities in the War on Drugs (New York: Human Rights Watch, 2000).

8. Marc Mauer and T. Huling, *Young Black Men and the Criminal Justice System: A Growing National Problem* (Washington, DC: The Sentencing Project, 1995).

9. New York State Uniform Crime Report and New York State Department of Correctional Services, cited in Alan Rosenthal, *Racial Disparities in the Local Criminal Justice System: A Report to the NAACP Syracuse/Onondaga Chapter* (Syracuse, NY: Center for Community Alternatives, 2001).

10. Lisa Feldman, Vincent Schiraldi, and Jason Ziedenberg, *Too Little Too Late: President Clinton's Prison Legacy* (Washington, DC: The Justice Policy Institute, 2001).

11. Alan Rosenthal, *Racial Disparities.*

12. Alan Rosenthal, *Racial Disparities.*

13. Alan Rosenthal, *Racial Disparities.* The statistical analyses below for Onondaga County were conducted by the authors, with data reported by Rosenthal, 2001.

14. Odds ratio 3.92, 95 percent CI 3.43–4.47.

15. Alan Rosenthal, *Racial Disparities.*

16. "Profiling Problems: Still Waiting for the Three-Year Project to Bring Results," *Syracuse Post Standard,* August 27, 2004.

17. Pam Greene, "Loitering Tickets: 93.6% Blacks. Syracuse Police Say They Respond to Complaints, Not Racial Profiling," *Syracuse Post-Standard,* July 18, 2002.

18. Eric Brenner, *Fathers in Prison: A Review of the Data* (Philadelphia, PA: National Center on Fathers and Families, 2003); B. Western and S. McLanahan, *Fathers Behind Bars: The Impact of Incarceration on Family Formation* (Princeton, NJ: Center for Research on Child Wellbeing, 2000).

19. Marsha Weissman, *Children of Incarcerated Parents: Consequences and Alternatives* (Syracuse, NY: Center for Community Alternatives, 2000).

20. Fragile Families Project, *Incarceration and Bonds among Parents* (Princeton, NJ and New York, NY: The Center for Research on Child Wellbeing, Princeton University, and The Social Indicators Survey Center, Columbia University, 2002).

21. L. M. Maruschak, "HIV in Prisons and Jails, 1999." *Bureau of Justice Statistics Bulletin* (July 2001): 1–12.

22. T. M. Hammett, M. P. Harmon, and W. Rhodes, "The Burden of Infectious Disease among Inmates of Releasees from US Correctional Facilities, 1997," *American Journal of Public Health* 92, no. 11 (2002): 1789–94.

23. J. E. Robertson, "Rape among Incarcerated Men: Sex, Coercion and STDs," *AIDS, Patient Care, and STDs* 17, no 8 (2003): 423–30.

24. A. R. Wohl, D. Johnson, W. Jordan, et al., "High-Risk Behaviors during

Incarceration in African-American Men Treated for HIV at Three Los Angeles Public Medical Centers," *Journal of Acquired Immune Deficiency Syndrome* 24 (2000): 386–92.

25. T. M. Hammett, P. Harmon, and L. Maruschak, *1996-1997 Update: HIV/AIDS, STDs and TB in Correctional Facilities* (Cambridge, MA; Abt Associates, Inc., 1999); A. R. Wohl, D. Johnson, W. Jordan, et al., "High-Risk Behaviors In and Out of Incarcerated Settings for African-American Men Treated for HIV at Three Los Angeles Public Medical Centers" (paper presented at the Seventh Conference on Retroviruses and Opportunistic Infections, San Francisco, CA, January, 2000).

26. Elisa Ledwig, "A Public Health Disaster," *Philadelphia Weekly*, July 25, 2001, http://www.philadelphiaweekly.com/view.php?id=3567.

27. T. M. Hammett and L. M. Maruschak, *1996–1997 Update: HIV/AIDS, STDs, and TB in Correctional Facilities* (Washington, DC: National Institutes of Justice, July 1999).

28. Centers for Disease Control, "Hepatitis B Outbreak in a State Correctional Facility 2000," *Morbidity and Mortality Weekly Report* 50, no. 25 (2001): 529–32.

29. William Speed Weed, "Incubating Disease: Prisons Are Rife with Infectious Illnesses—and Threaten to Spread Them to The Public," *Mother Jones*, July 10, 2001. The CDC study cited in this reference was obtained by *Mother Jones* through a Freedom of Information Act and is not otherwise published.

30. "HIV Transmission among Male Inmates in a State Prison System—Georgia, 1992–2005," *MMRW* 55, no. 15 (April 21, 2006): 421–26.

31. "HIV Transmission among Black Women—North Carolina, 2004," *MMWR* 54, no. 4 (February 4, 2005): 89–94.

32. Table 7.2: Logistic Regression. Exposure variable: father missing from birth certificate. Controlling for maternal race, maternal age (teen vs. age twenty and older), receipt of public assistance, and Medicaid insurance. Postneonatal mortality (infant death after twenty-eight days and before the first birthday) odds ratio 3.841 (1.305–11.294) p<0.014.

33. Arturo Escobar, *Encountering Development: The Making and Unmaking of the Third World* (Princeton, NJ: Princeton University Press, 1994): 11.

34. D. R. White and M. L. Burton, "Causes of Polygyny: Ecology, Economy, Kinship and Warfare," *American Anthropologist* 90 (1988): 871–87; M. Ember, "Warfare, Sex Ratio, and Polygyny," *Ethnology* 13 (1974): 197–206; J. Q. Wilson, *The Marriage Problem* (New York: Harper Collins Publishers, 2002).

35. E. O. Laumann, S. Ellingson, J. Mahay, A. Paik, and Y. Youm, *The Sexual Organization of The City* (Chicago: University of Chicago Press, 2004).

36. A. A. Adimora, V. J. Schoenbach, D. M. Bonas, et al., "Concurrent

Sexual Partnerships among Women in the United States," *Epidemiology* 13, no. 3 (2002): 320–27.

37. Marcia Guttentag and Paul Secord, *Too Many Women? The Sex Ratio Question* (Newbury Park, CA: Sage, 1983).

38. J. Q. Wilson, *The Marriage Problem.*

39. John O'Brien, "Jailers Disconnect Inmates' Free Calls: Jump in Calls to Advocacy Group Indicated Service Abuse at County Jail," *Syracuse Post-Standard,* sec. B, March 18, 2005.

40. Article 33 of the Geneva Convention states, "No protected person may be punished for an offence he or she has not personally committed." http://www.icrc.org/ihl.nsf/c525816bde96b7fd41256739003e636a/72728b6de56c7a68c12563cd0051bc40?OpenDocument.

Chapter 8

Food Is Just Decoration

This chapter examines urban retail food markets and health in Syracuse. The questions addressed in this chapter came directly from focus groups of community members brought together by the Syracuse Healthy Start project in March and July 1999. At those meetings community members expressed concerns about the local access to healthy foods; they called attention to the lack of supermarkets in much of urban Syracuse and reported that small corner stores were predominately selling pagers, beer, and non-food items. According to the community participants, the food items that the corner stores sold were overpriced and often spoiled. Most troubling to the community members was that the stores were venues for illegal activities, which the store owners seemed to encourage by selling drug paraphernalia.

In light of the community focus group findings we systematically investigated the marketing of health-promoting food and non-food items such as cigarettes, alcohol, and lottery tickets in urban Syracuse. Through the use of individual-level and census tract-level quantitative data we compared the presence or absence of a full-service supermarket in a given census tract and the per capita sale of lottery tickets to a specific type of low birth weight—intrauterine growth restriction (IUGR). This analysis examined two types of urban food markets: (1) Supermarkets, which sell fresh produce and low-fat dairy in addition to a variety of other items, and (2) Corner stores, which sell very little fresh produce or low-fat dairy, but which market lottery tickets, tobacco products, and alcohol.

Five health risks are associated with the location and business practices of retail food outlets in Syracuse. First, there is a paucity of fruits, vegetables, and low-fat dairy in many neighborhoods; to purchase these items consumers who do not own cars must take city buses or arrange for help with transportation to reach supermarkets. Second, the corner stores rack up extensive sales of the New York State–run lottery. Per capita lotto purchases are significantly higher in census tracts with greater poverty. Third, the corner stores aggressively market tobacco products, often the most dangerous mentholated cigarettes, which some sell illegally to underage children. Fourth, the corner stores typically devote more shelf space to alcohol than to dairy, including malt liquor in 40 oz. containers, which some sell illegally to underage children. Finally, the corner stores are often the locus of neighborhood violence, causing stress to local residents and making many reluctant to take the risk of purchasing even the meager offerings within the store at certain times of day.

Urban Retail Food Availability

Store owners argue that new supermarkets require substantial amounts of land that are often not available in inner-city neighborhoods and inner-city store owners argue that their overhead costs are substantially higher than suburban store owners, thus legitimizing higher prices.[1] Owners of small corner markets also claim that their food costs are higher due to the lack of space available to inventory surplus foods and the fact that produce and other perishables have short shelf lives.[2] Moreover, corner store owners with limited space report that they must focus on selling products that have the strongest demand, which, unfortunately, may mean alcohol, tobacco, and unhealthy snack foods. As supermarkets left the inner city for the suburbs, therefore, the cost of food in urban areas increased. Analyses of food prices showed identical or highly similar items cost more in inner-city corner markets than in larger supermarkets. Because healthy foods are often more expensive and less available in poor areas, low-income households often select cheaper and lower quality food in order to save on food costs. As in many other urban areas, the food prices in Syracuse were higher in the poorest areas than in the suburbs.[3]

Marketing of Non-food Items

The marketing of cigarettes, alcohol, and drug paraphernalia by corner stores has been found to be a potential risk factor for the racial/ethnic disparity in low birth weight.[4] Both alcohol and tobacco abuse can lead to poor fetal growth and consequent low birth weight.[5] As described in Chapter 4, since the 1970s tobacco companies have aggressively marketed mentholated cigarettes to people of color. Malt liquor in 40 oz. containers is another feature of the offerings at inner-city corner stores in many parts of the United States; it is not only cheaper than other types of alcohol, but also, the 40 oz. container of malt liquor provides the drinker with the ethanol equivalent of five shots of whiskey. Rap artists are employed to shill malt liquor to youth of color by extolling the efficacy of the product at putting women in the mood for sex.[6] One of our focus group participants said of the marketing of 40 oz. malt liquor to inner city areas, "You're not gonna find a 40 oz. out there [in the suburbs]."

Newspaper Analysis of Reporting on Corner Stores

Using the Nexus/Lexus search engine, we conducted a content analysis of the Syracuse *Post-Standard* (2000–2002), Syracuse's major daily newspaper, for the key words "corner store, convenience store, violence, gun shots, drugs, and arrest." This search yielded forty articles. The texts of these articles were entered into an NVivo electronic database for content analysis.[7] The news articles substantiated the community members' allegations that the corner stores in Syracuse have become the locus for drugs and violence.[8] Nine episodes of gunshots being fired, often by drive-by shooters, were described in *Post-Standard* articles in this three-year period.[9] In addition to the apparent intended victims, bullets hit both store clerks and shoppers and sometimes store clerks fired back at robbers. Five articles describe drug arrests in, or in front of, corner stores; one store was identified as the location of seventeen and a second store the location of twenty-two previous drug arrests.[10]

Residents interviewed by news reporters complained that due to the criminal activity they feared leaving their homes and feared retaliation if they reported details of this criminal activity to police.[11] For example, an item in the March 31, 2000, edition of the paper noted "The vast majority [of drug dealers] have scared off all the clientele"; and a June 1, 2002, article stated, "Convenience stores on the city's south and west sides have become "hot corners" for drugs, violence, loitering and litter." Several articles documented evidence of undercover sting operations that found illegal sales of tobacco and alcohol to minors, as well as the flavored single cigars known as "blunts," which are almost exclusively used with marijuana.[12] Many corner stores have been cited by the New York State Department of Agriculture and Markets for selling spoiled food, using dirty equipment, being unsanitary, and operating without appropriate licenses.[13] In 2002, Syracuse United Neighbors, a community action group, released a list of the top ten "Worst Corner Stores," based on the New York State food inspectors' findings. In February of 2003, Syracuse United Neighbors successfully convinced the Syracuse Common Council to pass a bill regulating corner stores. As a result of this bill, in 2005, twenty-four corner stores were closed; many, however, reopened immediately. Community members with whom we have spoken remain skeptical about whether this bill will result in substantial improvement in the situation of the corner stores.

Supermarket Map Analysis

We assessed the impact of residential proximity to a full-service supermarket on a specific type of low birth weight. We considered a retail outlet to be a supermarket if it sold many types of food, produce, low-fat dairy, and often other items such as cookware, cosmetics, and household products. Syracuse during 2000–2001 had seven supermarkets within the city boundary and an additional four supermarkets immediately outside of the city limits. Using maps from the 2000 U.S. Census Web site we plotted a one-half mile radius around each of these supermarkets. If this one-half mile radius fell within the boundary of a census tract it was categorized as a "supermarket census tract" and if it did not it was categorized as a "non-supermarket census tract." A more precise analysis would be to use the actual addresses of the pregnant women in each census tract. However, we were not able to obtain the actual addresses because of patient confidentiality restrictions.

Structured Observations of Corner Stores

We conducted structured observations of thirty-six randomly selected small retail outlets (eighteen in the high-risk and eighteen in the low-risk census tracts) that are licensed to sell food, lottery tickets, tobacco, and alcohol. The corner stores comprise two types of establishments, according to the National Association of Convenience Stores: "convenience stores" and "grocery markets." The community residents refer to these businesses interchangeably as "corner stores," a term which we use in this article to distinguish the small local stores from supermarkets. In the structured observations we found that these two types of stores were nearly indistinguishable in terms of size, location, and sale products. In each group of eighteen stores in the high and low categories, there were five convenience stores and thirteen grocery markets. The structured shopping analysis was conducted as follows: We defined variables for observation based on the earlier ethnographic work and reviews of the literature, conducted pre-tests, and added more variables based on pre-tests (e.g., the presence of ATMs, the sale of lottery tickets). After the initial pre-testing of each variable measurement, we developed data collection instruments and field-tested the data collection instruments, following which we developed a coding framework for recording and analyzing the observational data.

Lottery Sales

Our research team obtained data from the New York State Lottery, by way of a Freedom of Information Act request, for all lottery sales by retail outlet for Syracuse for the years 2000, 2001, and 2002. These data were entered into a database at the level of retail outlet. They were also coded by census tract and entered into the environmental database described above. In Syracuse each year from 2000 to 2002, more than $40 million in lottery tickets were sold. The small corner and convenience stores sold 68 percent of lottery tickets, supermarkets 5 percent, and all other outlets 27 percent. The two zip codes with the highest level of health risks, described in Chapter 3, boast the highest lottery sales. Per year, zip code 13205 averaged $6,304,561 and zip code 13204 averaged $5,998,919 in lottery ticket sales.

Full-Term Intrauterine Growth Restriction (IUGR)

We assessed the impact of the health risks associated with supermarket and convenience stores on low birth weight in newborn infants who were not born prematurely. Low birth weight is a key aspect of the disparity in birth outcomes between white babies and babies of color.[14] Obstetricians count the pregnancy gestational period as lasting forty weeks; a pregnancy that lasts until the end of the thirty-seventh week is said to be "full term," and a baby that emerges prior to thirty-seven weeks is said to be "premature." A baby who weighs less than 2,500 g (about 5.5 lbs) at birth is considered "low birth weight." Babies whose growth falls below the tenth percentile for their gestational age (on standardized growth charts) have Intrauterine Growth Restriction, or IUGR.[15]

IUGR is associated with future learning problems if the growth of the fetal brain is restricted.[16] A growing body of literature suggests that IUGR may lead to heart disease, high blood pressure, and type II diabetes in adulthood.[17] As presented more fully in Chapter 3, among the known etiological factors for IUGR are maternal hypertension (preeclampsia), maternal substance use (tobacco, alcohol, cocaine), and multiple births (twins, triplets). Two additional factors have been found in human and animal studies to impede fetal growth: (1) maternal malnutrition, particularly inadequate intake of micronutrients[18] and (2) maternal exposure to stressors.[19] The data presented in this chapter describe three potential etiological factors for IUGR that are associated with retail food outlets in Syracuse: (1) inadequate access to healthful food, (2) stress caused by violence in and around the corner stores, and (3) mentholated cigarette sales to minors.

In order to control for the potential bias of premature or multiple births, all analyses use only full-term singleton births of infants born after thirty-seven completed weeks of gestation. We performed initial analyses to identify variables that were associated with full-term IUGR in the database of Syracuse births (2000–2001) described above. The following variables were significantly associated with full-term IUGR: the mother's race (African Americans have higher IUGR); receipt of Medicaid (a proxy for low income); preeclampsia (a medical condition associated with high blood pressure during pregnancy); medications to treat infertility; and tobacco, alcohol, or cocaine use during pregnancy. Receiving public assistance and being a teenager were not associated with full-term IUGR. To control for the known biological causes associated with fetal growth restriction we removed all births from the database in which a mother had preeclampsia, had taken fertility medications, or had used tobacco, cocaine, or alcohol. The low birth weight births in the resulting sample we call "full-term unexplained IUGR."

Supermarket Analysis

In the map (8.1) showing the location of supermarkets in Syracuse, each circle denotes the location of a supermarket and approximately a one-half mile radius around the supermarket. The striped crosses mark the former locations of supermarkets that had closed by the mid-1970s.

Table 8.1 compares the twenty-four supermarket census tracts with the thirty-three non-supermarket census tracts.

We performed a logistic regression analysis with residence in a supermarket or non-supermarket census tract as the risk factor, full-term unexplained IUGR as the outcome, and controlled for both mother's race (African American, white) and Medicaid insurance (yes, no). Infants whose mothers resided in a non-supermarket census tract during pregnancy had *three and one-third times* the full-term unexplained IUGR, compared with those living in a supermarket census tract. The second important finding in this analysis is that

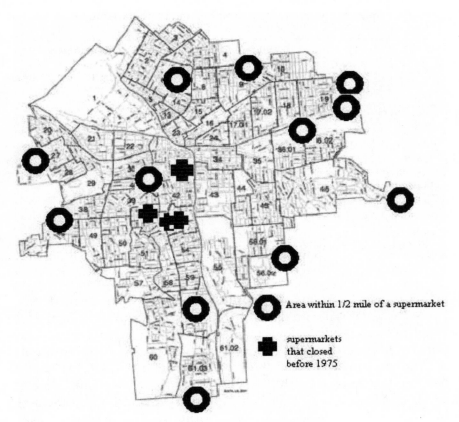

Map 8.1 Supermarkt locations, Syracuse, 2000–2001

by including supermarkets as a variable, race and Medicaid were no longer statistically significant. Access to healthy food may thus "explain" much of the racial and poverty disparities in fetal growth among mothers without any other risk factors.

When I initially spoke about this analysis to some of my colleagues, many speculated that perhaps the results of the association between supermarkets and IUGR was simply due to poverty. To investigate whether or not poverty was a main predictor of IUGR, I examined three census tracts in the most impoverished parts of

Table 8.1 Income, Demographic and Birth Variables, by Supermarket Proximity

	Supermarket census tracts N=24	Non-supermarket census tracts N=33
Median family income	$36,136*	$31,701*
Proportion of residents of color	32%*	34%*
Singleton full term births**	900	943
Actual # of full term unexplained IUGR babies**	10	23

* No statistically significant difference between supermarket and non-supermarket census tracts.

** Births with preeclampsia, fertility medications, tobacco, cocaine, and/or alcohol have been removed from the sample; singleton births only.

Syracuse, which are served by a full-service supermarket called "Nojaims." Nojaims is not an upscale suburban emporium, but it offers a range of fresh produce, low-fat dairy, fresh baked goods, and meats. One could purchase food only at Nojaims and eat a health-promoting diet. I compared the full-term unexplained IUGR in the three Nojaims census tracts with IUGR in three census tracts immediately south of Nojaims, which lacked supermarket access. As presented in Table 8.2, the median income in the three non-supermarket census tracts is more than $6,000 greater than the Nojaims' census tracts, but the proportion of unexplained IUGR is one-third higher in the non-supermarket census tracts, although this result was not statistically significant.

Table 8.2 Is It Just Poverty?
Unexplained IUGR, Median Household Income, and Presence of a Supermarket

	Median household income	% Unexplained Full Term IUGR
Nojaims supermarket*	$12,513	2.5%
No supermarket*	$18,736	3.7%

* Each area covers three contiguous census tracts

Corner Store Analysis

We chose eighteen randomly selected corner stores in each of the high- and low-risk groups of census tracts. As presented in Table 8.3, the median family income of the high-risk census tracts is about 60 percent below the median family income in the low-risk census tracts, a finding that is expected because poverty was one of the variables in the definition of high and low risk. Although race/ethnicity was not a variable to determine the categories of high and low risk, people of color comprise nearly three times the proportion of residents in the high risk compared with the low risk census tracts. The higher proportion of people of color in the high risk census tracts reflects their much higher rates of poverty in Syracuse.

Table 8.3 High- and Low-Risk Census Tracts, Median Household Income and Residents of Color

	High social and health-risk census (n=6 census tracts)	Low social and health-risk census tracts (n=25 census tracts)
Median household income	$17,632	$44,572
Proportion of residents of color	47%	16%

Below is a composite description of the qualitative observations of the corner stores from my field notes:

Metal bars, layered over the exterior of the corner store's cracked windows, partially obscure an ad featuring a pair of red female lips expectantly pouting toward a cigarette. Entering the store, our research team members looked for milk, infant formula, and fresh produce. A patina of dust covered the cereal. The milk cost more than twice what one would pay in the suburbs. There was no fresh produce. The employee was conducting a lively business, however, selling 40 oz. malt liquor, cigarettes, and lottery tickets. Thick wads of scratched-off losing tickets littered the floor. Multi-flavored cigars—in banana, strawberry, and honey—known as "blunts" and typically used to roll marijuana, were prominently displayed. In the neighborhoods where more African Americans live the stores featured huge displays of Newport cigarettes. As we left one of the stores a member of the research team exclaimed, "The food in there is just decoration … it's not what they are really selling."

We found very few differences in the corner stores in high- and low-risk census tracts. Frankly, in neither area could the stores be characterized as contributing to the health of the neighborhoods in which they were located. About a quarter of the stores in each area sold produce, although the type of produce was very limited (e.g., two tomatoes in one store) and was sometimes rotten. More stores in the high-risk area sold 1 percent milk and in both high- and low-risk areas the price of milk was more than twice the cost than in suburban areas. A majority of corner stores in both areas also sold blunts, which are flavored cigars that are commonly used to wrap marijuana for smoking. The only statistically significant difference among the variables in Table 8.4 was that more stores in the high-risk area sold infant formula.

My colleagues and I were struck by the lively business in lottery tickets and tobacco products; fifteen of the eighteen corner stores

Table 8.4 High- and Low-Risk Census Tracts by Corner Markets' Products

	High-risk census tracts (n=18 stores)	Low-risk census tracts (n=18 stores)
Produce—any	27.8%	22.2%
1% milk	22.2%	11.1%
2% milk	66.7%	66.7%
Whole milk	94.4%	94.4%
Milk out of date	11.1%	11.1%
Whole milk—mean price	$3.72 per ½ gal.	$3.63 per ½ gal.
Cheerios—mean price	$3.44	$3.96
Infant formula	61.1%*	27.8%*
Alcohol products up front by cashier	33.3%	38.9%
Cigarettes prominently displayed by cashier	83.3%	88.9%
Cigarette ads prominently displayed	88.9%	94.4%
Blunts	94.4%	94.4%
Lottery tickets	83.3%	83.3%
ATM machine in store	44.4%	50%
Dust on food boxes	44.4%	44.4%

*$p<0.05$

in each of the high- and low-risk areas sold lottery tickets. The mean yearly lottery ticket sales *per corner store* in the high-risk census was $249,904, compared with $167,501 in the low-risk census tracts. In the poorer neighborhoods, therefore, corner store clientele were spending considerably more on the lottery than in the more well-off areas. Likewise, the corner stores located in neighborhoods with more residents of color featured extensive menthol cigarette ads and large, prominent glass menthol cigarette displays on the front counters.

Community Members' Perspectives

Parents interviewed for the family case studies; almost all initially reported that they do not shop in the corner stores. They said that they shop for food in the supermarkets, but since few of them owned cars, they needed to take the bus or ask a friend or family member for a ride. When the interviewers asked specifically how often they bought items from the corner stores, most of the parents reported that they purchased milk, bread, or cigarettes from the corner stores two or three times per week. With regard to the offerings at the local corner store, one parent stated, "No fresh fruit or vegetables, but they do sell cheese, milk, bread. You do have to look at the dates from time to time; you can't leave it up to the owners of these stores to make sure it is quality."

Several of the case study parents reported feeling discriminated against by store clerks, as this African American parent described:

> For one thing even if you are a regular customer, as soon as you walk in they follow you with their eyes wherever you go in that store ... As far as [the store personnel] going out of their way to do something kind for another person, I've never seen that happen.

Several of the case study parents also described the corner stores as being unsafe. Fathers in particular mentioned discomfort with the environment for themselves and their families, as illustrated by the following comments from an African American father:

> There be fights going on just about every other day. Basically I don't want to have to go to the store, I have to keep looking around me ... They [drug dealers] make drug transactions inside and outside the

store, in the aisles, out back, anywhere around the store there are activities and transactions.

Other community members told us that drug dealing was a serious problem in and around the corner stores, as described by an older Latino resident,

> The worst drugs that I know [of] that are on the streets right now: heroin and crack cocaine. I believe that the neighborhood is infected with that pretty much everywhere you go. I walked in the store the other day and a young kid, he must have been sixteen, seventeen, he showed me that he had some crack to sell. That's pretty sad, you know.

Another neighborhood resident said, "Ninety-eight percent of the stores in that area, there is someone selling drugs ... They sell alcohol to underage kids." Parents also told us that the corner stores sell loose cigarettes to minors as well as drug paraphernalia. They described how individual cigarettes—called loosies—are sold for 50 cents each to children. Another commented on the stores' sales of drug paraphernalia,

> [Some corner stores sell] little bottles, you might see someone by the road you know they buying crack, then you see a little brown bag, now the baggies, they raided the stores, you can't buy them alone but buy a bundle now.

A former drug user also described how some stores sell "make-up-bags," which he described as baggies filled with the equipment needed to smoke crack cocaine.

Lottery Sales and Household Income

I divided the Syracuse census tracts into three groups based on the per capita yearly lottery purchases and compared that to the proportion of full-term unexplained IUGR in the census tract. As presented in Table 8.5, where household income was lower, lottery sales were higher, differences that were statistically significant. Census tracts with higher per capita lottery purchases also had higher full-term unexplained IUGR, but these differences did not reach statistical significance.

**Table 8.5 Per Capita Lottery Purchases, Median Household Income
and Full-Term IUGR**

Lotto and IUGR 55 census tracts* Mean per capita yearly lotto purchases**	Median household income	% Minority residents	% census tracts within ½ mile of a supermarket	% Unexplained full-term IUGR
$595	$22,942	46.1%	21%	2.50%
$185	$24,682	29.5%	55%	2.02%
$ 49	$33,942	20.9%	53%	1.04%

*Excluding the central downtown census tract, with city, county, and federal governmental offices and the mall census tract.
** Median household income and per capita lotto purchases, $p<0.0001$ between each stratum.

The three groups of census tracts presented above, however, are considerably different with regard to the proportion of minority residents. To control for this source of bias, I conducted a second analysis in the fifteen census tracts with more than 50 percent minority residents, as presented in Table 8.6. I divided the fifteen census tracts by per capita yearly lottery purchases (more than $400 versus less than $400), a division that resulted in the two groups of census tracts being quite similar in terms of median household income, proportion of minority residents, and access to a supermarket. Although the differences did not reach statistical significance, in the census tracts with higher lottery purchases, residents spent nearly four times as much per person on lottery tickets and the full-term unexplained IUGR was doubled.

Table 8.6 Per capita lottery purchases by IUGR

Lotto and IUGR 15 census tracts Mean per capita yearly lotto purchases	Median household income	% Minority residents	% Census within ½ mile of a supermarket	% Unexplained term IUGR
$503	$19,772	75.5%	44%	2.79%
$135	$19,338	70.6%	50%	1.34%

Discrimination and Store Owners

Corner stores are the locus of ethnic conflict, pitting immigrants from the Middle East against impoverished people of color. As mentioned earlier, I lived in Egypt for five years and speak Arabic, which helped me to understand each side's perspectives in this clash with painful clarity. An excerpt from my field notes on the corner store observations describes an interaction of one of the store cashiers with three young African American research assistants:

> These three young women, all gorgeous twenty-somethings, entered the first store just before me and asked the clerk at the cash register the whereabouts of milk, produce, baby formula, and the like. With narrowed eyes, he answered their queries. Several questions he appeared not to understand and the young women rephrased their requests. He seemed mistrustful and close to contemptuous, clearly wondering what they were up to. I stepped into his field of vision and as he turned toward me—a chubby, middle-aged, European American blond—he smiled deferentially. I repeated the question again and he stammered. Thinking he did not sufficiently understand English, I switched to Arabic, asking where he was from. His entire demeanor changed and an older man emerged from a back room to join the conversation in Arabic. The clerk's initial manner toward our African American research assistants was unfriendly and close to rude for American culture, but was far beyond rude according to Arabic cultural norms. I was also very puzzled by the condition of the stores; most were filthy and entirely lacked fresh produce. I recalled the small corner shops in Egypt and Jordan, for example, in which luscious fruits were piled in careful pyramids to tempt the buyer. Why, in the United States, did the shopkeepers abandon such wonderful aspects of their culture, I wondered.

The store owners have been criticized in the press and at community meetings for contributing to the problem of poor service, violence, and unsafe conditions in their stores. In the context of post–September 11, and in the wake of anti-Arab and anti-Muslim discrimination, many of the store owners see this criticism as xenophobia. For example, a store owner wrote in the Syracuse *Post-Standard,* "Blame the Arabs for everything. Inner-city violence—blame the Arab store owners. The current drug problem—blame the Arab store owners. Especially after the September 11 attacks, Arabs have been an easy target for any shortcomings in our society."[20] I believe that the conflict has little to do with the Middle Eastern origin of many of the Syracuse shopkeepers. New immigrant owners of local markets have frequently clashed with native-born minority groups; historically Jewish grocers, and more recently Korean store owners in Los Angeles, similarly clashed with local impoverished, mostly African American residents. The new immigrant proprietors often face violence, which occurs all too frequently around corner markets, and may be afraid of being harmed. What appears to be suspicion of their customers of color may in fact be difficulty in understanding English. But also, the immigrant shop keepers may be influenced by the same racism that pervades our society and may respond to that bias in their interactions with their clients of color.

Corner Store Case Study

One of the corner stores where my colleagues and I conducted observations is located on the city's near South side, where the mean household income for that census tract in 2000 was $8,974 and yearly lottery sales were $545,829. The corner store across from a low-income housing project sold 32 percent of all lottery tickets in the entire census tract. In addition to lottery sales, the corner store featured a two-foot by three-foot display of menthol cigarettes on the front counter and multiple flavors of blunts, and the store's alcohol section was larger than the dairy section. With regard to produce, the store offered a couple heads of cabbage and a few onions; there was no 1 percent milk for sale, and the price of 2 percent and whole milk was more than double the cost in suburban stores. In 2004, an 8:00 a.m. drive-by shooting into a crowded group buying coffee occurred at the store and wounded three customers. According to a news report, an adolescent male who was grazed by a bullet said that he was "coming out [of the] store when he heard gunshots and dropped to the ground and crawled back into the store." A female customer who was buying coffee when her son was shot said, "[I heard a] pop and I looked up and saw my baby with blood all over his face and started crying and said 'Baby, you been shot.'" The store owner claimed, "I keep chasing them [the drug dealers] away and telling them to leave my property

... We have elderly people who live right there. They don't even want to come over and get a loaf of bread because they're scared."[21]

Supermarkets, Corner Stores, Lottery Sales, Illicit Drug-Related Violence, and Vacant Houses

Chapter 3 described the association between neighborhood destruction, vacant houses, and health risks. This chapter adds four additional neighborhood-level risk factors: the absence of supermarkets, corner stores that sell non-food items, lottery tickets marketed to and purchased disproportionately by the poor, and drug-related violence in and around corner stores. I wondered to what extent this complex mix of neighborhood health hazards were themselves related and conducted an analysis on this point. I found that non-supermarket census tracts have nearly three times the per capita lottery sales, nearly twice the drug-related arrests, and 30 percent more vacant houses. Table 8.7 shows that these neighborhood risks overlap considerably. What this means is that residents of these devastated communities face multiple, at times perhaps insurmountable, obstacles to their health and their children's health and survival.

Infants of color are at risk for low birth weight as a result of poor fetal growth. It takes healthy food to grow a baby and part of the risk of poor fetal growth appears to be the lack of supermarkets that sell

Table 8.7 Intersecting Neighborhood Risks

	Lack of supermarkets	Drug arrests	Per capita lotto	Vacant houses
Lack of supermarkets	—	Not significantly correlated	XX	X
Drug arrests	Not significantly correlated	—	X	XX
Per capita lotto	XX	X	—	XX
Vacant houses	X	XX	XX	—

Based on 55 Syracuse census tracts, excluding the central downtown census tract, with city, county, and federal governmental offices; XX=p<0.01, X=p<0.05.

fresh produce, low-fat dairy, and other health-promoting foods. On the face of it, this may look like a simple matter of personal choice. Yet, there are a number of environmental structural barriers to women making those choices. Investing in healthy food seems a simple choice of how to dispose of one's income, however limited. This individual choice takes place, however, in a social context in which two factors limit that choice severely. First, our observations of corner stores show that marketing of lottery tickets is nearly universal in these stores. But, the stores are only the final end of a larger system designed to market aggressively the lottery to poor communities and communities of color. Many of the advertisements and press releases produced by the New York State Lottery feature people of color and glowing stories of winners whose jackpots helped them to get out of financial difficulties. A community member, when we were discussing the lottery sales, explained, "Folks are buying hope." I cannot help but think, however, that the abysmally low graduation rates in Syracuse are connected to the prodigious Lotto sales. Those with fewer math skills may be more likely to believe the state-run propaganda promoting the lottery.

Also exploitative of the community, and conditioning individual choice, is the way in which tobacco is sold. More highly addictive mentholated cigarettes are heavily promoted to communities of color. As described above, entering a corner store in Syracuse is to be exposed to extensive advertisements for tobacco products, especially mentholated cigarettes. The practice of the corner stores of selling individual cigarettes, or "loosies," compounds the effects of such advertising. Moreover, it is well documented that loosies are sold to minors illegally. Such sales increase the risk that a minor in this community will become addicted to tobacco products, perpetuating into the next generation the use of limited financial resources on unhealthy "choices."

Corner stores are the site of social conflict, including fights, shootings, and drug use. This violence is encouraged, in part, by the practice of selling blunts and paraphernalia for drug-related purposes. These activities make some residents wary of going to the store for fear of harm. Can we separate the impact of the stress of constant violence from the lack of healthy food on fetal growth? No, I don't think so. These factors are intertwined and overlapping in a negative synergy.

Notes

1. D. Cassady and V. Mohan, "Doing Well by Doing Good? A Supermarket Shuttle Feasibility Study," *Journal of Nutrition Education and Behavior* 36 (March/April 2004): 67–70; R. W. Cotterill and A. W. Franklin, "The Urban Grocery Store Gap," *Food Marketing Policy Center Issue* (paper no. 8, Storrs, CT: University of Connecticut, 1995); B. Hall, "Neighborhood Differences in Retail Food Stores: Income versus Race and Age of Population," *Economic Geography* 59, no. 3 (1983): 282–95.

2. B. Hall, "Neighborhood Differences."

3. G. Crockett, K. Clancy, and J. Bowering, "Comparing the Cost of a Thrifty Food Plan Market Basket in Three Areas of New York State," *Journal of Nutrition Education* 24, no. 1 (1992): 71–78.

4. S. Y. Shiao, C. M. Andrews, and R. J. Helmreich, "Maternal Race/ Ethnicity and Predictors of Pregnancy and Infant Outcomes," *Biological Research for Nursing* 7, no. 1 (2005): 55–66.

5. W. A. Visscher, M. Feder, A. M. Burns, et al., "The Impact of Smoking and Other Substance Use by Urban Women on the Birthweight of Their Infants," *Substance Use and Misuse* 40, no. 11 (2004): 1749–50.

6. R. N. Bluthenthal, D. Browntaylor, N. Guzman-Becerra, et al., "Characteristics of Malt Liquor Beer Drinkers in a Low-Income Racial Minority Community Sample," *Alcohol, Clinical and Experimental Research* 29, no. 3 (2005): 402–9; J. D. Allen-Taylor, "The Malt Liquor Industry, Drunk on High-Octane Sales to the Black Hip-Hop Nation, Has Set Its Sights on the Latino Youth Market," *Sonoma County Independent*, October 2–8, 1997.

7. NVivo2, QSR International, Melbourne, Australia, 2002.

8. S. Weibezahl, "Powder in Her Sock Is for the Nose, Not the Toes," *Syracuse Post-Standard*, May 8, 2003.

9. "Man Wearing Stocking on Head Robs Corner Store," *Syracuse Post-Standard*, Sunday Final Edition, sec. B, 2000; "Man, Shot Leaving Store, Now in Fair Condition," *Syracuse Post-Standard*, Monday Final Edition, sec. B, 2001; "Would-Be Robber, Shot by Store Owner, Dies," *Syracuse Post-Standard*, Wednesday Final Edition, sec. B, 2001; "Man Hit by Stray Bullet While in Front of Store," *Syracuse Post-Standard*, Friday Final Edition, sec. B, 2002; "One of 10 Shots Strikes Man in Arm Outside Store," *Syracuse Post-Standard*, Thursday Final Edition sec. B, 2002; M. Breidenbach and N. M. Harris, "Man Shot to Death Outside City Store," *Syracuse Post-Standard*, Saturday Final Edition, sec. A, 2002; D. Clarke and S. A. Gray Jr., "City Records 2 New Shootings with Injuries: Syracuse Police Investigate Whether Morning, Afternoon Incidents Are Related," *Syracuse Post-Standard*, Sunday Final Edition, sec. B, 2002; S. Errington, "Store Owner Shoots Robbery Suspect: Police Say They Won't Charge the Gifford Street

Shop Proprietor Who Fired Gun," *Syracuse Post-Standard,* Tuesday Final Edition, sec. C, 2001; P. Greene, "Quiet" Store Clerk Shot in Robbery: Paul Colby Remains in Fair Condition at Hospital After Pair Hold Up A-Plus," *Syracuse Post-Standard,* Friday Final Edition, sec. D, 2001; S. Weibezahl, "City Man Charged in Store Shooting: Wounded Clerk Released from Hospital. Police Are Looking for Second Suspect in Case," *Syracuse Post-Standard,* Wednesday Final Edition, sec. B, 2001; S. Weibezahl, "City Boy, 15, Grazed by Bullet: Youth Told Police He Was Leaving Store When He Heard Shots and Dropped to Ground," *Syracuse Post-Standard,* Wednesday Final Edition, sec. B, 2002.

10. "Police Arrest Store Clerk on Drug-Possesion Counts," *Syracuse Post-Standard,* Wednesday Final Edition, sec. B, 2000; "City Takeover: Must City Hall Shut Down a Business to Keep a Neighborhood Safe?" *Syracuse Post-Standard,* Friday Final Edition, sec. A, 2000; M. Sieh, "City Grocery Faces Closure: Boss Market, Closed Last Summer Because of Drug Arrests, Is Cited Again," *Syracuse Post-Standard,* Thursday Final Edition, sec. B, 2000; M. Sieh, "Police Order Store Closed: Boss Market in Syracuse Will Be Shut for a Year Under a Nuisance Abatement Law," *Syracuse Post-Standard,* Friday Final Edition, sec. B, 2000; S. Weibezahl, "City Man Bound with Tape, Shot," *Syracuse Post-Standard,* Wednesday Final Edition, sec. B, 2000.

11. S. Weibezahl, "Guns on The Corner: 'It's Pop, Pop, Pop,' Shots Are Common Here, City Resident Says," *Syracuse Post-Standard,* sec. B, June 11, 2002; C. Clark, "I Looked Up and Saw My Baby with Blood All Over His Face," *Syracuse Post-Standard,* sec. A, November 14, 2004.

12. S. A. Gray, "City Police to Speak to SUN: Group Hears Reassurances That 'Targeted' Anti-Gang Efforts Will Continue," *Syracuse Post-Standard,* sec. B, March 28, 2003; S. A. Gray, "Troopers: 3 Sold Alcohol to Minor," *Syracuse Post-Standard,* sec. B, March 2, 2003; S. Weibezahl, "Underage Cigarette Sales Lead to Fines for Sellers: Ten Businesses Caught When Onondaga County Sends Minors in to Buy Tobacco," *Syracuse Post-Standard,* sec. B, June 7, 2002; D. LaMattina, "Sweep Nets 18 Arrests; Stores Sold Alcohol, Tobacco to Minors, City Police Say," *Syracuse Post-Standard,* sec. B, September 30, 2004.

13. P. Riede, "SUN Burns Over What It Calls 'City's Apathy': Neighborhood Group Claims Problems at Corner Stores Are Being Ignored," *Syracuse Post-Standard,* sec. B, June 1, 2002; C. Clark, "Set to Take Action Against Noncompliant Businesses: Stores Under 20,000 Square Feet Have Until Wednesday to Comply With New Law," *Syracuse Post-Standard,* sec. B, September 14, 2004.

14. S. D. Lane, S. Teran, C. Morrow, et al., "Racial and Ethnic Disparity in Low Birth Weight in Syracuse, NY," *American Journal of Preventive Medicine* 24, supp. 4 (2003): S128–32.

15. D. K. Steward and D. K. Moser, "Intrauterine Growth Retardation

in Full-Term Newborn Infants with Birth Weights Greater Than 2,500 g.," *Research on Nursing in Health* 27, no. 6 (2004): 406–12.

16. V. Frisk, R. Amsel, and H. E. Whyte, "The Importance of Head Growth Patterns in Predicting the Cognitive Abilities and Literacy Skills of Small-for-Gestational-Age Children," *Acta Paediatrica* 94, no. 7 (2002): 819–24.

17. P. D. Gluckman and M. A. Hanson, "Maternal Constraint of Fetal Growth and Its Consequences," *Seminars in Fetal and Neonatal Medicine* 9, no. 5 (2004): 419–25.

18. J. F. Ludvigsson and J. Ludvigsson, "Milk Consumption during Pregnancy and Infant Birthweight," *Acta Paediatrica* 93, no. 11 (2004): 1474–8; E. A. Mitchell, E. Robinson, P. M. Clark, et al., "Maternal Nutritional Risk Factors for Small for Gestational Age Babies in a Developed Country: A Case-Control Study," *Archives of Disease in Childhood Fetal and Neonatal* 89, no. 5 (2004): F431–5; R. J. Sram, B. Binkova, A. Lnenickova, et al., "The Impact of Plasma Folate Levels of Mothers and Newborns on Intrauterine Growth Retardation and Birth Weight," *Mutation Research* 591, nos. 1–2 (December 2005): 302–10; G. Wu, F. W. Bazer, T. A. Cudd, et al., "Maternal Nutrition and Fetal Development," *Journal of Nutrition* 134, no. 9 (2004): 2169–72.

19. M. F. Schreuder, M. Fodor, J. A. Van Wijk, et al., "Association of Birth Weight with Cardiovascular Parameters in Adult Rats during Baseline and Stressed Conditions," *Pediatric Research* 59, no 1 (2006): 126–30; J. Lesage, F. Del-Favero, M. Leonhardt, H. Louvart, et al., "Prenatal Stress Induces Intrauterine Growth Restriction and Programmes Glucose Intolerance and Feeding Behaviour Disturbances in the Aged Rat," *Journal of Endocrinology* 181, no. 2 (2004): 291–96; P. J. Landrigan, P. J. Lioy, G. Thurston, et al., "Health and Environmental Consequences of the World Trade Center Disaster," *Environmental Health Perspectives* 112, no. 6 (2004): 731–39.

20. A. Amar, "Arab-Americans Unfairly Blamed," *Syracuse Post-Standard,* sec. A, August 23, 2002.

21. J. Read and C. Clark, "Suspect Charged in Wounding of 3: Two Victims of 8 a.m. Drive-By Shooting at Convenience Store Remain in Hospital," *Syracuse Post-Standard,* sec. B, August 4, 2004.

Chapter 9

Plenty Blame to Go Around

Infants are the most vulnerable group in any society. Internationally, we use a country's infant mortality rate to assess its level of development. The shameful fact of Syracuse's history of having among the highest rates of infant death in the United States indicates that Syracuse's level of development—the access of its residents to health-promoting resources—is poor.

As a graduate student, I learned about the ecosystem approach to understanding health and illness. My professors typically focused on the developing world, where, for instance, cutting down the rainforest in West Africa left clear pools of rainwater for mosquitoes to breed, thus creating the ideal conditions for malaria to proliferate. I remember discussions about how dam construction in Egypt or Tanzania increased the spread of the schistosomiasis parasite. In these examples, alterations in the environment increased or decreased the risk of disease. In the preceding chapters, I have used this ecosystem approach to understand the environmental and social conditions that lead to unequal infant death for poor babies, largely African Americans and Latinos.

In Syracuse, the clearing of whole neighborhoods during urban renewal, coupled with an economic downturn due to the collapse of industry, brought unintended consequences. Dilapidated rental housing, abandoned houses, and empty lots provide the conditions for lead poisoning, gonorrhea, and illicit drug use to grow. White flight to the suburbs, the closure of small businesses, and expanding governmental offices and university facilities slash property tax revenues available to fund city public schools. Inadequate education, unemployment, the Rockefeller drug laws, and racially biased arrest and sentencing underpin the epidemic of African American male incarceration. Inmate fathers cannot provide financial support and the emotional support they can offer during collect calls from jail or prison is limited. Neighborhood violence, likely a key reason that full-service supermarkets left the inner city, now clusters around corner stores that sell cigarettes, malt liquor, lottery tickets, and drug paraphernalia in place of healthy food. Residents' diets suffer when there are barriers of distance and expense to fresh produce, low-fat dairy, and other good food. Fear of gunshots, assault, or being targeted by police keep residents indoors; children kept indoors lack vigorous exercise, with dramatically rising obesity as a result.

But the ecosystem model of health cannot completely account for the gap in infant death between people of color and their white neighbors in Syracuse. Structural violence, in the form of hidden disadvantage and imbedded racism, forms the crucible in which African Americans and Latinos die too soon of largely preventable or treatable causes. Since 1960 Syracuse's population has shrunk by one third, but the county jail was enlarged. More than 90 percent of loitering arrests are of African Americans. Unemployment, incarceration, and poor health do not afflict all groups equally. Families of color in Syracuse have more than twice the rate of poverty of white families. African American males become inmates at more than seven times the white rate. If African Americans in Onondaga County had the same death rates as their white counterparts, about 125 would not die each year, based on an analysis I conducted for the year 2000. Every two years, therefore, the equivalent of an airliner full of African American residents of Onondaga County crashes, everyone dies, and no one notices.

I imagine that some readers are thinking: What about individual responsibility? Obviously individual efforts in health promotion are important. I struggle to eat the right foods to keep my cholesterol under control and I encourage my smoking friends to quit. I monitor my daughter's intake of junk food. I think a lot about how to be healthy and I often drive my family and friends to distraction with my suggestions. The analyses in this book, however, make it clear that there are limits to how much individual will can accomplish. A baby cannot make sure the house in which he or she learns to crawl is free of lead paint dust. A young mother cannot compel her baby's father to be involved with his child if he is incarcerated. Parents surviving on low-wage jobs cannot create a supermarket in their neighborhoods; they cannot stop the gunshots or drug dealing surrounding their local corner stores.

Within this context of community stress, worsening economy, Welfare reform, and cuts in public health funding, Syracuse Healthy Start was successful in three key areas. First, pregnant and parenting teens in Syracuse had generally good birth outcomes and lower rates of infant death than adult women. Because we had designed such a comprehensive package of teen services, however, we cannot say what part of the care made the difference. Second, adult women who had not graduated from high school and were served by SHS had significantly lower postneonatal infant death than comparable women who were not SHS participants. Third, our screening and treatment protocol for bacterial vaginosis during pregnancy led to lower rates of premature births. I cannot, however, make recommendations advising other communities to undertake bacterial vaginosis screening and treatment. The protocol will need to be studied further before such policy recommendations can be made.

So much remains to be done. In writing this book, I wanted to offer suggestions of key areas on which my research shows that we should focus. Disproportionate incarceration of young males of color and the abysmal high school graduation rates are two factors that make me worry the most about the future of Syracuse. I cannot offer simple solutions to these enormous and complex problems, but I believe they are two roots of the problem of infant death as well as many of our other social ills.

Fortunately, some issues might lend themselves to more doable resolutions. We need to change the law in New York State on lead in rental housing. Presently we wait until a child is exposed to dangerous levels of lead before addressing the home conditions. Landlords may go above and beyond the law to ensure that their properties are lead-free, but we cannot expect the majority of landlords to go beyond what the law requires. In the past few months I have been speaking with my colleagues and students to encourage their interest in strengthening the law regarding lead hazards in New York State.

Many Syracuse neighborhoods have among the highest rates of elevated lead in children in the state. Our research demonstrates that lead poisoning among babies and toddlers alters the life chances of poisoned individuals many years later.

A second relatively doable suggestion is to better fund STD screening and treatment services. Presently, the lone public STD clinic in Syracuse is open only eleven hours per week. Despite the fact that the group with the highest rates of STDs is teen females ages fifteen through nineteen, the clinic's only after-school hours are Thursday until 4:30 p.m. If we better funded STD screening and treatment, so that infected individuals could get treatment the day they noticed their symptoms, we would potentially decrease new sexually transmitted HIV infections. Decreasing HIV would not only decrease unnecessary suffering and death, but would also save tax dollars in Medicaid costs.

Third, the New York State Lottery should stop preying on the hopes of the poor. The research presented in this book demonstrates that the very poorest citizens spend the most on the lottery. About $40,000,000 per year of lottery tickets are sold in Syracuse. I believe that the abysmally low graduation rates in Syracuse are connected to the prodigious lotto sales. Those with fewer math skills may be more likely to believe the State-run propaganda promoting the likelihood of winning the lottery.

Two issues that are beginning to be resolved, although not yet completely, are vacant houses and the absence of supermarkets. A coalition of groups is busy refurbishing abandoned homes and building new homes on empty lots on the South and Southwest sides of Syracuse. To date they have only made a dent in the number of boarded-up, broken-down properties, but some whole blocks are beginning to look trim and cared for. The newly available homes are also priced within the economic capacity of the original low income residents of the neighborhood. Second, Syracuse University is developing a supermarket in downtown Syracuse.[1] Of course, one supermarket is insufficient to reach all of the Syracuse neighborhoods that lack healthy food, but it is a start.

It is tempting, but wrong, to blame one group or another for these problems. Some people blame the poor themselves for not taking sufficient personal responsibility. Others, looking at the racial disparity in incarceration, blame the police. Still others, looking at the poor graduation rates, blame the teachers or school administrators. It is comforting to try to find someone to blame, and it gives the accuser a feeling of self-righteousness. But these problems are not the product of one group. The police or teachers or physicians work in large systems that are beyond individual control. When I was speaking to a group of African American clergy in Syracuse, I was struggling to explain that while police or teachers or elected officials bore some responsibility, they did not create these conditions and the fault does not entirely reside with any one group. One of the ministers nodded knowingly and said, "There's plenty blame to go around."

Notes

1. "Prime the Pump: City and College Leaders Can Do More for Downtown Growth," April 5, 2006, *Rochester, NY Democrat and Chronicle.*

Bibliography

"A Closer Look at Sudanese Refugee Resettlement," 2001, http://gbgm-umc.org/UMCOR/update/lostboys.stm.

"Abstinence-Only Programs Challenged." *AIDS Patient Care STDs* Nov 19 (11): 783–84 (2005).

Acevedo-Garcia, D., L. F. Berkman, and M. J. Soobader. "The Differential Effect of Foreign-Born Status on Low Birth Weight by Race/Ethnicity and Education." *Pediatrics* Jan 115 (1): e20–30 (2005).

"Achievements in Public Health, 1900–1999: Healthier Mothers and Babies." *MMWR* 48 (38): 849–58 (1999).

Adamek, R., A. Anholcer, E. Florek, E. Kaczmarek, and W. Piekoszewski. "Effect of Exposure to Tobacco Smoke and Selected Socioeconomic Factors in Occurrence of Low Birth Weight." *Przegl Lek* 62 (10): 965–9 (2005).

Adimora, A. A., V. J. Schoenbach, D. M. Bonas, et al. "Concurrent Sexual Partnerships among Women in the United States." *Epidemiology* 13 (3): 320–7 (2002).

Agustines, L. A., Y. G. Lin, P. J. Rumney, M. C. Lu, R. Bonebrake, T. Asrat, and M. Nageotte. "Outcomes of Extremely Low-Birth-Weight Infants between 500 and 750g.," *American Journal of Obstetric Gynecology* 182 (5): 1113–16 (2000).

Alexander, R. T., and D. Radisch. "Sudden Infant Death Syndrome Risk Factors with Regard to Sleep Position, Sleep Surface, and Co-Sleeping." *Journal of Forensic Science* 50 (1): 147–51 (2005).

Allen-Taylor, J. D. "The Malt Liquor Industry, Drunk on High-Octane Sales to the Black Hip-Hop Nation, Has Set Its Sights on the Latino Youth Market." *The Sonoma County Independent* (1997), http://www.metroactive.com/papers/sonoma/10.02.97/latino-drinking-9740.html.

Aluoch, J. R. "Higher Resistance to Plasmodium Falciparum Infection in Patients with Homozygous Sickle Cell Disease in Western Kenya." *Tropical Medicine & International Health* 2 (6): 568–71 (1997).

Amar, A. "Arab-Americans Unfairly Blamed." *Syracuse Post-Standard*, August 23, 2002, A1.

American Academy of Pediatrics, Committee on Child Abuse and Neglect. "Distinguishing Sudden Infant Death Syndrome from Child Abuse Fatalities." *Pediatrics* 107 (2): 437–41 (2001).

American Anthropological Association Statement on "Race." http://www.aaanet.org/stmts/racepp.htm.

Apgar, Virginia. "A Proposal for a New Method of Evaluation of The Newborn Infant." *Current Researches in Anesthesia and Analgesia* 32 (4): 260–7 (1953).

Aral, S. O. "Determinants of STD epidemics: Implications for Phase Appropriate Intervention Strategies." *Sexually Transmitted Infections* Apr 78 (Suppl 1): i3–13 (2002).

Aral, S. O., W. Cares Jr., and W. D. Mosher. "Vaginal Douching among Women of Reproductive Age in the United States: 1988." *American Journal of Public Health* 82 (2): 210–14 (1992).

Ariadli, M., Elizabeth Arias, Kenneth D. Kochanek, M. Minino, Sherry L. Murphy, and Betty L. Smith. *Deaths: Final Data for 2000* (National Vital Statistics Reports, 2002).

Arnold, C. L., T. C. Davis, H. J. Berkel, R. H. Jackson, I. Nandy, and S. London. "Smoking Status, Reading Level, and Knowledge of Tobacco Effects among Low-Income Pregnant Women." *Preventive Medicine* 32 (4): 313–20 (2001).

Arnold, Jacqueline. "Inmate in Coma after She Collapses. Justice Center Officials Say the Inmate Had Been Checked on Regularly after She Complained of Pain." *Syracuse Post-Standard*, March 14, 1996, sec. C.

"Arson Fire Damages Vacant South Side House." *Syracuse Post-Standard*, May 15, 2000, sec. B.

Baker, D. W., R. M. Parker, M. V. Williams, W. S. Clark, and J. Nurss. "The Relationship of Patient Reading Ability to Self-Reported Health and Use of Health Services." *American Journal of Public Health* 87 (6): 1027–30 (1997).

Balbach, E. D., E. M. Barbeau, and R. J. Gasior. "R.J. Reynolds' Targeting of African Americans: 1988–2000." *American Journal of Public* Health 93 (5): 822–27 (2003).

Barnes P. M., and C. A. Schoeborn. "Physical Activity among Adults: United States, 2000: Advance Data from Vital and Health Statistics, no. 333." (Hyattsville, Maryland: National Center for Health Statistics, 2003).

Barth, A., W. Osterode, A. W. Schaffer, et al. "Reduced Cognitive Abilities in Lead-Exposed Men." *International Archives of Occupational and Environmental Health* 75 (6): 394–98 (2002).

Bashir, S. A. "Home Is Where the Harm Is: Inadequate Housing as Public Health Crisis." *American Journal of Public Health* 92 (5): 733–38 (2002).

Basso, B., F. Gimenez, and C. Lopez. "IL-1beta, IL-6 and IL-8 Levels in

Gyneco-Obstetric Infections." *Infectious Diseases Obstetric Gynecology* 13 (4): 207–11 (2005).

Bateson, Gregory, et al. "Toward a Theory of Schizophrenia." *Behavioral Science* (1956).

Beigi, R. H., S. L. Hillier, M. A. Krohn, T. Straw, and H. C. Wiesenfeld. "Factors Associated with Absence of H2O2-Producing Lactobacillus among Women with Bacterial Vaginosis." *Journal of Infectious Diseases* 191 (6): 924–29 (2005).

Bellinger, D. C. "Lead." *Pediatrics* 113 (Suppl 4): 1016–22 (2004).

Bennett, S. E., and N. P. Assefi. "School-Based Teenage Pregnancy Prevention Programs: A Systematic Review of Randomized Controlled Trials." *Journal of Adolescent Health* 36 (1): 72–81 (2005).

Benowitz, N. L., B. Herrera, and P. Jacob. "Mentholated Cigarette Smoking Inhibits Nicotine Metabolism." *Journal of Pharmacology and Experimental Therapeutics* 310 (3): 1208–15 (2004).

Bertranpetit, J., and F. Calafell. "Genetic and Geographical Variability in Cystic Fibrosis: Evolutionary Considerations." *Ciba Found Symp.* 197: 97–114 (1996).

Bluthenthal, R. N., D. Browntaylor, N. Guzman-Becerra, et al. "Characteristics of Malt Liquor Beer Drinkers in a Low-Income Racial Minority Community Sample." *Alcohol, Clinical and Experimental Research* 29 (3): 402–9 (2005).

Board on Health Sciences Policy, Institute of Health. *Unequal Treatment: Confronting Racial and Ethnic Disparities in Health Care* (2003).

Bolen, E., and K. Hecht. *Neighborhood Groceries: New Access to Healthy Food in Low-Income Communities* (San Francisco, CA: California Food Policy Advocates, 2003).

Borawski, E. A., T. Block, N. Colabianchi, L. D. Lovegreen, and E. S. Trapl. "Effectiveness of Abstinence-Only Intervention in Middle School Teens." *American Journal of Health Behavior* 29 (5): 423–34 (2005).

Boulding, Elise. *Cultures of Peace: The Hidden Side of History* (Syracuse University Press, 2000).

Bourdieu, Pierre. *Outline of a Theory of Practice* (1977).

———. *The Logic of Practice* (1990).

Bradshaw, C. S., C. K. Fairley, S. M. Garland, J. Hocking, L. B. Horvath, I. Kuzevska, M. B. Morris, A. N. Morton, and L. M. Moss. "High Recurrence Rates of Bacterial Vaginosis over the Course of 12 Months after Oral Metronidazole Therapy and Factors Associated with Recurrence." *Journal of Infectious Diseases* 193 (11): 1478–86 (2006).

Bradshaw, C. S., C. K. Fairley, S. M. Garland, M. B. Morris, A. N. Morton, and L. M. Moss. "Higher-Risk Behavioral Practices Associated with Bacterial Vaginosis Compared with Vaginal Candidiasis." *Obstetric Gynecology* 106 (1): 105–14 (2005).

Breidenbach, M., and N. M. Harris. "Man Shot to Death Outside City Store." *Syracuse Post-Standard,* March 30, 2002, A1.

Brenner, Eric. *Fathers in Prison: A Review of the Data* (Philadelphia, PA: National Center on Fathers and Families, 2003).

Brody, J. E. "With Tylenol and Children, Overdosing Is Perilously Easy." *New York Times,* January 25, 2000.

Brunett, Dana. "Supermarket Access in Low Income Communities." Prevention Institute for the Center for Health Improvement (CHI), Oakland, California, 2002, http://www.preventioninstitute.org/CHI_supermarkets.html.

Burgio, G. R., P. Gancia, A. Paganelli, and P. Sampaolo. *Ethics in Perinatology* (2006).

CDC Infant Death Investigation, Sudden Infant Death Syndrome (SIDS), http://www.cdc.gov/SIDS/index.htm.

Canfield, R. L., C. Cornwall, D. A. Kreher, et al. "Low-Level Lead Exposure, Executive Functioning, and Learning in Early Childhood." *Neuropsychology, Development, and Cognition* 9 (1): 35–53 (2003).

Canfield, R. L., D. A. Cory-Slechta, and M. H. Gendle. "Impaired Neuropsychological Functioning in Lead-Exposed Children." *Developmental Neuropsychology* 26 (1): 513–40 (2004).

Canfield, R. L., D. A. Cory-Slechta, C. R. Henderson, et al. "Intellectual Impairment in Children with Blood Lead Concentrations below 10 mcg per Deciliter." *New England Journal of Medicine* 348 (16): 1517–26 (2003).

Carter, Emmanuel J. "ESF Projects Aim to Revitalize American Cities," http://fla.est.edu/people/faculty/carter/revitalize.htm.

Cassady, D., and V. Mohan. "Doing Well by Doing Good? A Supermarket Shuttle Feasibility Study." *Journal of Nutrition Education and Behavior* 36 (2): 67–70 (2004).

"Cause of Merriman Fire Still Being Investigated." *Syracuse Post-Standard,* October 29, 2000, sec. B.

Centers for Disease Control. Hepatitis B Outbreak in a State Correctional Facility 2000. *Morbidity and Mortality Weekly Report* 50 (25): 529–32 (2001).

Centers for Disease Control and Prevention. *The Fry Readability Scale.* March 14, 2001.

Champion, L. "Two Firefighters Injured in Early-Morning City Blaze. Arson Suspected as Fire Spreads from Vacant House to Home Next Door." *Syracuse Post-Standard,* May 28, 1997, sec. A.

———. "Vacant City Home Damaged by Arson." *Syracuse Post-Standard,* July 25, 1996, sec. D.

Charmaine, D. M., Royal Dunston, and Georgia M. Dunston. "Changing the Paradigm from 'Race' to Human Genome Variation." *Nature Genetics* 36 (Suppl 11): S5–7 (2004).

Chiaffarino, F., P. De Besi, M. Lavezzari, and F. Parazzini. "Risk Factors for Bacterial Vaginosis." *European Journal of Obstetric Gynecology and Reproductive Biology* 117 (2): 222–26 (2004).

Children's Defense Fund. "More Than 1 out of 3 Syracuse Children Live in Poverty—Nearly Twice the Rate in New York." (press release, 2004).

Chiodo, L. M., J. L. Jacobson, and S. W. Jacobson. "Neurodevelopmental Effects of Postnatal Lead Exposure at Very Low Levels." *Neurotoxicology and Teratology* 26 (3): 359–71 (2004).

"City Takeover. Must City Hall Shut Down a Business to Keep a Neighborhood Safe?" *Syracuse Post-Standard*, January 14, 2000, A12.

Clark, C. "I Looked Up and Saw My Baby with Blood All over His Face." *Syracuse Post-Standard*, November 14, 2004, sec. A.

———. "Set to Take Action against Noncompliant Businesses: Stores under 20,000 Square Feet Have until Wednesday to Comply with New Law." *Syracuse Post-Standard*, September 14, 2004, B3.

Clarke, D., and S. A. Gray Jr. "City Records 2 New Shootings with Injuries. Syracuse Police Investigate Whether Morning, Afternoon Incidents Are Related." *Syracuse Post-Standard*, July 28, 2002, B1.

Cohen, D., R. Scribner, S. Spear, et al. "Broken Windows and the Risk of Gonorrhea." *American Journal of Public Health* 90 (2): 230–36 (2000).

Coin, G. "Man Warned Someone Would Start House Fire Early Morning. Fire Damages Vacant House and Home Next Door." *Syracuse Post-Standard*, September 15, 1996, C3.

Commonwealth Fund National Scorecard on U.S. Health System Performance, 2006, http://www.commonwealthfund.org/usr_doc/Schoen_natscorecard_chartpack_955.pdf?section=4039.

Connors, Dennis J. *Syracuse, NY, Images of America* (Arcadia Publishing, 1997).

"Convicted Felons in NYS Cannot Vote While Serving Their Sentences." Felony Disenfranchisement, The Sentencing Project, http://www.sentencingproject.org/issues_03.cfm.

Cory-Slechta, D. A. "Lead-Induced Impairments in Complex Cognitive Function: Offerings from Experimental Studies." *Neuropsychology, Development, and Cognition* 9 (1): 54–75 (2003).

Coster, William. "Purity, Profanity and Puritanism. The Churching of Women, 1500–1700." In *Women in the Church*, edited by W. J. Sheils and Diana Wood (Oxford: Blackwell, 1990).

Cotterill, R. W., and A. W. Franklin. *The Urban Grocery Store Gap* (Storrs: Food Marketing Policy Center, University of Connecticut, Food Marketing Policy Issue Paper No. 8, 1995).

Cottrell, B. H. "Vaginal Douching Practices of Women in Eight Florida Panhandle Counties." *Journal of Obstetric Gynecology Neonatal Nursing* 35 (1): 24–33 (2006).

Cottrell, B. H., M. Shannahan. "Maternal Bacterial Vaginosis and Fetal/Infant Mortality in Eight Florida Counties, 1999 to 2000." *Public Health Nursing* 21 (5): 395–403 (2004).

Cox, D. N., A. S. Anderson, M. D. Lean, et al. "UK Consumer Attitudes, Beliefs and Barriers to Increasing Fruit and Vegetable Consumption." *Public Health and Nutrition* 1 (1): 61–8 (1998).

Crawford, J. A., T. M. Hargrave, A. Hunt, C. C. Liu, R. D. Anbar, G. E. Hall, D. Naishadham, M. H. Czerwinski, N. Webster, S. D. Lane, and J. L. Abraham. "Issues in Design and Implementation of an Urban Birth Cohort Study: The Syracuse AUDIT Project." *The Journal of Urban Health* 83 (4): 741–59 (2006).

Crawford, Judith A., Jerrold L. Abraham, Ran D. Anbar, Maria H. Czerwinski, Geralyn E. Hall, Teresa M. Hargrave, Andrew Hunt, Sandra D. Lane, Chien-Chih Liu, Deepa Naishadham, and Noah Webster. "Issues in Design and Implementation of an Urban Birth Cohort Study: The Syracuse AUDIT Project." *The Journal of Urban Health* 83 (4): 741–59 (2006).

Crockett, G., J. Bowering, and K. Clancy. "Comparing the Cost of a Thrifty Food Plan Market Basket in Three Areas of New York State." *Journal of Nutrition Education* 24 (1) (1992).

Cross Cultural Health Care Program, "Interpreter Services," http://www.xculture.org/interpreter/overview/models.html.

Cubbin C., W. C. Hadden, and M. A. Winkleby. "Neighborhood Context and Cardiovascular Disease Risk Factors: The Contribution of Material Deprivation." *Ethnicity and Disease* 11 (4): 687–700 (2001).

Cunningham, Gary, Steven L. Bloom, John C. Hauth, and Kenneth J. Leveno. *Williams' Obstetrics, Edition 22* (McGraw-Hill Professional, March 31, 2005).

Currie, J. M. "Health Disparities and Gaps in School Readiness." *The Future of Children* 15 (1): 117–38 (2005).

Czerwinski, Maria, Don Cibula, Rob Keefe, Sandra D. Lane, Carla Liberatore, and Martha Wojtowycz. "Missing Fathers and Incarceration: Health Impacts of Structural Violence." *Social Justice: Anthropology and Human Rights* 4 (1–2): 147–67 (2003).

Da Silva, A. A., M. T. Alves, M. A. Barbieri, H. Bettiol, L. C. Coimbra, F. Lamy-Filho, and V. M. Simoes. "Young Maternal Age and Preterm Birth." *Pediatric Perinatal Epidemiology* 17 (4): 332–39 (Oct. 2003).

Dannelly, J. L., B. L. Hopkins, J. R. Kicklighte, et al. "Recommendations for Nutrition Interventions with Overweight African-American Adolescents and Young Adults of the Atlanta Jobs Corps Center." *Journal of Health Care for the Poor and Underserved* 16 (1): 111–26 (2005).

Davis, Barbara Sheklin. *Syracuse African Americans (Black America)* (Arcadia Publishing, 2006).

Davis, T. C., R. F. Holcombe, H. J. Berkel, S. Pramanik, and S. G. Divers.

"Informed Consent for Clinical Trials: A Comparative Study of Standard versus Simplified Forms." *Journal of the National Cancer Institute* 90: 668–74 (1998).

Dean, M., M. Carrington, and S. J. O'Brien. "Balanced Polymorphism Selected by Genetic versus Infectious Human Disease." *Annual Review Genomics Human Genetics* 3: 263–92 (2002).

Deb, K., M. M. Chaturvedi, and Y. K. Jaiswal. "Comprehending the Role of LPS in Gram-Negative Bacterial Vaginosis: Ogling into the Causes of Unfulfilled Child-Wish." *Arch Gynecology Obstetric* 270 (3): 133–46 (2004).

DeMott, Kathy. "Antenatal Risk Reduction: Effectiveness of a Community Based Public Health Initiative in Syracuse, New York." (doctoral dissertation, London School of Hygiene and Tropical Medicine, 2006).

Department of Health and Human Services. "Annual Update of the HHS Poverty Guidelines." *Federal Register* (2005).

DeTocqueville, Alexis. *Democracy in America* (1835), http://xroads.virginia.edu/~HYPER/DETOC/home.html.

Devi, C. B., R. P. Prasanthi, G. H. Reddy, et al. "Developmental Lead Exposure Alters Mitochondrial Monoamine Oxidase and Synaptosomal Catecholamine Levels in Rat Brain." *International Journal of Developmental Neuroscience* 23 (4): 375–81 (2005).

Diaz, V. A., F. J. Koopman, A. G. Mainous, et al. "Race and Diet in the Overweight: Association with Cardiovascular Risk in a Nationally Representative Sample." *Nutrition* 21 (6): 718–25 (2005).

Donovan, P. "Can Statutory Rape Laws Be Effective in Preventing Adolescent Pregnancy?" *Family Planning Perspectives* 29 (1): 30–34, 40 (1997).

"Don't Douche." *Mother Jones* (November/December 1997).

Douglass, Frederick, John W. Blassingame, Peter P. Hinks, and John R. McKivigan. *Narrative of the Life of Frederick Douglass, An American Slave: Written by Himself* (Yale University Press: New edition, March 1, 2001).

Dressler, William W. *Stress and Adaptation in the Context of Culture: Depression in a Southern Black Community* (Albany, NY: State University of New York Press, 1991).

Dressler, William W., and Jose Ernesto dos Santos. "Social and Cultural Dimensions of Hypertension in Brazil: A Review," *Cadernos de Saude Publica* 16: 303–15 (2000).

Drewnowski, A., and S. E. Specter. "Poverty and Obesity: The Role of Energy Density and Energy Costs." *American Journal of Clinical Nutrition* 79: 6–16 (2004).

Duffy, L. "City Firefighter Injures Back while Battling Blaze." *Syracuse Post-Standard*, April 14, 1995, C3.

Duggan, E. "Fire in Vacant House Started by Arson." *Syracuse Post-Standard,* July 27, 1998, B1.

Duggan, E. M. "City Firefighters Battle Blaze in Office Building. Authorities Say a Faulty Electrical Box in The Basement of 400 Montgomery St. Is to Blame for the Smoky Fire Sunday." *Syracuse Post-Standard,* March 16, 1998, B1.

Dye, T., S. D. Lane, and L. F. Novick. *A Population-Based, Race-Independent Public Health Assessment for Identifying Pregnant Women in Need of Healthy Start Services* (Centers for Disease Control and Prevention, 1998), http://www.uic.edu/sph/dataskills/liveconf/slideshows/IIIE2/IIIE21/sld001.htm.

Elster, A., and M. Fleming. "Abstinence and Abstinence-Only Education." *Journal of Adolescent Health* 39 (2): 150; discussion 152 (2006).

Ember, M. "Warfare, Sex Ratio, and Polygyny." *Ethnology* 13: 197–206 (1974).

Emerson, Ralph Waldo. *Self Reliance and Other Essays* (New York: Dover Publications, 1841/1993).

Errington, S. "Store Owner Shoots Robbery Suspect. Police Say They Won't Charge the Gifford Street Shop Proprietor Who Fired Gun." *Syracuse Post-Standard,* January 23, 2001, C1.

———. "City Fire Leaves Family Homeless. Syracuse Firefighters Face Fire on All Three Floors of Merriman Avenue House." *Syracuse Post-Standard,* November 24, 2000, sec. B.

Escobar, Arturo. *Encountering Development: The Making and Unmaking of the Third World* (Princeton, NJ: Princeton University Press, 1994).

Espy, K. A. "Using Developmental, Cognitive, and Neuroscience Approaches to Understand Executive Control in Young Children." *Developmental Neuropsychology* 26 (1): 379–84 (2004).

Farmer, Paul. "An Anthropology of Structural Violence: Sidney W. Mintz Lecture for 2001." *Current Anthropology* 45 (3): 305–25 (2004).

———. *Infections and Inequalities* (Berkeley, California: University of California Press, 2004).

Fawcett, J., T. Blakely, and A. Kunst. "Are Mortality Differences and Trends by Education Any Better or Worse in New Zealand? A Comparison Study with Norway, Denmark and Finland." *European Journal of Epidemiology* 20 (8): 683–91 (2005).

Fazli-Tabaei, S., M. Fahim, and M. R. Zarrindast. "Effect of Acute and Chronic Lead Exposure on Apomorphine-Induced Sniffing in Rats." *Pharmacology & Toxicology* 92 (2): 88–93 (2003).

Feldman, L., V. Schiraldi, and J. Ziedenberg. *Too Little Too Late: President Clinton's Prison Legacy* (Washington, DC: The Justice Policy Institute, 2001).

Fellner, Jamie. *Cruel and Usual: Disproportionate Sentences for New York Drug Offenders* (New York: Human Rights Watch, 1997).

————. *Punishment and Prejudice: Racial Disparities in the War on Drugs.* New York: Human Rights Watch, 2000.

"Fire at Valley Home Was Set, Firefighters Say." *Syracuse Post-Standard,* October 15, 1998, sec. B.

"Firefighters Douse Blaze at Vacant Syracuse House." *Syracuse Post-Standard,* August 4, 1999, sec. B.

"Firefighters Put out Fire at Vacant Syracuse Home." *Syracuse Post-Standard,* July 31, 1999, sec. A.

"First Measured Century," http://www.pbs.org/fmc/book/11government8. htm.

Fiscella, K. "Racial Disparities in Preterm Births. The Role of Urogenital Infections." *Public Health Report* 111 (2): 104–13 (1996).

Flagal, K. M., M. Carroll, R. J. Kuczmarski, et al. "Overweight and Obesity in the United States: Prevalence and Trends, 1960–1994." *International Journal of Obstetrics* 22: 39–47 (1998).

Fleming, D. T., and J. N. Wasserheit. "From Epidemiological Synergy to Public Health Policy and Practice: The Contribution of Other Sexually Transmitted Diseases to Sexual Transmission of HIV Infection." *Sexually Transmitted Infections* 75 (1): 3–17 (1999).

Formica, M. K., J. R. Palmer, L. Rosenberg, et al. "Smoking, Alcohol Consumption, and Risk of Systemic Lupus Erythematosus in the Black Women's Health Study." *The Journal of Rheumatology* 30 (6): 1222–26 (2003).

Fragile Families Project. *Incarceration and Bonds among Parents* (Princeton, NJ and New York, NY: The Center for Research on Child Wellbeing, Princeton University and the Social Indicators Survey Center, Columbia University, 2002).

Franz, Adolph. *Die kirchlichen Benediktionen im Mittelalter.* 2 vols. (Freiburg, Germany: Herder, 1909).

Freire, Paulo. *Pedagogy of the Oppressed* (New York: Continuum, 1970).

Fried, P. A., R. Gray, and B. Watkinson. "Neurocognitive Consequences of Cigarette Smoking in Young Adults—A Comparison with Pre-Drug Performance." *Neurotoxicological Teratology* 28 (4): 517–25 (2006).

————. "Neurocognitive Consequences of Marijuana—A Comparison with Pre-Drug Performance." *Neurtoxicological Teratology* 27 (2): 231–9 (2005).

Frisk, V., R. Amsel, and H. E. Whyte. "The Importance of Head Growth Patterns in Predicting the Cognitive Abilities and Literacy Skills of Small-for-Gestational-Age Children." *Acta Paediatrica* 94 (7): 819–24 (2002).

Fullilove, M. T. *Root Shock: How Tearing up City Neighborhoods Hurts America, and What We Can Do about It* (New York: Ballantine, 2004).

Fumkin, H. "Health, Equity, and the Built Environment." *Environmental Health Perspectives* 113 (50): A290–91 (2005).

Galtung, J. "Violence, Peace, and Peace Research." *Journal of Peace Research* 6 (3): 167–91 (1969).

Gardiner, P. S. "The African Americanization of Menthol Cigarette Use in the United States." *Nicotine and Tobacco Research* 6 (Suppl 1): S55–65 (2004).

Garland, S. M., F. Ni Chuileannain, R. Robins-Browne, and C. Satzke. "Mechanisms, Organisms and Markers of Infection in Pregnancy." *Journal of Reproductive Immunology* 57 (1–2): 169–83 (2002).

Garten, S., and R. V. Falkner. "Role of Mentholated Cigarettes in Increased Nicotine Dependence and Greater Risk of Tobacco-Attributable Disease." *Preventative Medicine* 38 (6): 793–98 (2004).

Geneva Convention, Article 33, http://www.icrc.org/ihl.nsf/c525816bde96b7fd41256739003e636a/72728b6de56 c7a68c12563c d0051bc40?OpenDocument.

Genzel-Boroviczeny, O., S. MacWilliams, M. Von Poblotzki, and L. Zoppelli. "Mortality and Major Morbidity in Premature Infants Less than 31 Weeks Gestational Age in the Decade after Introduction of Surfactant." *Acta Obstetric Gynecology Scandinavia* 85 (1): 68–73 (2006).

Giovanni, J. "Come to Cancer Country, USA." *The Times of London*, 1992.

Giovino, G. A., J. C. Gfroerer, S. Sidney, et al. "Epidemiology of Menthol Cigarette Use." *Nicotine Tobacco Research* 6 (Suppl 1): S67–81 (2004).

Gluckman, P. D., and M. A. Hanson. "Maternal Constraint of Fetal Growth and Its Consequences." *Seminars in Fetal and Neonatal Medicine* 9 (5): 419–25 (2004).

Goerlitz, D. B. "Steven R. Arch et al. vs. The American Tobacco Company, et al. Videotape Deposition of David B. Goerlitz, Exhibits 1–17." August 6, 1997, http://tobaccodocuments.org/rjr/517706191-6708.html.

Golden, A. L. "Abstinence and Abstinence-Only Education." *Journal of Adolescent Health* 39 (2): 151–52; discussion 152; author reply 152–54 (2006).

Gravlee, Clarence C., and William W. Dressler. "Skin Pigmentation, Self-Perceived Color, and Arterial Blood Pressure in Puerto Rico." *American Journal of Human Biology* 17: 195–206 (2005).

Gray, S. A. "City Police to Speak to SUN: Group Hears Reassurances that 'Targeted' Anti-Gang Efforts Will Continue." *Syracuse Post-Standard*, March 28, 2003, sec. B.

———. "Troopers: 3 Sold Alcohol to Minor." *Syracuse Post-Standard*, March 2, 2003, sec. B.

Great State of New York Golden Snowball Contest Weather Website, http://www.goldensnowball.com/.

Greene, P. "Loitering Tickets: 93.6% Blacks. Syracuse Police Say They

Respond to Complaints, Not Racial Profiling," *Syracuse Post-Standard*, July 18, 2002, sec. A.

Greene, P. "Quiet Store Clerk Shot in Robbery. Paul Colby Remains in Fair Condition at Hospital after Pair Hold up A-Plus." *Syracuse Post-Standard*, September 21, 2001, D3.

Guttentag, M., and Secord, P. *Too Many Women? The Sex Ratio Question* (Newbury Park, CA: Sage, 1983).

Gutman, Herbert. *The Black Family in Slavery and Freedom, 1750-1925* (New York: Vintage Books, 1976).

Hacker, Andrew. *Two Nations: Black, and White, Separate, Hostile, Unequal* (New York: Scribners, 1992).

Hafstrom, O., J. Milerad, and H. W. Sundell. "Prenatal Nicotine Exposure Blunts the Cardiorespiratory Response to Hypoxia in Lambs." *American Journal of Respiratory Critical Care Medicine* 166 (12 Pt 1): 1544–49 (2002).

Hafstrom, O., J. Milerad, K. L. Sandberg, and H. W. Sundell. "Cardiorespiratory Effects of Nicotine Exposure during Development." *Respiratory Physiology Neurobiology* 149 (1–3): 325–41 (2005).

Haley, V. B., and T. O. Talbot. "Geographic Analysis of Blood Levels in New York State Children Born 1994–1997." *Environmental Health Perspectives* 112 (15): 1577–82 (2004).

Hall, B. "Neighborhood Differences in Retail Food Stores: Income versus Race and Age of Population." *Economic Geography* 59 (3): 282–95 (1983).

Hammett, T. M., M. P. Harmon, and W. Rhodes. "The Burden of Infectious Disease among Inmates or Releasees from US Correctional Facilities, 1997." *American Journal of Public Health* 92 (11): 1789–94 (2002).

Hammett, T. M., P. Harmon, and L. Maruschak. *1996-1997 Update: HIV/AIDS, STDs and TB in Correctional Facilities* (Cambridge, MA: Abt Associates Inc., 1999).

Hann, C. S., I. King, C. L. Rock, et al. "Validation of the Health Eating Index Using Plasma Biomarkers in Clinical Sample of Adult Females." *American Journal of Clinical Nutrition* (2001).

Hanna, B., H. Jarman, and S. Savage. "The Clinical Application of Three Screening Tools for Recognizing Post-Partum Depression." *International Journal of Nurse Practitioners* 74: 479–86 (2004).

Hardy, Sarah. *Mother Nature: A History of Mothers, Infants, and Natural Selection* (Pantheon, 1999).

Hayes, K. S. "Literacy for Health Information of Adult Patients and Caregivers in a Rural Emergency Department." *Clinical Excellence for Nurse Practitioners* 4 (1): 35–40 (2000).

Health and Human Services. *Guidance to Federal Financial Assistance Recipients Regarding Tital VI Prohibition against National Origin Discrimination Affecting*

Limited English Proficient Persons. 2000, http://www.hhs.gov/ocr/lep/revisedlep.html.

Healthy People 2010. http://wonder.cdc.gov/.

Hegaard, H. K., H. Kjaergaard, L. F. Moller, B. Ottesen, and H. Wachmann. "The Effect of Environmental Tobacco Smoke during Prenancy on Birth Weight." *Acta Obstetric Gynecology Scand.* 85 (6): 675–81 (2006).

Hendler, I., S. N. Caritis, R. L. Goldenberg, J. D. Iams, C. A. MacPherson, K. M. Menard, P. J. Meis, B. M. Mercer, M. S. Miodovnik, A. H. Moawad, Y. Sorokin, and G. R. Thurnau. "The Preterm Prediction Study: Association between Maternal Body Mass Index and Spontaneous and Indicated Preterm Birth." *American Journal of Obstetric Gynecology* 192 (3): 882–86 (2005).

Hillier, S. L. "The Vaginal Microbial Ecosystem and Resistance to HIV." *AIDS Resistant Human Retroviruses* 14 (suppl 1): S17–21 (1998).

Hillier, S. L., M. F. Cotch, R. Edelman, D. A. Eschenbach, R. S. Gibbs, M. A. Krohn, D. H. Martin, R. P. Nugent, J. G. Pastorek II, A. V. Rao, et al. "Association between Bacterial Vaginosis and Preterm Delivery of a Low-Birth-Weight Infant." *New England Journal of Medicine* 333 (26): 1737–42 (1995).

"HIV Transmission among Male Inmates in a State Prison System—Georgia, 1992–2005," *MMRW* 55 (15): 421–26 (2006).

"HIV Transmission among Black Women—North Carolina, 2004, History of Male Partner Incarceration," *MMRW* 54 (4): 89–94 (2005).

Hosono, S., K. Harada, H. Kimoto, T. Ohno, and M. Shimizu. "Morbidity and Mortality of Infants Born at the Threshold of Viability: Ten Years' Experience in a Single Neonatal Intensive Care Unit." *Pediatric Int.* 48 (1): 33–39 (2006).

Human Rights Watch. "United States. Ignorance Only: HIV/AIDS, Human Rights and Federally Funded Abstinence-Only Programs in the United States, Texas: A Case Study," *Human Rights Watch Report* 14 (5), http://hrw.org/reports/2002/usa0902/.

Hunter College. "How Can Students Meet City University's Basic Skills Requirements?" http://rwc.hunter.cuny.edu/cuny-act/overview.html.

Inhorn, M. C. *Infertility and Patriarchy: The Cultural Politics of Gender and Family Life in Egypt* (University of Pennsylvania Press, 1996).

Jacobs, J. "Tipp Hill House Fire Called Suspicious. The House at Willis Avenue and Cayuga Street Was Vacant and Had No Power." *Syracuse Post-Standard*, December 7, 2000, sec. B.

———. "Fire Damages Merriman Ave. Vacant House." *Syracuse Post-Standard*, October 28, 2000, sec. B.

Jackson, V. "Arson Linked to Blaze in Vacant East Side House." *Syracuse Post-Standard*, September 13, 1998, sec. B.

———. "Arson Charged in North Side Fire." *Syracuse Post-Standard,* July 14, 1998, sec. C.

Jackson, V., and P. Ortiz. "Man Charged in Court Street Arson. Police Say Ernest B. Mosier Jr., 36, Set a Couch on Fire in A Building at 312 Court St. (13208) that Damaged Two Adjacent Houses." *Syracuse Post-Standard,* July 15, 1998, sec. B.

Jaffee, D. H., Z. Eisenbach, O. Manor, and Y. D. Neumark. "Effects of Husbands' and Wives' Education on Each Other's Mortality." *Social Science Medicine* 62 (8): 2014–23 (2006).

Johnson, K. H., M. Bazargan, and C. J. Cherpitel. "Alcohol, Tobacco, and Drug Use and the Onset of Type 2 Diabetes among Inner-City Minority Parents." *The Journal of the American Board of Family Practice* 14 (6): 430–36 (2001).

Johnson, R. L. "Gender Differences in Health-Promoting Lifestyles of African Americans." *Public Health Nursing* 22 (2): 130–37 (2005).

Jones, E. Michael. *The Slaughter of Cities: Urban Renewal as Ethnic Cleansing* (St. Augustine's Press, 2003).

Kaiser Family Foundation. "Overview of Medicaid Managed Care Provisions in the Balanced Budget Act of 1997." New York State Department of Health.

Kalchbrenner. Clinical Review of Home Uterine Activity Monitoring. *JAOA* 101 (2): 18–24 (2001).

Karaer, A., A. F. Avsar, and M. Boylu. "Vaginitis in Turkish Women: Symptoms, Epidemiologic-Microbiologic Association." *European Journal of Obstetric Gynecology and Reproductive Biology* 121 (2): 211–15 (2005).

Kaufman, P. R., S. M. Lutz, J. M. MacDonald, et al. *Do the Poor Pay More for Food? Item Selection and Price Differences Affect Low-Income Household Food Costs* (Agricultural Economics Report No. [AER759], 1997).

Kavic, S. M., E. J. Frehm, and A. S. Segal. "Case Studies in Cholera: Lessons in Medical History and Science." *Yale Journal of Biological Medicine* 72 (6): 393–408 (1999).

Kickbusch, I. S. "Health Literacy: Addressing the Health and Education Divide." *Health Promotion International* 16, 289–97 (2001).

Kieffer, R. S., J. Loveluck, A. M. Odoms-Young, J. Two Feathers, and S. K. Willis. "Reducing Disparities in Diabetes among African-American and Latino Residents of Detroit: The Essential Role of Community Planning Focus Groups." *Ethnicity and Disease* 14 (3 Suppl 1): S27–37 (2004).

Kingston, R. S., and J. P. Smith. "Socioeconomic Status and Racial and Ethnic Differences in Functional Status Associated with Chronic Diseases." *American Journal of Public Health* 87 (5): 805–10 (1997).

Kittredge, D. "Abstinence and Abstinence-Only Education." *Journal of Adolescent Health* 39 (2): 150–51; discussion 152; author reply 152–54 (2006).

Klaus, H. "Abstinence and Abstinence-Only Education." *Journal of Adolescent Health* 39 (2): 151; discussion 152; author reply 152–54 (2006).

Klebanoff, M., W. W. Andrews, R. M. Brotman, S. P. Cliver, T. R. Nansel, J. R. Schwebke, K. F. Yu, and J. Zhang. "A Pilot Study of Vaginal Flora Changes with Randomization to Cessation of Douching." *Sexually Transmitted Diseases* 33 (10): 610–13 (2006).

Klebanoff, M. A., J. C. Carey, M. P. Dombrowski, M. Harper, C. A. Hauth, S. L. Hillier, O. Langer, K. J. Leveno, C. A. MacPherson, M. Miodovnik, A. Moawad, R. P. Nugent, J. J. O'Sullivan, B. M. Sibai, W. Trout, J. P. Vandorsten, M. Varner, and R. J. Wapner. "Is Bacterial Vaginosis a Stronger Risk Factor for Preterm Birth When It Is Diagnosed Earlier in Gestation?" *American Journal of Obstetric Gynecology* 192 (2): 470–77 (2005).

Klonoff-Cohen, H. S., J. C. Chang, S. L. Edelstein, D. Kaegi, E. S. Lefkowitz, I. P. Srinivasan, and K. J. Wiley. "The Effect of Passive Smoking and Tobacco Exposure through Breast Milk on Sudden Infant Death Syndrome." *Journal of the American Medical Association* 273 (10): 795–98 (1995).

Kotsias, B. A. "The Advantage of Heterozygotes." *Medicina* 64 (1): 79–83 (2004).

Koumans, Emilia, Sandra Lane, Richard Aubry, Noah Webster, Brooke Levandowski, Martha Wojtowycz, Stuart Berman, and Lauri Markowitz. "Bacterial Vaginosis Screening and Treatment in Syracuse." (12th Annual CDC Maternal and Child Health Conference section Infections among Women of Reproductive Age (A2), Atlanta, GA, December 6, 2006).

Kreiger, J., and D. Higgins. "Housing and Health: Time Again for Public Health Action." *American Journal of Public Health* 92 (5): 758–68 (2002).

LaMattina, D. "Sweep Nets 18 Arrests; Stores Sold Alcohol, Tobacco to Minors, City Police Say." *Syracuse Post-Standard*, September 30, 2004, sec. B.

Landrigan, P. J., P. J. Lioy, G. Thurston, et al. "Health and Environmental Consequences of the World Trade Center Disaster." *Environmental Health Perspectives* 112 (6): 731–39 (2004).

Lane, Sandra D., R. Aubry, B. Bourgeois, D. Cibula, K. Demott, K. Dygert, R. Gregg, L. P. Milano, D. Milton, L. F. Novick, F. Schweitzer, M. Shaw, C. Steiner, N. Webster, and K. Wilson. "Racial and Ethnic Disparities in Infant Mortality: Risk in Social Context." *Journal of Public Health Management and Practice* 7 (3): 30–46 (2001).

Lane, S. D., and D. Cibula. "Gender and Health." In *Handbook of Social Studies in Health and Medicine,* edited by S. Scrimshaw and G. Albrecht (London: SAGE Publications, 2004).

Lane, Sandra D., Don Cibula, Maria Czerwinski, Michael Freedman, Robert Keefe, Brooke Levandowski, and Robert A. Rubinstein. "Marriage Promotion and Missing Men: African American Women in a Demographic Double Bind." *Medical Anthropology Quarterly* 18 (4): 405–28 (2004).

Lane, Sandra D., Don Cibula, Jesse Dowdell, Rob Keefe, Alan Rosenthal, Robert A. Rubinstein, and Noah Webster. "Structural Violence and Racial Disparity in Heterosexual HIV Infection." *Journal of Health Care for the Poor and Underserved* 15 (3): 319–35 (2004).

Lane, Sandra D., Don Cibula, Robert A. Rubinstein, and Noah Webster. "Toward a Public Health Approach to Bioethics. Ethics and Anthropology: Facing Future Issues in Human Biology, Globalism, and Cultural Property." *Annals of the New York Academy of Sciences* 925: 25–36 (2000).

Lane, Sandra D, R. H. Keefe, R. A. Rubinstein, B. A. Levandowski, N. J. Webster, D. A. Cibula, A. K. Boahene, O. Dele-Michael, D. Carter, T. Jones, M. Wojtowycz, and J. Brill. "Structural Violence, Urban Retail Food Markets, and Low Birth Weight." *Health and Place*, forthcoming.

Lane, Sandra D., C. Morrow, L. F. Novick, and S. Teran. "Racial and Ethnic Disparity in Low Birth Weight in Syracuse, New York." *American Journal of Preventive Medicine* 24 (Suppl 4): 128–32 (2003).

Lane, Sandra D. and Robert A. Rubinstein. "International Health: Problems and Programs in Anthropological Perspective." In *Medical Anthropology: Contemporary Theory and Method, Second Edition*, edited by C. F. Sargent and T. M. Johnson (Westport, CT: Praeger, 1996).

Lane, Sandra D., N. J. Webster, B. A. Levandowski, R. A. Rubinstein, R. H. Keefe, M. Wojtowycz, D. A. Cibula, J. A. Kingson, and R. A. Aubry. "Environmental Injustice: Childhood Lead Poisoning, Teen Pregnancy, and Tobacco." *Journal of Adolescent Health*, forthcoming.

Larson, Tom. "Why There Will Be No Chain Supermarkets in Inner City Neighborhoods." *California Politics and Policy* 7 (1) (June 2003).

"Latinos in Syracuse." http://www.archives.nysed.gov/projects/legacies/Syracuse/S_Latino/histories/.

Laumann, E. O., S. Ellingson, J. Mahay, A. Paik, and Y. Youm. *The Sexual Organization of the City* (Chicago: University of Chicago Press, 2004).

Leavitt, J. W. "The Wasteland: Garbage and Sanitary Reform in the Nineteenth-Century American City." *Journal of Historical Medical Allied Science* 35 (4): 431–52 (1980).

Ledwig, Elisa. "A Public Health Disaster," *Philadelphia Weekly*, July 25, 2001.

Lee, R. E., and C. Cubbin. "Neighborhood Context and Youth Cardiovascular Health Behaviors." *American Journal of Public Health* 92 (3): 428–36 (2002).

Lesage, J., F. Del-Favero, M. Leonhardt, H. Louvart, et al. "Prenatal Stress

Induces Intrauterine Growth Restriction and Programs Glucose Intolerance and Feeding Behavior Disturbances in the Aged Rat." *Journal of Endocrinology* 181 (2): 291–96 (2004).

Leung, A. K., J. E. Fagan, W. L. Robson, et al. "Attention Deficit Hyperactivity Disorder: Getting Control of Impulsive Behavior." *Journal of Postgraduate Medicine* 95 (2): 153–60 (1994).

Levandowski, B., D. Buchanan, S. D. Lane, B. Paul, F. Schweitzer, and S. Teran. "Obstetrical Care Coordination for Incarcerated Women." (Presentation at the National Centers of Excellence in Women's Health: Second National Forum, "Understanding Health Differences and Disparities in Women: Closing the Gap," Virginia, May 13–14, 2003).

Levandowski, B., D. Cibula, S. Huntington, S. D. Lane, A. Nestor, P. Sharma, and N. Webster. "Parental Literacy and Infant Health: An Evidence-Based Healthy Start Intervention." *Health Promotion Practice* 7 (1): 95–102 (2006).

"Listeriosis." CDC website, http://www.cdc.gov/ncidod/dbmd/diseaseinfo/listeriosis_g.htm.

Lobel, M., C. Dunkel-Schetter, and S. C. M. Scrimshaw. "Prenatal Maternal Stress and Prematurity: A Prospective Study of Socioeconomically Disadvantaged Women." *Health Psychology* 11 (1): 32–40 (1992).

Lower Mississippi Delta Nutrition Research Consortium. "Self-Reported Health of Residents of the Mississippi Delta." *Journal of Health Care of the Poor and Underserved* 15 (4): 645–62 (2004).

Lu, M. C., G. R. Alexander, N. Halfon, M. Kotelchuck, and V. Tache. "Preventing Low Birth Weight: Is Prenatal Care the Answer?" *Journal of Maternal Fetal Neonatal Medicine* 13 (6): 362–80 (2003).

Lu, M. C., and N. Halfon. "Racial and Ethnic Disparities in Birth Outcomes: A Life-Course Perspective." *Maternal Child Health* 7 (1): 13–30 (2003).

Lu, M. C., Y. G. Lin, T. J. Garite, and N. M. Prietto. "Elimination of Public Funding of Prenatal Care for Undocumented Immigrants in California: A Cost/Benefit Analysis." *American Journal of Obstetric Gynecology* 182 (1 Pt 1): 233–39 (2000).

Ludvigsson, J. F., and J. Ludvigsson. "Milk Consumption during Pregnancy and Infant Birthweight." *Acta Paediatrica* 93 (11): 1474–78 (2004).

Majewska, M. D. "Cocaine Addiction as a Neurological Disorder: Implications for Treatment." *NIDA Research Monograph* 163: 1–26 (1996).

"Malaria in Pregnancy: An Overview," *MJM* 8: 66–71 (2004).

"Man Hit by Stray Bullet While in Front of Store." *Syracuse Post-Standard*, May 3, 2002, B1.

"Man, Shot Leaving Store, Now in Fair Condition." *Syracuse Post-Standard*, August 6, 2001, B1.

"Man Wearing Stocking on Head Robs Corner Store." *Syracuse Post-Standard*, April 23, 2000, B3.

Marrazzo, J. M., P. Coffey, and M. N. Elliott. "Sexual Practices, Risk Perception and Knowledge of Sexually Transmitted Disease Risk among Lesbian and Bisexual Women." *Perspectives on Sexual & Reproductive Health* 37 (1): 6–12 (2005).

Maruschak L. M. "HIV in Prisons and Jails, 1999." *Bureau of Justice Statistics Bulletin* 1–12 (July 2001).

"Maternal Mortality—United States, 1982–1996." *MMRW* 47 (34): 705–7 (1998).

Matthews, T. J., Marian F. MacDorman, and Fay Menacker. "Infant Mortality Statistics from the 2002 Period Linked Birth/Infant Death Data Set." Division of Vital Statistics National Vital Statistics Reports 53 (10) (2004).

Mathews, T. J., and Marian F. MacDorman. "Infant Mortality Statistics from the 2004 Period Linked Birth/Infant Death Data Set." *National Vital Statistics Report* 55 (14) (2004).

Mauer, M. *Race to Incarcerate* (New York: The New Press, 1999).

Mauer, M., and Huling, T. *Young Black Men and the Criminal Justice System: A Growing National Problem.* (Washington, DC: The Sentencing Project, 1995).

Mbizvo, M. E., Z. Chirenje, A. Hussain, S. E. Musya, and B. Stray-Pedersen. "Bacterial Vaginosis and Intravaginal Practices: Association with HIV." *Central African Journal of Medicine* 50 (5–6): 41–46 (2004).

McKenna, J. J., and T. McDade. "Why Babies Should Never Sleep Alone: A Review of the Co-Sleeping Controversy in Relation to SIDS, Bedsharing and Breast Feeding." *Pediatric Respiratory Review* 6 (2): 134–52 (2005).

McKenna, J. "A Message from James McKenna," http://www.armsreach.com/article.php?ID=9.

Mebane, F. E., B. K. Rimer, and E. A. Yam. "Sex Education and the News: Lessons from How Journalists Framed Virginity Pledges." *Journal of Health Communications* 11 (6): 583–606 (2006).

Medline Plus. "Fetal Development," http://www.nlm.nih.gov/medlineplus/ency/article/002398.htm.

Merculief, J. S. "Vacant House Gutted by Fire. Firefighters Search Flaming Building after Being Told Children Had Been Inside." *Syracuse Post-Standard*, November 22, 2000, sec. B.

———. "Vacant City House Damaged by Flames." *Syracuse Post-Standard*, July 11, 1999, sec. B.

Milerad, J., S. H. Opdal, T. O. Rognum, and A. Vege. "Objective Measurements of Nicotine Exposure in Victims of Sudden Infant Death Syndrome and in Other Unexpected Child Deaths." *Journal of Pediatrics* 133 (2): 232–36 (1998).

Mitchell, E. A., P. M. Clark, E. Robinson, et al. "Maternal Nutritional Risk

Factors for Small for Gestational Age Babies in a Developed Country: A Case-Control Study." *Archives of Disease in Childhood Fetal and Neonatal Edition* 89 (5): F431–35 (2004).

Moynihan, Daniel P. *The Negro Family: The Case for National Action* (Washington, DC: Office of Policy Planning and Research, U.S. Department of Labor, 1965).

Moolchan, E. T. "Adolescent Menthol Smokers: Will They Be a Harder Target for Cessation?" *Nicotine and Tobacco Research* 6 (Suppl 1): S93–95 (2004).

Morland, K., A. D. Roux, S. Wing. "The Contextual Effect of the Local Food Environment on Residents' Diets: The Atherosclerosis Risk in Communities Study." *American Journal of Public Health* 92 (11): 1761–67 (1992).

Murphy, M., M. Bobak, M. Marmot, A. Nicholson, and R. Rose. "The Widening Gap in Mortality by Educational Level in the Russian Federation." *American Journal of Public Health* 96 (7): 1293–99 (2006).

Myer, L., L. Denny, L. Kuhn, Z. A. Stein, and T. C. Wright Jr. "Intravaginal Practices, Bacterial Vaginosis, and Women's Susceptibility to HIV Infection: Epidemiological Evidence and Biological Mechanisms." *Lancet Infectious Diseases* 5 (12): 786–94 (2005).

Nation, J. R., G. R. Bratton, and K. R. Smith. "Early Developmental Lead Exposure Increases Sensitivity to Cocaine in a Self-Administration Paradigm." *Pharmacology Biochemistry and Behavior* 77 (1): 127–35 (2004).

Nation, J. R., A. L. Cardon, H. M. Heard, et al. "Perinatal Lead Exposure and Relapse to Drug-Seeking Behavior in the Rat: A Cocaine Reinstatement Study," *Psychopharmacology* 168 (1–2): 163–74 (2003).

National Kidney and Urologic Diseases Clearinghouse, http://kidney.niddk.nih.gov/kudiseases/pubs/kustats/index.htm, 2003.

National Work Group on Literacy and Health. "Communicating with Patients Who Have Limited Literacy Skills. Report of the National Work Group on Literacy and Health." *Journal of Family Practice* 46, 168–76 (1998).

Needleman, H. L. "Childhood Lead Poisoning: The Promise and Abandonment of Primary Prevention." *American Journal of Public Health* 88 (12): 1871–77 (1998).

Needleman, H. L., C. McFarland, R. B. Ness, et al. "Bone Lead Levels in Adjudicated Deliquents: A Case Control Study." *Neurotoxicology and Teratology* 24 (6): 711–17 (2002).

Ness, R. B., D. C. Bass, S. L. Hillier, K. E. Kip, J. A. McGregor, P. Rice, H. E. Richter, D. E. Soper, C. A. Stamm, and R. L. Sweet. "Douching, Pelvic Inflammatory Disease, and Incident Gonococcal and Chlamydial Genital Infection in a Cohort of High-Risk Women." *American Journal of Epidemiology* 161 (2): 186–95 (2005).

Neumark-Sztainer, D., P. J. Hannan, M. Storey, et al. "Overweight Status and Eating Patterns among Adolescents: Where Do Youths Stand in Comparison with the Healthy People 2010 Objectives?" *American Journal of Public Health* 92 (5): 844–51 (2002).

New York History Net, The Jerry Rescue, http://www.nyhistory.com/gerritsmith/jerry.htm.

New York History Net, The Harriet Tubman home, http://www.nyhistory.com/harriettubman/.

New York Immigrant Coalition Press Release. "A Matter of Life and Death: State Creates Patient Protections to Overcome Hospital Communication Barriers. Civil Rights Complaints Bring about Reforms." 2006.

"New York Schools Ruling: Overview, State Underfinancing Damages City Schools, New York Court Finds," by Greg Winter. *New York Times*, June 27, 2003.

New York State Department of Health. "Eliminating Childhood Lead Poisoning in New York State by 2010." 2004, http://www.health.state.ny.us/nysdoh/environ/lead/finalplantoc.html.

New York State Department of Health. "HIV/AIDS Related Costs and Expenditures in New York State, Annual Medicaid Expenditures for People with HIV/AIDS, New York State, Federal Fiscal Years 1986–2002," http://www.health.state.ny.us/diseases/aids/reports/2001/docs/section20.pdf.

New York State Department of Labor. "Welfare-To-Work Policy and Program Framework." Welfare-To-Work Division, NYS Department of Labor, 2000.

New York State District Report Card Comprehensive Information Report, http://www.emsc.nysed.gov/repcrd2003/cir/4218000100000.pdf.

New York State, "State Plan, Outline of the general provisions of its Temporary Assistance for Needy Families (TANF) Program," http://www.otda.state.ny.us/tanf/09_06/TANF0609Plan.

New York State Rules and Regulations, Title 10: Public Health Law, Section 206(1)(n) and 1370-a Subpart 67-2, Environmental Assessment And Abatement (Statutory authority: Public Health Law, Section 206(1)(n) and 1370-a), http://www.health.state.ny.us/nysdoh/phforum/nycrr10.htm.

New York State School Boards Association, http://www.nyssba.org/.

Nusselder, W. J., B. Deboosere, S. Gadeyne, M. Huisman, A. E. Kunst, C. W. Looman, J. P. Mackenbach, and H. Van Oyen. "The Contribution of Specific Diseases to Educational Disparities in Disability-Free Life Expectancy." *American Journal of Public Health* 95 (11): 2035–41 (2005).

O'Brien, John O. "Jailers Disconnect Inmates' Free Calls. Jump in Calls to Advocacy Group Indicated Service Abuse at County Jail." *Syracuse Post-Standard*, March 18, 2005, sec. B.

———. "Mom Who Killed 5 Children Dies in Jail. Waneta Hoyt's Story Was a Landmark SIDS Case Before It Became a Homicide Investigation." *Syracuse Post-Standard*, August 11, 1998, A1.

———. "State Faults Care of Inmate. A Report Cites a Doctor and Three Nurses at the Justice Center Jail for Ignoring Signs That Lucinda Batts Was Seriously Ill Before She Collapsed and Died." *Syracuse Post-Standard*, November 2, 1996, sec. A.

O'Brien, John, Jacqueline Arnold, and Maureen Sieh. "Inmate Described Bleeding in Note as Part of Their Review of Lucinda Batts' Death. County Officials Are Looking at What Happened to Her Note to a Nurse." *Syracuse Post-Standard*, March 20, 1996, sec. A.

Okosun, I. S., M. Glodener, and G. E. Dever. "Diagnosed Diabetes and Ethnic Disparities in Adverse Health Behaviors of American Women." *Journal of the National Medical Association* 95 (7): 523–32 (2003).

Okuyemi, K. S., J. S. Ahluwalia, M. Ebersole-Robinson, et al. "Does Menthol Attenuate the Effect of Bupropion among African-American Smokers?" *Addiction* 98 (10): 1387–93 (2003).

Okuyemi, K. S., M. Ebersol-Robinson, N. Nazir, et al. "African-American Menthol and Nonmenthol Smokers: Differences in Smoking and Cessation Experiences." *Journal of the National Medical Association* 96 (9): 1208–11 (2004).

Olson, C. M. "Nutrition and Health Outcomes Associated with Food Insecurity and Hunger." *Journal of Nutrition* 129: 521–24 (1999).

"One of 10 Shots Strikes Man in Arm outside Store." *Syracuse Post-Standard*, May 2, 2002, B1.

Onondaga Nation. "History," http://www.onondaganation.org/history.html.

Onondaga County Health Department. *Youth Risk Behavior Survey.* (1999).

Oppenheimer, S., and G. Lefevre. *Introduction to Embryonic Development, 3rd Edition* (Prentice Hall, 1996).

Ortiz, P. "Fire Damages House in City's South Side." *Syracuse Post-Standard*, September 8, 1998, sec. B.

———. "Arson Suspected in Early Morning Fire at Vacant City Home." *Syracuse Post-Standard*, January 8, 1998, sec. B.

———. "Garfield Ave. Fire Is Called Arson." *Syracuse Post-Standard*, April 9, 1997, sec. C.

———. "Arson Suspected in Fire That Burned Porch of City Home." *Syracuse Post-Standard*, April 9, 1997, sec. B.

Paeratakul, S., J. C. Loverjoy, D. H. Ryan, et al. "The Relation of Gender, Race and Socioeconomic Status to Obesity and Obesity Comorbidities in a Sample of U.S. Adults." *International Journal of Obstetric Related Metabolic Disorders* 26: 1205–10 (2002).

Panaretto, K., P. Buettner, S. Larkins, H. Lee, V. Manessis, M. Mitchell, and D. Watson. "Risk Factors for Pre-Term, Low Weight and Small for

Gestational Age Birth in Urban Aboriginal and Torres Strait Islander Women in Townsville." *Australia. New Zealand Journal of Public Health* 30 (2): 163–70 (2006).

Parker, R. M., D. W. Baker, M. V. Williams, and J. R. Nurss, "The Test of Functional Health Literacy in Adults: A New Instrument for Measuring Patients' Literacy Skills." *Journal of General Internal Medicine* 10: 537–41 (1995).

Parker, R. M., M. V. Williams, D. W. Baker, and J. R. Nurss. "Literacy and Contraception: Exploring the Link." *Obstetrics and Gynecology* 88: 72S–77S (1996).

Paul, D. A., L. Bartoshesky, K. H. Leef, R. G. Locke, J. L. Stefano, J. Walrath. "Increasing Illness Severity in Very Low Birth Weight Infants over a 9-Year Period." *BMC Pediatric* 6 (6): 2 (2006).

Perez, L. "Owners Slow Getting the Lead out. Painting over Danger." *Syracuse Post-Standard*, July 24, 2001, sec. A.

Perrizo, K., and S. Pustilnik. "Association between Sudden Death in Infancy and Co-Sleeping: A Look at Investigative Methods for Galveston County Medical Examiners Office from 1978–2002." *American Journal Forensic Medical Pathology* 27 (2): 169–72 (2006).

Pierce, F. "Arson Is Suspected in Vacant House Fire." *Syracuse Post-Standard*, August 3, 1998, sec. B.

———. "System Fails Kids: Hundreds of CNY Children Afflicted by Lead Poisoning Every Year." *Syracuse Post-Standard*, July 22, 2001, sec. A.

———. "Grace Street's Children Have Poison in Blood: Homes There Have One of the Highest Concentrations of Lead-Poisoned Children." *Syracuse Post-Standard*, July 22, 2001.

———. "Blaze Damages Two-Story House. Arson Suspected." *Syracuse Post-Standard*, January 12, 1998, sec. B.

———. "Vacant House in City Damaged by Suspicious Fire." *Syracuse Post-Standard*, December 29, 1997, sec. B.

Pinto, V. M., C. M. Buchalla, A. Neto, and M. V. Tancredi. "Sexually Transmitted Disease/HIV Risk Behavior among Women Who Have Sex with Women." *AIDS* 19 (Suppl 4): S64–69 (2005).

"Police Arrest Store Clerk on Drug-Possession Counts." *Syracuse Post-Standard*, November 15, 2000, B1.

"Police: Three Youths Tried to Set Fire in Empty House." *Syracuse Post-Standard*, May 26, 2000, sec. B.

"Prime the Pump. City and College Leaders Can Do More for Downtown Growth." *Rochester. NY Democrat & Chronicle*, April 5, 2006.

"Profiling Problems: Still Waiting for the Three-Year Project to Bring Results." *Syracuse Post-Standard*, August 27, 2004.

Promises of Medicaid Managed Care, Consumer's Union. www.consumersunion.org/health/txmedicaid/txmed-5.htm.

Putnam, J., J. Allshouse, and L. S. Kantor. "US per Capita Food Supply Trends: More Calories, Refined Carbohydrates, and Fats." *Food Review* 25: 2–15 (2002).

Rauh, V. A., J. F. Culhane, and V. K. Hogan. "Bacterial Vaginosis: A Public Health Problem for Women." *Journal of American Medical Womens Association* 55 (4): 220–24 (2000).

Read, J., and C. Clark. "Suspect Charged in Wounding of 3: Two Victims of 8 A.M. Drive-By Shooting at Convenience Store Remain in Hospital." *Syracuse Post-Standard*, August 4, 2004, sec. B.

"Redlining in the Past, Syracuse Then and Now." http://www.syracusethenandnow.net/Redlining/Redlining.htm.

Reime, B., A. Kelly, P. A.Ratner, B. A. Schuecking, S. N. Tomaselli-Reime, and P. Wenzlaff. "The Role of Mediating Factors in the Association between Social Deprivation and Low Birth Weight in Germany." *Social Science Medicine* 62 (7): 1731–44 (2006).

Renton, A. M., M. Riddlesdell, and L. Whitaker. "Heterosexual HIV Transmission and STD Prevalence: Predictions of a Theoretical Model." *Sexually Transmitted Infections* 74 (5): 339–44 (1988).

Riede, P. "SUN Burns over What It Calls 'City's Apathy.' Neighborhood Group Claims Problems at Corner Stores Are Being Ignored." *Syracuse Post-Standard*, June 1, 2002, sec. B.

Riede, P., and Maureen Nolan. "Schools Undercount Dropouts. Central New York High Schools Fail to Graduate About 7,000 Students." *Syracuse Post-Standard*, July 3, 2002, sec. A.

Riffenburgh, A. "Joint Commission of Accreditation of Healthcare Organizations (JCAHO)." *Health Literacy Toolbox*, 2000, http://www.prenataled.com/ healthlit/hlt2k/script/ht2_a_7.asp.

Robertson, J. E. "Rape among Incarcerated Men: Sex, Coercion and STDs." *AIDS Patient Care STDs* 17 (8): 423–30 (2003).

Roe v. Wade. http://www.sacred-texts.com/wmn/rvw/rvw06.htm.

Rogers, L. "Firefighters Try to Stop Fires by Children. Vacant Houses Are Favorite Targets for Teenagers and Children." *Post-Standard*, April 28, 1995, sec. B.

Romero, R., T. Chaiworapongsa, J. Espinoza, and K. Kalache. "Infection and Prematurity and the Role of Preventive Strategies." *Seminars on Neonatology* 7 (4): 259–74 (2002).

Rosenbaum, P. F., J. L. Abraham, R. Anbar, J. A. Crawford, G. Hall, T. Hargrave, A. Hunt, S. D. Lane, C. Liu, and D. Naishadham. "Risk Factors for Wheeze in the First Year of Life in Inner-City Infants at Risk for Asthma." *Proceedings of the American Thoracic Society*, A694 (Presented at the American Thoracic Society Meeting, May 2005. Published online by the American Thoracic Society, 2005, *ATS Abstracts2 View*, http://www.abstracts2view.com/atsall/).

Rosenberg, Merri. "Suit Filed to Challenge Disparities in Schools." *New York Times,* January 17, 1999, sec. 14WC.

Rosenberg, T. J., M. A. Chiasson, S. Garbers, and H. Lipkind. "Maternal Obesity and Diabetes as Risk Factors for Adverse Pregnancy Outcomes: Differences among 4 Racial/Ethnic Groups." In *American Journal of Public Health* 95 (9): 1545–51 (2005).

Rosenthal, Alan. *Racial Disparities in the Local Criminal Justice System: A Report to the NAACP Syracuse/Onondaga Chapter* (Syracuse, NY: Center for Community Alternatives, 2001).

Rothstein, Richard. "The Challenge: The Unforeseen Costs of Raising Academic Standards." *New York Times,* January 11, 2001.

Sangani, P., G. Rutherford, and D. Wilkinson. "Population-Based Interventions for Reducing Sexually Transmitted Infections, Including HIV Infection." In *The Cochrane Library* (Chichester, UK: John Wiley & Sons, Ltd., 2004).

Santelli, J., M. Lyons, M. A. Ott, J. Rogers, and D. Summers. "Abstinence-Only Education Policies and Programs: A Position Paper of the Society for Adolescent Medicine." *Journal of Adolescent Health* 38 (1): 83–87 (2006).

Santelli, J., M. Lyons, M. A. Ott, J. Rogers, R. Schleifer, and D. Summers. "Abstinence and Abstinence-Only Education: A Review of U.S. Policies and Programs." *Journal of Adolescent Health* 38 (1): 72–81 (2006).

Scanlon, Scott. "Inmate's Death Linked to Rupture of Fallopian Tube." *Syracuse Post-Standard,* March 16, 1996, sec. A.

Schizophr, Bull. "A Summary of Important Documents in the Field of Research Ethics." *Schizophr, Bull* 32 (1): 69–80, 2006.

Schreuder, M. F., M. Fodor, J. A. Van Wijk, et al. "Association of Birth Weight with Cardiovascular Parameters in Adult Rats during Baseline and Stressed Conditions." *Pediatric Research* 59 (1): 126–30 (2006).

Schwartz, B. S., K. Bandeen-Roche, B. K. Lee, et al. "Occupational Lead Exposure and Longitudinal Decline in Neurobehavioral Test Scores." *Epidemiology* 16 (1): 106–13 (2005).

Schwartz, B. S., K. I. Bolla, W. F. Stewart, et al. "Past Adult Lead Exposure Is Associated with Longitudinal Decline in Cognitive Function." *Neurology* 55 (8): 1144–50 (2000).

Schwebke, J. R., and R. Desmond. "Risk Factors for Bacterial Vaginosis in Women at High Risk for Sexually Transmitted Diseases." *Sexually Transmitted Diseases* 32 (11): 654–58 (2005).

Scrimshaw, S. C. M. "Infant Mortality and Behavior in the Regulation of Family Size." *Population and Development Review* 4 (3): 383–403 (1978).

Shearer, D. L., L. V. Klerman, B. A. Mulvihill, et al. "Association of Early Childbearing and Low Cognitive Ability." *Perspectives on Sexual and Reproductive Health* 34 (5): 236–43 (2002).

Shiao, S. Y., C. M. Andrews, and R. J. Helmreich. "Maternal Race/Ethnicity and Predictors of Pregnancy and Infant Outcomes." *Biologicial Research for Nursing* 7 (1): 55–66 (2005).

SIECUS. "Revamped Federal Abstinence-Only-Until-Marriage Programs Go Extreme, Bush Administration Approach to Healthier Youth: Get Married," http://www.siecus.org/media/press/press0124.html..

Sieh, M. "City Grocery Faces Closure. Boss Market, Closed Last Summer Because of Drug Arrests, Is Cited Again." *Syracuse Post-Standard*, March 23, 2000, B3.

———. "Urban Renewal, Syracuse Then and Now, 15th Ward Stood Tall, Fell." *Syracuse Post-Standard*, September 21, 2003, B1.

———. "Few FHA Loans Go to Minorities, Study Says: Over Four Years, 78.1 Percent Went to City's White Neighborhoods, Group Finds." *Syracuse Post-Standard*, May 21, 2002.

———. "Police Order Store Closed. Boss Market in Syracuse Will Be Shut for a Year under a Nuisance Abatement Law." *Syracuse Post-Standard*, 2000, sec. B.

———. "Tire Dumpers Wear on City. Thousands of Tires Left on Vacant Properties Pose Fire Threat, Syracuse Officials Say." *Syracuse Post-Standard*, June 9, 2000, sec. B.

Silverman, J. G., M. R. Decker, A. Raj, and E. Reed. "Inmate Partner Violence Victimization Prior to and during Pregnancy among Women Residing in 26 U.S. States: Associations with Maternal and Neonatal Health." *American Journal of Obstetric Gynecology* 195 (1): 140–48 (2006).

Simeoni, U., and R. Zetterstrom. "Long-Term Circulatory and Renal Consequences of Intrauterine Growth Restriction." *Acta Paediatrica* 94 (7): 819–24 (2005).

Simpson, E. "Immunology: Why the Baby Isn't Thrown Out..." *Current Biology* 6 (1): 43–44 (1996).

Singer, M., Ed. *The Political Economy of AIDS* (Amityville, New York: Baywood Publishing Co., 1997).

Singer, M. C., T. Abraham, L. Badiane, R. Diaz, P. I. Erickson, A. M. Nicolaysen, and D. Ortiz. "Syndemics, Sex and the City: Understanding Sexually Transmitted Diseases in Social and Cultural Context." *Social Science and Medicine* 63 (8): 2010–21 (2006).

Singer, M., D. Buchanan, R. Heimer, K. Khoshnood, C. Santelices, S. Shaw, T. Stopka, and W. Teng. "Lessons from the Field: From Research to Application in the Fight Against AIDS Among Injection Drug Users in Three New England Cities." *Human Organization* 64 (2): 179–91 (2005).

Smedley, Audrey, and Brian D. Smedley. "Race as Biology Is Fiction, Racism as a Social Problem Is Real." *Anthropological and Historical Perspectives on the Social Construction of Race, American Psychologist* 60 (1): 16–26 (2005).

Smedley, Brian D., Alan R. Nelson, and Adrienne Y. Stith. *Unequal Treatment:*

Confronting Racial and Ethnic Disparities in Health Care (Board on Health Sciences Policy, Institute of Medicine, National Academy Press, 2003).

Smith, H. P., and Robert Joki. *Syracuse and Its Surroundings: A Victorian Photo Tour of New York's Salt City* (September 10, 2002).

Smith, J. L. "Foodborne Infections during Pregnancy." *Journal of Food Protection* 62 (7): 818–29 (1999).

"South-Siders Fearful; Need Help; Nobody Listens to Longtime Residents' Concerns." *Syracuse Post-Standard*, October 7, 1996, sec. A.

Spinillo, A., E. Fazzi, B. Gardella, E. Preti, M. Stronati, and S. Zanchi. "Rates of Neonatal Death and Cerebral Palsy Associated with Fetal Growth Restriction among Very Low Birthweight Infants. A Temporal Analysis." *American Journal of Obstetric Gynecology* 113 (7): 775–80 (2006).

Sram, R. J., B. Binkova, A. Lnenickova, et al. "The Impact of Plasma Folate Levels of Mothers and Newborns on Intrauterine Growth Retardation and Birth Weight." *Mutation Research* 591 (1–2): 302–10 (2005).

Stanton, Elizabeth Cady. *The Declaration of Sentiments.* 1848, http://www.libertynet.org./edcivic/stanton.html (accessed April 9, 2000).

Stein, J. A., M. C. Lu, and L. Gelberg. "Severity of Homelessness and Adverse Birth Outcomes." *Health Psychology* 19 (6): 524–34 (2000).

Steinberg, Steven. *Turning Back: The Retreat from Racial Justice in American Thought and Policy* (Boston: Beacon Press, 1995).

Steinschneider, A. "Prolonged Apnea and the Sudden Infant Death Syndrome: Clinical and Laboratory Observations." *Pediatrics* 50 (4): 646–54 (1972).

Steward, D. K., and D. K. Moser. "Intrauterine Growth Retardation in Full-Term Newborn Infants with Birth Weights Greater than 2,500 g." *Research on Nursing in Health* 27 (6): 406–12 (2004).

Steyn, K., T. de Wet, H. Nel, Y. Saloojee, and D. Yach. "The Influence of Maternal Cigarette Smoking, Snuff Use and Passive Smoking on Pregnancy Outcomes: The Birth to Ten Study." *Pediatric Perinatal Epidemiology* 20 (2): 90–99 (2006).

Swanson, Christopher B. "Who Graduates? Who Doesn't? A Statistical Portrait of Public High School Graduation, Class of 2001." Education Policy Center, The Urban Institute.

Syracuse City School District Report Cards. http://www.emsc.nysed.gov/repcrd2003/links/d_421800.html.

Tanne, J. H. "Abstinence Only Programs Do Not Change Sexual Behavior, Texas Study Shows." *BMJ* 330 (7487): 326 (2005).

"Teen Charged with Arson after Tuesday Night Fire." *Syracuse Post-Standard*, March 29, 2000, sec. B.

Terrell, K. "Gasoline used to start blaze that destroyed house." *Syracuse Post-Standard*, September 19, 1997, sec. B.

The Six Nations of the Iroquois. http://tuscaroras.com/pages/six_nations_ex.html.

Theodore, J. "City Firefighters Put out Blaze at Vacant House." *Syracuse Post-Standard*, May 18, 1995, sec. B.

Thoreau, Henry David. *Civil Disobedience and Other Essays* (New York: Dover Pubications, 1849/1993).

"Three Children Charged with Setting House Fire." *Syracuse Post-Standard*, July 14, 1999, sec. B.

"Today in History." *Syracuse Post-Standard*, November 17, 2000, sec. C.

Towne, B., J. Blangero, S. A. Czerwinski, E. W. Demerath, A. F. Roche, and R. M. Siervogel. "Heritability of Age at Menarche in Girls from the Fels Longitudinal Study." *American Journal of Physical Anthropology* 128 (1): 210–19 (2005).

UNICEF. 1997. http://www.unicef.org/sowc97/.

UNICEF. "Child Poverty in Perspective: An Overview of Child Well-Being in Rich Countries" (Florence: UNICEF Innocenti Research Centre, 2007).

U.S. Department of Health and Human Services, Administration of Children and Families, Office of Public Affairs. "Interim Final Regulations Fact Sheet," http://www.acf.hhs.gov/programs/ofa/regfact.htm.

U.S. Department of Health and Human Services, Office of Minority Health. "National Standards for Culturally and Linguistically Appropriate Services in Health Care" (2001).

U.S. Department of Health and Human Services. "State Success Stories and Examples of Savings using PARIS," http://www.acf/hhs.gov/nhsitrc/paris/succ_par.html.

"Varnished-Soaked Rags Blamed for Apartment Fire." *Syracuse Post-Standard*, May 18, 1999, sec. B.

Visscher, W. A., A. M. Burns, M. Feder, et al. "The Impact of Smoking and Other Substance Use by Urban Women on the Birthweight of Their Infants." *Substance Use and Misuse* 40 (11): 1749–50 (2004).

Wakefield, J. "Leading to Drug Abuse." *Environmental Health Perspectives* 109 (2): A68 (2001).

Wallace, D., and R. Wallace. *A Plague on Your Houses: How New York Was Burned Down and National Public Health Crumbled* (New York: Verso Press, 1998).

Wallace R., and M. T. Fullilove. "AIDS Deaths in the Bronx 1983–1988: Spatiotemporal Analysis from a Socioeconomic Perspective." *Environmental Planning* 23 (12): 1701–23 (1991).

Watcharotone, W., S. Chandanabodhi, G. Chiravacharadej, O. Kiriwat, N. A. Leckyim, P. Nukoolkarn, S. Pibulmanee, K. Kirimai, and O. Watcharaprapapong. "Prevalence of Bacterial Vaginosis in Thai Women Attending the Family Planning Clinic, Siriraj Hospital." *Journal of the Medical Association Thailand* 87 (12): 1419–24 (2004).

Wedekind, H., T. Bajanowski, B. Brinkmann, G. Breithardt, B. Engeland, P. Friederich, W. Haverkamp, G. Monnig, E. Schulze-Bahr, C. Siebrands, and T. Wulfing. "Sudden Infant Death Syndrome and Long QT Syndrome: An Epidemiological and Genetic Study." *International Journal of Legal Medicine* 120 (3): 129–37 (2006).

Weed, William Speed. "Incubating Disease: Prisons Are Rife with Infectious Illnesses—and Threaten to Spread Them to the Public." *Mother Jones* (2001).

Weibezahl, S. "Powder in Her Sock Is for the Nose, Not the Toes." *Syracuse Post-Standard*, May 8, 2003.

———. "City Man Charged in Store Shooting. Wounded Clerk Released from Hospital. Police Are Looking for Second Suspect in Case." *Syracuse Post-Standard*, October 3, 2001, B2.

———. "City Boy, 15, Grazed by Bullet. Youth Told Police He Was Leaving Store When He Heard Shots and Dropped to Ground." *Syracuse Post-Standard*, February 20, 2002, B3.

———. "City Man Bound with Tape, Shot." *Syracuse Post-Standard*, July 18, 2001, B3.

———. "Guns on the Corner: 'It's Pop, Pop, Pop,' Shots Are Common Here, City Resident Says." *Syracuse Post-Standard*, June 11, 2002, sec. B.

———. "Underage Cigarette Sales Lead to Fines for Sellers. Ten Businesses Caught When Onondaga County Sends Minors in to Buy Tobacco." *Syracuse Post-Standard*, June 7, 2002, sec. B.

———. "Fire Damages Salina St. House. Officials Are Still Searching for Cause in Blaze that Ruined the South Side Building." *Syracuse Post-Standard*, June 1, 2000, sec. B.

———. "Morning Fire Destroys Vacant House on South Side. More than 30 Firefighters Battled the 8:30 a.m. Blaze." *Syracuse Post-Standard*, May 31, 2000, sec. B.

———. "City Fire Appears Arson. Two Houses Burn on the South Side." *Syracuse Post-Standard*, November 17, 1999, sec. B.

———. "Fire Destroys Abandoned House." *Syracuse Post-Standard*, November 16, 1999, sec. C.

Weigert, K. M. "Structural Violence." *Encyclopedia of Violence, Peace, and Conflict, 3* (New York: Academic Press, 1999).

Weiner, M. "Arson Suspected in Fire that Damaged Vacant City Row House." *Syracuse Post-Standard*, July 4, 1998, sec. B.

Weisskopf, M. G., H. Hu, R. V. Mulkern, et al. "Cognitive Deficits and Magnetic Resonance Spectroscopy in Adult Monozygotic Twins with Lead Poisoning." *Environmental Health Perspectives* 112 (5): 620–25 (2004).

Weissman, Marsha. *Children of Incarcerated Parents: Consequences and Alternatives* (Syracuse, NY: 2000).

Welfare Reform. http://www.whitehouse.gov/infocus/welfarereform/.

Welych, Lilie, Don Cibula, Tracey Durham, Amy Fitzgerald, Sandra D. Lane, and Barbara Laws. "Formative Research for Public Health Interventions among Adolescents at High Risk for Gonorrhea and other STDs." *Journal of Public Health Management and Practice* 4 (6): 54–61 (1998).

"West Kennedy Street Fire Determined to Be Arson." *Syracuse Post-Standard*, April 7, 2000, sec. B.

Western, B., and S. McLanahan. *Fathers Behind Bars: The Impact of Incarceration on Family Formation* (Princeton, NJ: Center for Research on Child Wellbeing, 2000).

White D. R., and Burton M. L. "Causes of Polygyny: Ecology, Economy, Kinship and Warfare." *American Anthropologist* 90: 871–87 (1988).

Williams, M. V. "Recognizing and Overcoming Inadequate Health Literacy, A Barrier to Care." *Cleveland Clinic Journal of Medicine* 69: 415–18 (2002).

Wilson, J. Q. *The Marriage Problem* (New York: Harper Collins Publishers, 2002).

Wilcox, A. J., E. G. Armstrong, D. D. Baird, R. E. Canfield, B. C. Nisula, J. F. O'Connor, and C. R. Weinberg. "Incidence of Early Loss of Pregnancy." *New England Journal of Medicine* 319: 189–94 (1988).

Wilks, M., A. Corfield, E. Hennessy, M. Millar, S. Porter, S. Warwick, A. Whiley, and R. Wiggins. "Identification and H(2)O(2) Production of Vaginal Lactobacilli from Pregnant Women at High Risk of Preterm Birth and Relation with Outcome." *Journal of Clinical Microbiology* 42 (2): 713–17 (2004).

Williams, J. A. *Portrait of a City: Syracuse, the Old Home Town* (Syracuse, NY: Syracuse University Library Associates, 1994).

Williams, R. C. "The Mind of Primitive Anthropologists: Hemoglobin and HLA, Patterns of Molecular Evolution." *Human Biology* 75 (4): 577–84 (2003).

Wilson, Edward O. *Consilience: The Unity of Knowledge* (New York: Vintage Books, 1998).

Wohl A. R., D. Johnson, W. Jordan, et al. "High-Risk Behaviors in and out of Incarcerated Settings for African-American Men Treated for HIV at 3 Los Angeles Public Medical Centers." (Paper presented at the 7th Conference on Retroviruses and Opportunistic Infections, San Francisco, CA, January, 2000).

Wohl A. R., D. Johnson, W. Jordan, et al. "High-Risk Behaviors during Incarceration in African-American Men Treated for HIV at Three Los Angeles Public Medical Centers." *Journal of Acquired Immune Deficiency Syndrome* 24: 386–92 (2000).

"Would-Be Robber, Shot by Store Owner, Dies." *Syracuse Post-Standard*, January 21, 2001, B1.

Wu, G., F. W. Bazer, T. A. Cudd, et al. "Maternal Nutrition and Fetal Development." *Journal of Nutrition* 134 (9): 2169–72 (2004).

Xu, Y., C. Han, G. Li, et al. "Protective Effects of Hippophae Rhamnoides L. Juice on Lead-Induced Neurotoxicity in Mice." *Biological and Pharmaceutical Bulletin* 28 (3): 490–94 (2005).

Zambrana, R. E., C. Dunkel-Schetter, N. Collins, and S. C. Scrimshaw. "Mediators of Ethnic-Associated Differences in Infant Birth Weight," *Journal of Urban Health* 75 (1): 102–16 (March 1999).

Zuckerman, B., J. J. Alpert, E. Dooling, R. Hingson, H. Kayne, S. Morelock, and E. Oppenheimer. "Neonatal Outcome: Is Adolescent Pregnancy a Risk Factor." *Pediatrics* 71 (4): 489–93 (1983).

Index

About the Author

Sandra D. Lane is Chair of Health and Wellness and Professor of Social Work at Syracuse University, as well as Research Professor in the Department of Obstetrics and Gynecology at SUNY Upstate Medical University.